D1388722

Intellectual Trust in Oneself and Others

To what degree should we rely on our own resources and methods to form opinions about important matters? Conversely, to what degree should we depend on various authorities, such as a recognized expert or a social tradition?

In this novel and provocative account of intellectual trust and authority, Richard Foley argues that it can be reasonable to have intellectual trust in oneself even though it is not possible to provide a defense of the reliability of one's faculties, methods, and opinions that does not beg the question. Moreover, he shows how this account of intellectual self-trust can be used to understand the degree to which it is reasonable to rely on alternative authorities, as well as the degree to which it is reasonable for one's current opinions to be at odds with one's past or future opinions.

This book will be of interest to advanced students and professionals working in the fields of philosophy and the social sciences as well as anyone looking for a unified account of the issues at the center of intellectual trust.

Richard Foley is Professor of Philosophy and Dean of the Faculty of Arts and Sciences at New York University. He is the author of *The Theory of Epistemic Rationality* (1987) and *Working without a Net* (1993).

*This book is dedicated to my parents, William and Gladys Foley,
to whom I owe everything.*

Intellectual Trust in Oneself and Others

RICHARD FOLEY

New York University

CAMBRIDGE
UNIVERSITY PRESS

CAMBRIDGE UNIVERSITY PRESS
Cambridge, New York, Melbourne, Madrid, Cape Town, Singapore, São Paulo

Cambridge University Press
The Edinburgh Building, Cambridge CB2 8RU, UK

Published in the United States of America by Cambridge University Press, New York

www.cambridge.org
Information on this title: www.cambridge.org/9780521793087

First published 2001
This digitally printed version 2007

A catalogue record for this publication is available from the British Library

Library of Congress Cataloguing in Publication data
Foley, Richard.
Intellectual trust in oneself and others / Richard Foley.
p. cm. – (Cambridge studies in philosophy)
Includes bibliographical references and index.
ISBN 0-521-79308-4
1. Knowledge, Theory of. I. Title. II. Series.
BD161 .F565 2001
121'.6–dc21
00-065171

ISBN 978-0-521-79308-7 hardback
ISBN 978-0-521-03910-9 paperback

Contents

Acknowledgments

Chapter 1

§1.4 draws upon Richard Foley, "Locke and the Crisis of Post-Modern Epistemology," *Midwest Studies in Philosophy*, vol. 22, ed. Wettstein, French, and Uehling, and on two talks presented at the 1995 Wheaton College Philosophy Conference. §1.5 draws upon material from my *Working Without a Net* (New York: Oxford University Press, 1993), especially 75–85.

Chapter 2

The account of epistemic rationality defended in §2.2 is a revision and extension of the account presented in *Working Without a Net*; compare especially with 94–101.

Chapter 3

The principal arguments of Chapter 3 were first presented to a conference on philosophical intuitions held at the University of Notre Dame. The proceedings of that conference, including my "Rationality and Intellectual Self-Trust," were published as *Rethinking Intuition*, ed. M. DePaul and W. Ramsey (London: Rowman and Littlefield, 1998). Revised versions of the arguments were presented at a Montreal conference on Philosophical Approaches to Irrationality, October 1997, and at Brown University, February 1998.

Chapter 4

Versions of Chapters 4, 5, and 6 were the bases for three University of Notre Dame Perspectives Lectures, delivered in November 1998. §4.1, §4.4, and §4.5 make use of material from Richard Foley, "Epistemic

Egoism," in *Socializing Epistemology*, ed. F. Schmitt (London: Rowman and Littlefield, 1994), 53–73. §4.2, §4.7, and §4.8 draw upon an American Philosophical Association address on Nicholas Wolterstorff's book, *John Locke and the Ethics of Belief*, and on Richard Foley, "Locke and the Crisis of Post-Modern Epistemology," *Midwest Studies in Philosophy*, vol. 22, ed. Wettstein, French, and Uehling.

Chapter 5
The principal arguments of §5.3 through §5.6 were first presented at an American Philosophical Association session in April 1993, and were published as "How Should Future Opinion Affect Current Opinion?" *Philosophy and Phenomenological Research* (1994), 747–766. These arguments benefited from the contributions of the other participants at the above APA session – Brad Armendt, David Christenson, and Bas van Fraassen – and from the comments of people in the audience, including Marion David, Richard Fumerton, Jon Kvanving, William Lycan, and John Pollock.

Chapter 6
Early versions of the arguments in Chapter 6 were presented at the University of Vermont, the Graduate Center at the City University of New York, Northern Illinois University, and the University of Massachusetts.

In writing and revising this work, I have benefited greatly from exchanges with numerous individuals, but the following provided especially useful comments: Jonathan Adler, Phil Bricker, David Christenson, Marion David, Mike DePaul, Mic Detlefsen, Richard Feldman, Richard Fumerton, John Greco, Peter Klein, Hilary Kornblith, Jon Kvanvig, Ernest Lepore, William Lycan, Eileen O'Neill, Al Plantinga, Phil Quinn, Frederick Schmitt, Ernest Sosa, Stephen Stich, Fritz Warfield, Nicholas Wolterstorff, and Jay Wood.

One

Intellectual Trust in Oneself

1

The Importance of Intellectual Self-Trust

1. CLASSICAL FOUNDATIONALISM AND INTELLECTUAL TRUST

To what extent should we intellectually trust ourselves? Questions of trust arise about our opinions, and they also arise about the faculties, practices, and methods that generate these opinions. Moreover, there is a relation between the two. If I have trust in the reliability of my faculties, practices, and methods, I will tend also to have trust in the overall accuracy of my opinions, and vice-versa. Trust in one tends to transfer to the other.

Questions of intellectual trust also arise about other people's opinions and faculties, and they can even arise about one's own past or future opinions and faculties. Moreover, there is a relation between these questions and question of self-trust, for whenever one's current opinions conflict with those of others, or with one's own past or future opinions, there is an issue of whom to trust: one's current self, or the other person, or one's past or future self? However, one of the central claims of this work is that there is also an interesting theoretical relation between the two sets of questions. I argue in Part Two that the trust it is reasonable to have in one's current opinions provides the materials for an adequate account of the trust one should have in the opinions of others and in one's own past and future opinions. But in Part One, my focus is more limited. I am concerned with intellectual trust in one's current self.

Most of us do intellectually trust ourselves by and large. Any remotely normal life requires such trust. An adequate philosophical account of intellectual trust will go beyond this observation, however, and say

3

something about what necessitates intellectual trust, how extensive it should be, and what might undermine it.

I approach these issues from an epistemological point of view, which is to say I am concerned with the degree of self-trust it is appropriate for individuals to have insofar as their goal is to have accurate and comprehensive opinions. Opinions and the faculties that generate them can also be evaluated in terms of how well they promote other intellectual goals. They can be assessed, for example, on their informativeness, explanatory power, simplicity, testability, theoretical fruitfulness, and countless other intellectual dimensions. In addition, they can be assessed with respect to whether they further one's practical goals. The assessments that traditionally have been of the most interest to epistemologists, however, are those that are concerned with what I call 'the epistemic goal', that of now having accurate and comprehensive beliefs.

I am especially interested in investigating issues of intellectual self-trust from an internal, first-person perspective. My primary concern is not to look at inquirers from the outside and ask whether their opinions have the characteristics required for knowledge. Instead, I examine how issues involving self-trust look from the perspective of someone who wants to be invulnerable to self-criticism insofar as his or her goal is to have accurate and comprehensive beliefs. In previous work, I argued that there are various senses of rational belief, but that one especially important sense is to be understood in terms of making oneself invulnerable to intellectual self-criticism.[1] In what follows, I defend, extend, and occasionally revise this position. However, the account of intellectual self-trust I defend is independent of this account of rational belief; the former does not presuppose the latter. For convenience, I often use the language of epistemic rationality to report my conclusions, but my principal interest, to repeat, is in how issues involving self-trust look from the perspective of someone who wants to be invulnerable to self-criticism insofar as his or her goal is to have accurate and comprehensive beliefs.

Issues of self-trust are important in epistemology, I argue, because there is no way of providing non–question-begging assurances of the reliability of one's faculties and beliefs. Of course, much of modern epistemology has been devoted to the search for just such assurances. Descartes's project is perhaps the most notorious example, but there are

---

1 See especially Richard Foley, *Working Without a Net* (New York: Oxford University Press, 1993).

numerous, more recent examples as well. For the first half of the twentieth century, most of the philosophical community thought that classical foundationalism was capable of providing assurances of the overall reliability of our beliefs. A roster of the great philosophical figures of this period is also a roster of the great proponents of classical foundationalism: Russell, (the early) Wittgenstein, Ayer, Carnap, and C. I. Lewis. These philosophers had their disputes with one another, but they gave remarkably similar answers to the core questions of epistemology: some beliefs are basic and as such their truth is assured; other beliefs are justified by virtue of being deductively entailed or inductively supported by these basic beliefs; we can determine with careful enough introspection whether our beliefs are justified, and if they are, we can be assured that they are also for the most part true; and we are justified in relying upon the opinions of others only to the extent that we have good inductive evidence of their reliability.

These positions came under withering attacks in the last half of the twentieth century, with the result that classical foundationalism is now widely rejected.[2] As classical foundationalism has waned, a variety of movements and trends have taken its place. Indeed, the most salient feature of contemporary epistemology is its diversity. The demise of classical foundationalism has brought with it a bewildering but also intoxicating array of new views, approaches, and questions. There have been fresh attempts to refute skepticism; coherentism, probabilism, reliabilism, and modest foundationalism have staked their claims to be the successors of classical foundationalism; and naturalized epistemologies and socialized epistemologies have proposed novel approaches to epistemological questions.

Epistemology is a field in transition, and one potential benefit of the move away from classical foundationalism is that it should be easier to appreciate the importance of self-trust. Classical foundationalism masked the issue with a trio of powerful but ultimately unacceptable proclamations: there are basic beliefs that are immune from the possibility of error; rationality demands that our beliefs either be basic or appropriately supported by basic beliefs; and if we are rational in regulating our opinions, we can be assured that our beliefs are not deeply mistaken.

---

2 Not every philosopher has disavowed classical foundationalism. See Richard Fumerton, *Metaphysical and Epistemological Problems of Perception* (Lincoln: University of Nebraska Press, 1985); and Fumerton, *Metaepistemology and Skepticism* (London: Rowman and Littlefield, 1995).

Once classical foundationalism fell, the way was cleared for discussions of the role of self-trust in our intellectual lives, but surprisingly little of this discussion has occurred. Issues of intellectual self-trust have still not received the full attention they deserve. In the sections that follow, I cite and express qualms about three trends in contemporary epistemology that help explain why this is so: the tendency to regard skeptical challenges as ill-formed; the popularity of externalist accounts of epistemic justification; and the assumption that evolutionary considerations provide assurances of the overall reliability of our intellectual faculties.

In subsequent chapters in Part One (Chapters 2 and 3), I discuss the grounds and limits of self-trust; but then in Part Two, I discuss its extension to other domains: trust in the intellectual faculties and opinions of others (Chapter 4); trust in one's own past intellectual faculties and opinions (Chapter 5); and trust in one's own future intellectual faculties and opinions (Chapter 6).

2. ATTEMPTS TO REFUTE SKEPTICISM

One of the primary attractions of classical foundationalism was that it calmed our worst skeptical fears. Even if Cartesian certainty was not to be obtained, we could at least be assured that if we are careful enough, our beliefs will be justified, and assured as well that if our beliefs are justified, they are mostly accurate. Since the fall of classical foundationalism, epistemologists have had schizophrenic attitudes toward skepticism. On the one hand, they often complain that one of the most glaring mistakes of classical foundationalists was to treat skeptical hypotheses too seriously. The evil demon and the brain-in-the-vat hypotheses come in for special scorn as being too far-fetched to be worthy of attention. On the other hand, epistemologists are more drawn than ever to proving that skeptical hypotheses cannot possibly be correct. We belittle those who stop and gawk at gruesome accidents, but when we ourselves witness an accident, we too stop and gawk. We cannot help ourselves, it seems. So it is with epistemologists and skepticism. More and more epistemologists say that radical skeptical hypotheses are not worthy of serious philosophical attention, but at the same time more and more cannot help but try their hand at refuting them. Because the refutations of classical foundationalists no longer seem promising, epistemologists are looking elsewhere to refute skepticism.

One strategy is to argue that radical skepticism is self-referentially incoherent, because in raising their worries, would-be skeptics inevitably make use of the very intellectual faculties and methods about which they are raising doubts. In so doing, they are presupposing the general reliability of these faculties and methods. Hence, it is incoherent for them to entertain the idea that these same faculties and methods might be generally unreliable.[3]

The problem with this line of argument is that it fails to appreciate that the strategy of skeptics can be wholly negative, having the form of a reductio. Skeptics can conditionally assume, for the sake of argument, that our faculties, procedures, and methods are reliable and then try to illustrate that if employed rigorously enough, these same faculties, procedures, and methods generate evidence of their own unreliability and hence undermine themselves. Skeptics may or may not be right in making this charge, but there is nothing self-referentially incoherent about it.

A second strategy is to argue that the nature of belief, reference, or truth makes skeptical hypotheses metaphysically impossible. For example, Hilary Putnam argues that in thinking about the world it is impossible to separate out our conceptual contributions from what is "really" there. Accordingly, plausible theories of reference and truth leave no room for the possibility that the world is significantly different from what our beliefs represent it to be.[4] Donald Davidson defends an analogous position. He argues that at least in the simplest of cases, the objects of our beliefs must be taken to be the causes of them and that thus the nature of belief rules out the possibility of our beliefs being largely in error.[5]

Whatever the merits of such theories of belief, reference, and truth as metaphysical positions, they cannot lay skeptical worries completely to rest. Intricate philosophical arguments are used to defend these metaphysical theories, and these arguments can themselves be subjected to skeptical doubts. Moreover, the metaphysical positions cannot be used to dispel these doubts without begging the question.

Descartes is notorious for having attempted to use a theistic metaphysics to dispel skepticism. He claimed to have shown that God's

---

3   See Stanley Cavell, *The Claim of Reason* (Oxford: Oxford University Press, 1979); Michael Williams, *Groundless Belief* (Oxford: Basil Blackwell, 1977); and Barry Stroud, *The Significance of Philosophical Scepticism* (Oxford: Oxford University Press, 1984).

4   Hilary Putnam, *The Many Faces of Realism* (LaSalle, IL: Open Court, 1987).

5   Donald Davidson, "A Coherence Theory of Truth and Knowledge," in E. LePore ed., *The Philosophy of Donald Davidson* (London: Basil Blackwell, 1986), 307–19.

existence is indubitable and then went on to claim that it is also indubitable that God would not permit the indubitable to be false. Not many readers of Descartes have thought that these two claims really are indubitable, but even if they were, this still would not be enough to dispel all skeptical worries, because they do not rule out the possibility of our being psychologically constituted in such a way that we find some falsehoods impossible to doubt. Any argument which tries to use the metaphysics of God to dispel this worry – for example, an argument to the effect that God is omnipotent, omniscient, and perfectly good, and such a God would not create beings for whom falsehoods were impossible to doubt – begs the question, even if the metaphysics is itself indubitable. The lesson, which is widely noted in discussions of the Cartesian circle, is that Descartes's theistic metaphysics cannot provide non–question-begging protection against the possibility of error.[6]

It is less widely noted but no less true that contemporary attempts to use a theory of belief, truth, or reference to rule out the possibility of widespread error are in precisely the same predicament. We have no guarantee of the general reliability of the methods and arguments used to defend these metaphysical theories, and any attempt to use the theories themselves to provide the guarantees begs the question. The lesson, as with Descartes, is that these metaphysical systems cannot altogether extinguish skeptical worries. Regardless of how we marshal our intellectual resources, there can be no non–question-begging assurances that the resulting inquiry is reliable; and this constraint applies to metaphysical inquiries into the nature of truth, belief, and reference as much it does to any other kind of inquiry.

3. EXTERNALISM AND THE ANALYSIS OF KNOWLEDGE

In "Two Dogmas of Empiricism," W. V. O. Quine attacks the analytic/synthetic distinction and with it the conception of philosophy as a

---

6 Descartes himself occasionally seems to recognize this point. In his "Second Set of Replies," he says the following: "Now if this conviction is so firm that it is impossible for us ever to have any reason for doubting what we are convinced of, then there are no further questions for us to ask: we have everything we could reasonably want. What is it to us that someone may make out that the perception whose truth we are so firmly convinced of may appear false to God or an angel, so that it is, absolutely speaking, false? Why should this alleged "absolute falsity" bother us, since we neither believe in it nor have even the smallest suspicion of it?" J. Cottingham, R. Stoothoff, and D. Murdoch, trans., *The Philosophical Writings of Descartes*, vol. 2 (Cambridge: Cambridge University Press, 1985), 103–4.

discipline that seeks to uncover analytic truths.[7] According to Quine, there are no analytic truths and, hence, it cannot be philosophy's job to reveal them. Rather, philosophy is best understood as being continuous with science. Our theories and concepts are to be tested by how well they collectively meet the test of observation, and philosophy is a partner with science in this testing enterprise. This conception of philosophy helped initiate the movement to naturalize epistemology, but it also had the effect of nourishing suspicions about the project of defining knowledge, which was receiving an enormous amount of philosophical attention in the aftermath of Edmund Gettier's 1963 article, "Is Justified True Belief Knowledge?"[8]

Gettier presents a pair of counterexamples designed to illustrate that knowledge cannot be adequately defined as justified true belief. The basic idea behind both counterexamples is that one can be justified in believing a falsehood P from which one deduces a truth Q, in which case one has a justified true belief in Q but does not know Q. Gettier's article inspired a host of similar counterexamples, and the search was on for a fourth condition of knowledge, one that could be added to justification, truth, and belief to produce an adequate analysis of knowledge. However, during this same period, the influence of Quine's attack on the analytic/synthetic grew, spreading with it the idea that conceptual analysis was, if not impossible, at least uninteresting. The literature on defining knowledge came to be cited as the clearest illustration of just how uninteresting conceptual analysis is. The proposed analyses of knowledge were often clever, but critics questioned whether they told us anything significant about how cognition works or how it can be improved. At best the analyses only seem to tell us something about the intuitions of twentieth-century English speakers trained in philosophy as to what counts as knowledge.

The doubts about analysis persist today, but despite them, something which closely mimics conceptual analysis is still widely practiced in epistemology and in philosophy generally. Even epistemologists who think that no statement is analytically true go to great lengths to distinguish and elucidate epistemological concepts. The result is something that looks very much like analysis but without the pretense that one has given a list of precise necessary and sufficient conditions for the concept.

7   Quine, "Two Dogmas of Empiricism," in *From a Logical Point of View*, 2nd ed. (New York: Harper, 1961), 20–46.
8   Edmund L. Gettier, "Is Justified True Belief Knowledge?" *Analysis*, 25 (1963), 121–3.

On the other hand, what has changed significantly is the content of many of these close cousins of analyses. The movement to naturalize epistemology had a major role in encouraging this change, although a little historical background is needed to show how.

The initial response to Gettier's counterexamples was to look for ways of restricting or complicating the justification condition for knowledge. Some epistemologists proposed that knowledge is nondefectively justified true belief, where a justification is nondefective if (roughly) it does not justify any falsehood.[9] Others proposed that knowledge is indefeasibly justified true belief, where a justification is indefeasible if (roughly) it cannot be defeated by the addition of any true statement.[10] However, a secondary but ultimately more influential response to Gettier's counterexamples was to wonder whether something less explicitly intellectual than justification, traditionally understood, is better suited for elucidating knowledge. Justification is closely associated with having or being able to generate an argument in defense of one's beliefs, but in many instances of knowledge, nothing even resembling an argument seems to be involved.

Alvin Goldman played an especially interesting and important role in shaping this response. He was an early champion of a causal theory of knowledge. In a 1967 article, he contends that knowledge requires an appropriate causal connection between the fact that makes a belief true and the person's having that belief.[11] This proposal nicely handled the original cases described by Gettier, but it ran into other problems. Knowledge of mathematics, general facts, and the future proved particularly difficult to account for on this approach. Nevertheless, Goldman's recommendation captivated many epistemologists, in part because it fit well with the view of knowledge implicit in the emerging naturalized epistemology movement. According to this view, knowledge is best conceived as arising "naturally" from our complex causal interactions

9 See, for example, Roderick Chisholm, *Theory of Knowledge*, 2nd ed. (Englewood Cliffs, NJ: Prentice-Hall, 1977), 102–18; Ernest Sosa, "Epistemic Presupposition," in G. Pappas, ed., *Justification and Knowledge* (Dordrecht: Reidel, 1979), 79–92; and Ernest Sosa, "How Do You Know?" in E. Sosa, *Knowledge in Perspective* (Cambridge: Cambridge University Press, 1991), 19–34.

10 See, for example, Robert Audi, *The Structure of Justification* (Cambridge: Cambridge University Press, 1993); Peter Klein, *Certainty: A Refutation of Scepticism* (Minneapolis: University of Minnesota Press, 1981); Keith Lehrer, *Knowledge* (Oxford: Oxford University Press, 1974); John Pollock, *Contemporary Theories of Knowledge* (London: Rowman and Littlefield, 1986); and Marshall Swain, *Reasons and Knowledge* (Ithaca, NY: Cornell University Press, 1981).

11 Alvin Goldman, "A Causal Theory of Knowing," *The Journal of Philosophy*, 64, 357–72.

with our environment. To think of knowledge principally in terms of our having a justification for our beliefs is to overly intellectualize the notion. Some kinds of knowledge, especially highly theoretical knowledge, might involve justification, but other kinds typically do not, for example, simple perceptual knowledge. Our perceptual equipment collects and processes information from our environment and adjusts our opinions accordingly, all without argument or deliberation except in unusual cases.

Thus, in the eyes of many philosophers, Goldman's causal theory of knowledge, whatever its specific defects, had the virtue of shifting the focus away from questions of our being able to justify our beliefs intellectually and toward questions of our being in an appropriate causal or causal-like relation with our external environment. The philosophical task, according to this way of thinking about knowledge, is to identify the precise character of this relation. A simple causal connection between the fact that makes a belief true and the belief itself won't do. So, some other 'natural' relation needs to be found.

There has been no shortage of proposals,[12] but it was Goldman again who formulated the view that had the widest appeal, the reliability theory of knowledge. Contrary to what he had proposed earlier, Goldman here argues that for a person's belief to count as knowledge, it is not necessary that the belief be caused by the fact that makes it true, although this will often be the case. It is necessary, however, that the processes, faculties, and methods that produced or sustain the belief be highly reliable.[13]

Reliability theories of knowledge led in turn to new accounts of epistemic justification, specifically, externalist ones. Initially, reliabilism was part of a reaction against justification-driven accounts of knowledge, but an assumption drawn from the old epistemology tempted reliabilists to reconceive justification as well. The assumption is that, by definition, justification is that which has to be added to true belief to generate knowledge (with some fourth condition added to handle Gettier-style counterexamples). Goldman had already argued that knowledge is relia-

---

12 For example, see D. M. Armstrong, *Belief, Truth, and Knowledge* (Cambridge: Cambridge University Press, 1973); Fred Dretske, *Knowledge and the Flow of Information* (Cambridge, MA: MIT Press, 1981); Robert Nozick, *Philosophical Explanations* (Cambridge, MA: Harvard University Press, 1981); Alvin Plantinga, *Warrant: The Current Debate* (Oxford: Oxford University Press, 1993); and Ernest Sosa, *Knowledge in Perspective*, especially Chapters 13–16.

13 Alvin Goldman, *Epistemology and Cognition* (Cambridge, MA: Harvard University Press, 1986).

bly produced true belief. Relying on the above assumption, he further concludes that epistemic justification must also be a matter of one's beliefs having been produced and sustained by reliable cognitive processes. Because a cognitive process is reliable only if it is well suited to produce true beliefs in the external environment in which it is operating, this is an externalist account of epistemic justification. By contrast, most foundationalists and their traditional rivals, coherentists, are internalists, whose accounts of epistemic justification emphasize the perspectives of individual believers.

The proposals by Goldman and others provoked an enormous literature on the relative advantages and disadvantages of externalism and internalism in epistemology.[14] Most of this literature assumes that externalists and internalists are defending rival theories and that, hence, both cannot be right. However, a more interesting reading of the dispute is that they are not, or at least need not be, competitors at all. Rather, they are concerned with different issues, and each needs to acknowledge the legitimacy of the other's issues.

Externalists are principally interested in explicating knowledge, but along the way they see themselves as also offering an explication of epistemic justification, because justification, they stipulate, is that which has to be added to true belief in order to get a serious candidate for knowledge. Internalists, on the other hand, are principally interested in explicating a sense of justification that captures what is involved in having beliefs that are defensible from one's perspective; but along the way they see themselves as also providing the materials for an adequate account of knowledge, because they too assume that justification is by definition that which has to be added to true belief to get knowledge, with some fillip to handle Gettier problems.

It is easy to conflate these two very different ways of thinking about epistemic justification and the related notions of rational belief and reason, especially since some of the most influential figures in the history

---

14 For a summary and discussion of the relevant issues, see William Alston, *Epistemic Justification* (Ithaca, NY: Cornell University Press, 1989), especially chapters 8 and 9. Also see Robert Audi, "Justification, Truth and Reliability," *Philosophy and Phenomenological Research*, 49 (1988), 1–29; Laurence Bonjour, "Externalist Theories of Empirical Knowledge," in French, Uehling, Wettstein, eds., *Midwest Studies in Philosophy*, vol. 5 (Minneapolis: University of Minnesota Press, 1980), 53–71; Richard Fumerton, "The Internalism-Externalism Controversy," in J. Tomberlin, ed., *Philosophical Perspectives*, vol. 2 (Atasacadero, CA: Ridgeview, 1988); Alvin Goldman, "Strong and Weak Justification," in Tomberlin, ed., *Philosophical Perspectives*, vol. 2 (1988); and Ernest Sosa, "Knowledge and Intellectual Virtue," in E. Sosa, *Knowledge in Perspective*, 225–44.

of epistemology thought that one and the same notion could capture both ideas. Descartes, for example, urged his readers to believe only that which is altogether impossible to doubt and, hence, internally beyond the possibility of criticism. However, he also thought by doing so his readers could be altogether assured of acquiring knowledge.

Few epistemologists are so sanguine anymore. Descartes's search for an internal procedure that would provide an external guarantee of knowledge proved not to be feasible, but the lesson is not that either the internal or external aspect of the Cartesian project has to be abandoned. The lesson, rather, is that there are different, equally legitimate projects for epistemologists to pursue. One project, roughly put, is that of exploring what is required for one to put one's own intellectual house in order. Another, again roughly put, is that of exploring what is required for one to stand in a relation of knowledge to one's environment. It is not unusual for the results of both kinds of explorations to be reported using the language of justification and rationality, but the terms 'justified belief' and 'rational belief' have different senses when used by externalists than when used by internalists. The externalist sense tends to be closely connected with knowledge, whereas the internalist sense tends to be closely connected with internally defensible believing. Confusion occurs when epistemologists slide back and forth between the two, sometimes using the language of justification and rationality to report what has to be added to true belief to get a serious candidate for knowledge and other times to report what is involved in having beliefs that are defensible given the believer's perspective.

4. EPISTEMOLOGY, THEOLOGY, AND NATURAL SELECTION

For the medievals, religious authority and tradition were seen as repositories of wisdom. By contrast, Descartes and Locke regarded authority and tradition as potential sources of error and took reason to be the corrective. However, this did not prevent either from making liberal use of theological claims to undergird their epistemologies.

Descartes's use of theological assertions is well known. He claims that the existence of God is indubitable and that it is also indubitable that God would not permit the indubitable to be false. He concludes that if we follow the method of doubt and believe only that which is indubitable for us, we can be assured that of not falling into error.

Locke's reliance on theology is less bold than Descartes and hence less notorious, but it is no less essential to his epistemology. At the heart of

Locke's epistemology is the tenet that God has commanded us to have accurate opinions. As with all of God's commands, we have an obligation to do our best to obey this command. The resulting obligation, according to Locke, applies to all of our intellectual endeavors, but it is especially pressing to have accurate beliefs about matters of morality and religion, because with respect to these matters, the salvation of our souls is at stake.

These claims, like everything else in Locke's epistemology, are suffused with a spirit of intellectual optimism. Locke assumes that even ordinary people can have reliable beliefs about matters of morality and religion. They need only to make proper use of their intellectual faculties, which for Locke means believing claims with the degree of confidence that the evidence warrants.[15] Locke does not presume that one can be altogether assured of having only true beliefs if one regulates one's opinions in accordance with the evidence. On the contrary, he thinks that it is not possible to have certainty about matters of religion and morality. However, he does seem to think that one can be assured that one's beliefs about these matters are not wildly mistaken. I say 'seems' because Locke does not explicitly address this possibility. On the other hand, there is no hint in his discussions that one who follows one's evidence might possibly fall into massive error. A basic intellectual optimism is simply taken for granted.

The source of this optimism is the theological claim that God has provided us with intellectual faculties, most importantly the faculty of reason, which are well designed to generate accurate opinions. The following remarks are characteristic of Locke:

Every man carries about him a touchstone if he will make use of it, to distinguish substantial gold from superficial glittering, truth from appearances. . . . [T]his touchstone . . . is natural reason. (*Conduct of the Understanding*, §3)

Since our faculties are not fitted to penetrate into the internal fabric and real essence of bodies; but yet plainly discover to us the being of a God, and the knowledge of ourselves, enough to lead us into a full and clear discovery of our duty, and great concernment, it will become us, as rational creatures, to employ those faculties we have about what they are most adapted to, and follow the direction of nature, where it seems to point us out the way. For 'tis rational to conclude, that our proper employment lies in those enquiries, and in that sort of knowledge, which is most suited to our natural capacities, and carries in it

---

15 See §4.2 for a discussion of Locke's principles of evidence.

our greatest interest, i.e., the condition of our eternal state. Hence I think I may conclude, that morality is the proper science, and business of mankind in general; (who are both concerned, and fitted to search out their *Summum Bonum*). (*Essay Concerning Human Understanding*, IV, xii, 11).

Appeals to theology have a double purpose in Locke's epistemology. As in Descartes's epistemology, they provide assurances of reliability. God has properly equipped us for our intellectual tasks. All we need do is use our faculties for "what they are most adapted to, and follow the direction of nature, where it seems to point us out the way." But in addition, theology provides an explanation of why it is important for us to have accurate beliefs. We need accurate beliefs, especially in matters of religion and morality, because "the condition of our eternal state" is at stake.

Anyone familiar with twentieth-century thought is also familiar with its doubts about theism. One of the implications of these doubts for epistemology is that in general it is no longer thought appropriate to appeal to theological claims in trying to provide assurances that our beliefs are reliable or to explain the importance of our having reliable beliefs.[16] On the other hand, every age has its dominant assumptions that it is eager, sometimes overly eager, to employ to solve intellectual problems. Our age is no exception.

The question of why it is important to have reliable beliefs is not extensively discussed in contemporary epistemology, but when the question is raised, the answer is often placed in an evolutionary framework rather than the moral and theological framework in which Locke placed his answer. An especially familiar line of thought begins with the observation that it is important for one to have accurate beliefs if one is to make one's way about the world successfully. Without accurate opinions, one is unable to fashion effective strategies for satisfying one's needs and pursuing one's goals. Moreover, this observation is relevant not just to the prospects of individual human beings but also to the workings of natural selection on humans collectively. Natural selection has resulted in our having faculties that have allowed us to survive and prosper as a species, but according to this line of argument, if our faculties regularly misled us about our surroundings, we would not have survived, much less prospered. Natural selection thus provides assurances that our cognitive faculties are generally reliable and our beliefs for the most part accurate.

---

16 For a contrary view, see Alvin Plantinga, *Warrant: The Current Debate*, and Plantinga, *Warrant and Proper Function* (Oxford: Oxford University Press, 1993).

Locke's view was that God has provided us with the cognitive faculties needed for that inquiry "which is most suited to our natural capacities, and carries in it our greatest interest, i.e., the condition of our eternal state." The contemporary view, by contrast, is that the processes of natural selection have provided us with cognitive systems that are well designed for survival, and these systems would not be well designed for survival unless they were generally reliable.[17] In other words, the contemporary view has evolution playing a role in epistemology analogous to the role played by God in Locke's epistemology. Why is it important for us to have accurate beliefs? The answer is not salvation but survival. And, how can we be assured that our beliefs are in fact generally accurate? The answer is not natural theology but natural selection. Whereas Locke says that God has provided us with faculties suitable for our intellectual inquiries, the contemporary view is that natural selection has provided us with faculties suitable for our intellectual inquiries. It is evolution, rather than God, which provide the grounds for intellectual optimism.

Unfortunately, arguments from natural selection are no more capable than arguments from natural theology of providing guarantees that our opinions are accurate. The most obvious problem is that such arguments inevitably beg the question. The theory of natural selection is used to argue that our intellectual faculties and procedures are trustworthy, but the theory itself, and the implications drawn from it, are themselves the products of our intellectual faculties and procedures and, hence, are trustworthy only if these faculties and procedures are trustworthy.

On the other hand, naturalized epistemologists, who are often the most enthusiastic advocates of the above argument, tend to be unimpressed by the charge that they may be begging the question. They reject a priori epistemology and urge instead that epistemology be thought of as continuous with science. Thus, in making use of the theory of natural selection for epistemological purposes, they claim simply to be following their own advice.[18]

---

17   "There is some encouragement in Darwin. If people's innate spacing of qualities is a gene-linked trait, then the spacing that has made for the most successful inductions will have tended to predominate through natural selection. Creatures inveterately wrong in their inductions have a pathetic but praiseworthy tendency to die before reproducing their kind." W. V. O. Quine, "Natural Kinds," in *Ontological Relativity and Other Essays* (New York: Columbia University Press, 1969), 114–38. See also Nicholas Rescher, *A Useful Inheritance* (Totowa, NJ: Rowman and Littlefield, 1989).

18   For a further discussion of this claim, see Richard Foley, "Quine and Naturalized Episte-

An objection that is less easy to shrug off, however, is that the theory of natural selection does not have the implications it needs to have for the above argument to succeed. First, nothing in the theory implies that evolution is only caused by natural selection. Other factors, for example, random genetic drift, can also lead to changes in gene frequency, and these other factors need not exert pressure in the direction of well-designed systems. Second, nothing in the theory implies that the set of genetic options available for natural selection to choose among will be large and varied enough to include ones that will produce well-designed cognitive systems. The fact that humans have survived, and even prospered, for a relatively brief period of time is not in itself an adequate argument. Third, nothing in the theory implies that all, or even the majority, of our intellectual procedures, methods, and dispositions are products of biological evolution at all. They may instead be social and cultural products. Fourth, even if it is assumed that our most characteristic intellectual procedures, methods, and dispositions are the products of evolution, nothing in the theory implies that these procedures are well designed to generate accurate opinions in our current environment. At best the theory implies that they were well designed to enhance prospects for survival in the late Pleistocene, which, according to the best evidence, is when humans evolved, but what constitutes a good design for survival need not also be a good design for having accurate opinions.[19] A fortiori what constitutes a good design for survival in the Pleistocene need not be a good design for having accurate opinions in the twenty-first century.[20]

The moral is that despite the undeniable power of the theory of natural selection, appeals to it cannot provide ironclad assurances that our beliefs are for the most part accurate.

mology," in French, Uehling, and Wettstein, eds., *Midwest Studies in Philosophy* (Notre Dame, IN: University of Notre Dame Press, 1994), 243–60.

19 "[T]he selection pressures felt by organisms are dependent on the costs and benefits of various consequences. We think of hominids on the savannah as requiring an accurate way to discriminate leopards and conclude that parts of ancestral schemes of representation, having evolved under strong selection, must accurately depict the environment. Yet, where selection is intense the way it is here, the penalties are only severe for failures to recognize present predators. The hominid representation can be quite at odds with natural regularities, lumping together all kinds of harmless things with potential dangers, provided that the false positives are evolutionarily inconsequential and provided that the representation always cues the dangers." Philip Kitcher, *The Advancement of Science* (Oxford: Oxford University Press, 1993), 3000.

20 For a discussion of these and related issues, see Stephen Stich, *The Fragmentation of Reason* (Cambridge, MA: MIT Press, 1990), 55–74.

I have been expressing qualms about some trends in contemporary epistemology, but not out of nostalgia for classical foundationalism. Its day has come and gone. Had classical foundationalists been able to accomplish what they set out to do, which is nothing less than the discovery of methods and rules that would provide guarantees that our beliefs are generally accurate, it would have been a remarkable achievement. They were not able to do so, of course, and not from a lack of effort or intelligence, but rather because their project cannot be done.

However, epistemologists have found it difficult to acknowledge the full implications of the demise of classical foundationalism. One of these implications is that self-trust is an important and unavoidable element in all our intellectual projects. The above mentioned trends in contemporary epistemology mask the importance of intellectual self-trust.

Some epistemologists, for example, insist that skeptical worries are not to be taken seriously. As a result they tend not to concern themselves with whether a basic trust in the overall reliability of our most fundamental cognitive faculties and procedures is a necessary ingredient of our intellectual lives. They say that skeptical hypotheses are unnatural, or that they are self-refuting, or that they are metaphysically impossible or incompatible with what we know about the workings of natural selection. However, none of these positions is convincing.

There are deep, uncomfortable lessons to be learned from the failures of classical foundationalism. Among the most important of these lessons is that it is not unnatural to worry that our most fundamental faculties and methods might not be well suited to discover truths. Try as we may, we cannot entirely discredit this worry. In everyday contexts, entertaining general skeptical doubts is peculiar, because it requires distancing oneself from ordinary concerns. If your computer has just crashed for the third time in a week, you will not be disposed, even if you are a philosopher, to wonder whether your memories of its repeated breakdowns might be completely mistaken. A fortiori you will not discuss with the technician, except perhaps as a joke, whether there are convincing reasons for thinking that the computer really exists.[21] On the other hand, in the context of an inquiry into our role as inquirers, especially if the inquiry is a philosophical one that takes as little for

---

21 Compare with Michael Williams, *Unnatural Doubts* (Oxford: Basil Blackwell, 1991); Barry Stroud, *The Significance of Philosophical Scepticism*.

granted as possible, skeptical worries arise naturally. We worry whether our cognitive equipment and our ways of employing this equipment are well suited to produce accurate beliefs about our environment.

The proper reaction to such worries is to admit that they are unavoidable rather than to try to legislate against them. The ability that makes epistemology possible also makes skeptical concerns and questions inevitable; this is, namely, the ability to turn our methods of inquiry and the opinions they generate into objects of inquiry and to do so while taking as little for granted as possible. Within the context of such an inquiry, the worry that our beliefs might be widely mistaken is as natural as it is ineradicable. We want to defend our faculties and methods, but the only way to do so is by making use of these same faculties and methods, which means that we will never succeed in altogether ruling out the possibility that our beliefs might be broadly and deeply mistaken.

Moreover, it does not help to retreat to the claim that what is being sought are not so much assurances that our opinions are generally accurate but rather assurances that it is probable that our opinions are generally accurate, where 'probable' is given an objective interpretation, for instance, as a frequency or propensity of some sort. The retreat to probabilities leaves us in exactly the same predicament. The only way to argue that our most fundamental faculties, methods, and opinions are probably reliable is to make use of these same faculties, methods, and opinions. Just as there can be no non–question-begging guarantees that our opinions are true, and no non–question-begging guarantees that they are largely reliable, so too there can be no non–question-begging guarantees of its being probable that they are largely reliable.

This predicament is an extension of the familiar Cartesian circle, and it is a circle from which we can no more escape than could Descartes or Locke. Appeals to special methods, or to theories of belief, truth, or reference, or to the workings of natural selection are no more capable of helping us to break out of this circle than were the favored methods and theologies of Descartes and Locke.

Skeptical worries are inescapable, and the appropriate reaction to this fact about our intellectual lives is acceptance, not denial. Our lack of non–question-begging guarantees of our reliability is not a failing that needs to be corrected. It is a reality that needs to be acknowledged.[22] We must acknowledge our vulnerability to error, and acknowledge also

---

22 Ernest Sosa, "Philosophical Scepticism and Externalist Epistemology," *Proceedings of Aristotelian Society* (1994), 263–90.

that inquiry always involves a substantial element of trust in our own intellectual faculties and in the opinions they generate, the need for which cannot be eliminated by further inquiry. Significant inquiry requires an equally significant leap of intellectual faith. The faith need not, and should not, be unlimited; that is the path to dogmatism and irrationalism. But there does need to be such faith. The pressing questions for epistemologists are ones about its limits. How much trust is it appropriate for us to have in our faculties, especially our most fundamental faculties? Are there conditions under which this trust in the general reliability of our most basic faculties can be legitimately undermined? If so, what are they?

These questions are underappreciated in epistemology, in part because epistemologists have found it difficult to accept the conclusion that there are no non–question-begging assurances of our overall reliability.[23] This in turn has discouraged them from focusing upon the idea that our intellectual projects always require an element of intellectual faith and that among the most important questions in epistemology are ones about the limits of such faith. Instead, the tendency has been to look for ways of doing epistemology that bypass such questions.

This tendency has been encouraged by the unfortunate methodological assumption discussed in §1.3, namely, the assumption that the properties that make a belief rational (or justified) are by definition such that when a true belief has these properties, it is a good candidate to be an instance of knowledge, with some other condition added to handle Gettier-style counterexamples. I call this assumption 'unfortunate' because it is overly constraining. It places the theory of rational (justified) belief in service to the theory of knowledge. If it is assumed that the properties that make a belief rational must also be the very same properties that turn true belief into a good candidate for knowledge, then an account of rational belief is adequate only if it contributes to a successful account of knowledge. It is this assumption that has tempted reliabilists to stretch their proposed accounts of knowledge into accounts of epistemic justification, and that likewise has coaxed coherentists, modest foundationalists, and other internalists to regard these reliabilist accounts as competitors to their own accounts.

The remedy is for epistemologists of all persuasions, at least at the

---

23 Keith Lehrer is a notable exception. See Lehrer, *Self-Trust* (Oxford: Clarendon Press, 1997).

beginning of the enterprise, to be wary of the idea that knowledge can be adequately understood in terms of rational (justified) true belief plus some fillip to handle Gettier problems, and, correspondingly, to be wary also of the idea that there is a simple, necessary tie between the theory of rational belief and the theory of knowledge. Divorcing the theory of rational belief from the theory of knowledge is liberating for both partners. It leaves open the possibility that a belief need not be rational, in at least one important sense, to count as an instance of knowledge, and it thereby creates space for a theory of rational belief whose principal aim is to explore not what is needed for one to stand in a relation of knowledge to one's environment but rather what is required for one to have beliefs that are defensible from one's own perspective. Simultaneously, it frees the theory of knowledge from an overly intellectual conception of knowledge, thus smoothing the way for accounts that give due recognition to the fact that most people cannot provide adequate intellectual defenses for much of what they know. Such accounts can be introduced without embarrassment and without the need for awkward attempts to force back into the account some duly externalized notion of rational belief, because the definition of knowledge is thought to require it.[24]

The assumption that the conditions which make a belief rational are by definition conditions that turn a true belief into a good candidate for knowledge is needlessly limiting. It discourages the idea that there are different, equally legitimate projects for epistemologists to pursue. One project is to investigate what has to be the case in order to have knowledge. An externalist approach is well suited to this project. A distinct project, also important, is concerned with what is required to put one's own intellectual house in order. It is within this latter project that issues of intellectual self-trust most naturally arise.

The inescapability of skeptical worries is one way of illustrating the centrality of issues of intellectual self-trust, but there are more indirect ways of doing so, as well. Consider the view that one of the aims of epistemology is to improve intellectual performance. It would not have occurred to Descartes or Locke to question this assumption, but one

24 Compare with Hilary Kornblith, "Distrusting Reason," *Midwest Studies in Philosophy*, 22 (1998): "[T]he ability to form one's belief in a way which is responsive to evidence is not at all the same as the ability to present reasons for one's beliefs, either to others or to oneself."

implication of the failure of classical foundationalism is that epistemologists do not have a privileged role to play in handing out intellectual advice.

Neither Descartes nor Locke would have claimed that epistemologists are well positioned to give less than fundamental intellectual advice. The relevant experts, whether they be statisticians, medical doctors, or astronomers, are best placed to provide guidance on the issues within a given field, because they have the requisite specialized knowledge. Nor would have Descartes and Locke claimed that it is the role of epistemologists to formulate non–field-specific, intellectual rules of thumb. Such informal rules are best produced by reflection on as wide a range of data as possible. One can potentially use anything in fashioning these rules, from studies in cognitive psychology about our tendencies to make mistakes of statistical reasoning to mnemonic devices and other intellectual tricks, for example, carrying nines. Epistemologists can make contributions to the project of fashioning these rules of thumb, but qua epistemologists they are not in a specially privileged position.

On the other hand, classical foundationalists did think that they were in a special position to give useful advice about the most basic matters of inquiry. They were wrong, however. Epistemologists can provide interesting and revealing insights about the conditions of rational belief and knowledge, but it is a mistake to think that these conditions will provide us with useful guidance concerning the most basic matters of intellectual inquiry.

The lack of such guidance is a familiar complaint about externalist accounts of rational belief. For example, if an externalist account tell us that a necessary condition of being rational is that we use reliable methods, we will want to know how to determine which methods are reliable and which ones are not, but the proposed reliabilist account does not provide us with advice about how to make these determinations. What is insufficiently appreciated is that internalist accounts of rational belief are unable to do any better. Classical foundationalists thought otherwise, of course. For example, Descartes claimed that his method of doubt provides advice to inquirers that is both useful and fundamental. His recommended method is notorious for being overly demanding and, moreover, it fails to accomplish what he most wanted it to accomplish, which is a way of conducting inquiry that provides guarantees of truth. But for present purposes, it is another point that I am making. Namely, even if the method had been otherwise defensible, it would not have provided us with useful, fundamental advice. Descartes tells us to believe only those propositions whose truth we cannot doubt when we bring them clearly to mind. However, it is not always immediately obvious whether a proposition is in fact indubitable for us. Nor is it always immediately obvious whether we have succeeded in bringing a proposition clearly to mind. Thus, we can have questions about that which Descartes says is fundamental to our being rational, and these are questions that his account does not help us answer.

The proposals of coherentists, modest foundationalists, and other internalists fare no better. Coherentists, for example, say that our beliefs should cohere with one another. Suppose we grant that this is advice worth following. Then, we have to determine when our opinions are coherent and when they are not. However, the proposed conditions do not provide us with advice about how to make these determinations. Moreover, this is not an insignificant problem. It is not a simple matter to determine whether a set of beliefs is coherent, especially when the set is large.

The only way to avoid problems of this sort is to embrace an especially extreme version of foundationalism, one that insists that the conditions of rational belief are conditions to which we always have immediate and unproblematic access. Bertrand Russell defended such a view. He claimed that we are directly acquainted with certain truths and that these truths make various other propositions probable. If this kind of epistemology is to provide us with fundamental and useful intellectual advice, we must be capable of determining immediately and unproblematically when we are directly acquainted with something and when we are not. Likewise, we must be capable of determining immediately and unproblematically when a proposition is made probable by truths with which we are directly acquainted. Otherwise we will want advice as to how to make these determinations. According to Russell, we in fact do have these capabilities. We can be directly acquainted with the fact that we are directly acquainted with something. Similarly, we can be directly acquainted with the fact that one thing makes another probable.[25]

An epistemology of direct acquaintance or something closely resembling it is our only alternative if we expect the conditions of rational belief to provide us with useful advice about those matters that the conditions themselves imply are most fundamental to our being rational.

25   See Bertrand Russell, *The Problems of Philosophy* (Oxford: Oxford University Press), 1959. See also Richard Fumerton, *Metaphysical and Epistemological Problems of Perception*, especially 57–8.

It is also the kind of epistemology that few epistemologists are willing to take seriously anymore. But if we give up on this kind of epistemology, we must also give up the idea that epistemology is in the business of providing advice about the most fundamental matters of inquiry.

Correspondingly, and this returns to the main point I have been making, we must accept the idea that trust in our most basic cognitive faculties is a central part of our intellectual lives. In Russell's extreme version of foundationalism, there is no need for, indeed no room for, intellectual trust. Nothing whatsoever need be taken on trust or should be taken on trust. Once we give up on such an epistemology, we have no choice but to acknowledge that significant intellectual projects require correspondingly significant leaps of intellectual faith. The relevant question for epistemology thus becomes one of the proper limits of such faith.

2

Intellectual Self-Trust, Rational Belief, and Invulnerability to Self-Criticism

1. CONFIDENCE AND DEPTH

Part of the appeal of classical foundationalism is that it purported to provide the tools for a refutation of skepticism. With the fall of classical foundationalism, we can no longer pretend that such a refutation is possible. We must instead acknowledge that skeptical worries cannot be utterly banished and, as a result, inquiry always involves an element of trust, the need for which cannot be eliminated by further inquiry, whether it be scientific or philosophical.

The trust need not be and should not be unrestricted, however. Unquestioning faith in our faculties and in the opinions they generate is naïve and also risky, given what we know about our own fallibility. Thus, among the most pressing questions for epistemology are ones concerning the limits of self-trust. What degree of intellectual self-trust is it appropriate for us to have in our opinions and faculties, insofar as our goal is to have accurate and comprehensive beliefs? And, what kinds of considerations can undermine this trust?

An approximate answer to the first of these questions, I argue, is that trust in one's opinions ought to be proportionate to the degree of confidence one has in them and to what I call the 'depth' of this confidence. Correspondingly, trust in one's intellectual faculties, methods, and practices ought be proportionate to the degree of confidence one has in their reliability and to the depth of this confidence.

Sheer confidence is never a guarantee of truth or reliability, but for the first-person questions that are my principal concern, it is at least the place to begin. In deliberating about an intellectual issue from one's own perspective, one should begin with what one feels most sure of. Not just any kind of confidence will do, however. It is epistemic confidence that matters, that is, confidence in the accuracy of one's opinions. Epistemic confidence is to be distinguished from confidence that one can successfully defend one's opinions against attacks by others; with enough information and dialectical skills, one may be able to defend even that which one disbelieves. A fortiori, epistemic confidence is to be distinguished from confidence that an opinion is pragmatically useful (that it will have economic, social, or psychological benefits) or intellectually useful (that it will be theoretically fruitful or computationally convenient).[1]

Even epistemic confidence counts for little in and of itself, however. What does begin to count is deep confidence. Some opinions are confidently held but not deeply held. They are the doxastic counterparts of whims, impulses, and urges, which in practical reasoning are not to be treated with the same seriousness as full-blooded, less fleeting, and more deeply seated drives, preferences, and needs. An analogous point is true of theoretical reasoning. Hunches, inklings, and other shallow opinions are not to be treated with the same seriousness as deeply held convictions.

What distinguishes deeply held from shallowly held opinions is not mere revisability. Virtually all of our opinions are revisable over time. There are conceivable turns of events and evidence that would cause us to abandon or modify them. On the other hand, for some opinions, even some that are confidently held, new evidence is not needed to make one critical of them. All that is required is a little reflection.

Other opinions are not so shallow, however. Some are the products of such careful thinking that they are unlikely to be affected by further deliberation. Others are acquired with little thought but are nonetheless deeply held. For example, most perceptual beliefs are not the products of deliberation. We acquire them automatically, and yet many are such that reflection would not prompt us to revise them. They are reflectively stable, in the sense that we would continue to endorse them on reflection.

Like confidence, depth is a matter of degree, varying inversely with how vulnerable the opinion is to criticism on reflection. Some opinions

---

1 Compare with Keith Lehrer's distinction between belief and acceptance. 'Acceptance' is Lehrer's term for a positive evaluation of a belief from an epistemic point of view: "Beliefs . . . sometimes arise capriciously and sometimes perversely within me and contrary to my better judgement. . . . The objective of acceptance is to accept something if it is worth accepting as true and to avoid acceptance of what is not." Lehrer, *Self-Trust: A Study of Reason, Knowledge and Autonomy*, 3.

are such that even superficial reflection would be enough to undermine one's trust in them. Others are such that only lengthy or difficult reflection would undermine them. Still others are such that one would continue to endorse them even if one were to be ideally reflective.

So, to repeat, not every opinion is equally appropriate to trust and equally suitable for deliberating about what else to believe. The rough rule is that the more confidently and deeply held an opinion is, the more invulnerable to self-criticism it is and, hence, the more one is entitled to rely on it, at least until some new consideration or evidence arises that interferes with its credibility.

2. RATIONAL BELIEF AS INVULNERABILITY TO SELF-CRITICISM

My primary interest is to develop an account of intellectual self-trust from a first person, epistemological point of view, by which I mean an account of the degree of trust one can have in one's opinions and faculties without making oneself vulnerable to self-criticism, insofar as one's goal is to have accurate and comprehensive beliefs. The above rule, which recommends that trust be proportionate to the degree and depth of one's epistemic confidence in one's opinions and faculties, represents the beginnings of such an account; but in my view, it also represents the beginnings of an account of epistemically rational belief, because one important sense of rational belief can be understood in terms of invulnerability to self-criticism. Accordingly, I use the language of epistemic rationality to express and defend various claims about the degree of intellectual self-trust it is appropriate to have in one's opinions and faculties. Nevertheless, these claims are independent of my account of epistemically rational belief. One can reject the latter and still accept the former, although one would have to employ more cumbersome terminology. Instead of talking to the degree of self-trust it is epistemically rational for one to have in one's opinions and faculties, one would need to talk about the degree of self-trust one can have in one's opinions and faculties without making oneself vulnerable to self-criticism insofar as one's goals is to have accurate and comprehensive beliefs.

My principal goal, to repeat, is to develop an account of what necessitates intellectual trust, how extensive it should be, and what might undermine it. Later in this chapter, I discuss to what extent the discovery of inconsistency in one's belief system undermines self-trust, and in Chapter 3, I discuss how information about the tendency of people in

27

general to make mistakes of reasoning and judgement can raise questions about the trust one should have in one's own opinions. But because I express my conclusions about these and other issues in terms of the degree of trust it is epistemically rational to have in one's opinions and faculties, it will be useful to set issues of intellectual trust to one side for a moment and explain why I think that one important sense of rational belief can be understood in terms of invulnerability to self-criticism.

I say 'one sense' because 'rational belief' can be used in a variety of senses. In Chapter 1, I talk about two of the senses common in the literature, one which tends to be externalist and closely connected with what is required to turn true belief into a good candidate for knowledge, and the other which tends to be internalist and closely connected with what is required to have internally defensible beliefs. It is this second sense that can be understood in terms of making oneself invulnerable to intellectual self-criticism to the extent possible.

Epistemic rationality in this sense is a matter of having opinions that are capable of standing up to one's own, most severe scrutiny. For an opinion to pass this test, it must not be the case that one's other opinions could be used to mount what on reflection one would regard as a convincing critique of the accuracy of the opinion. Nor can it be the case that on reflection one could mount a convincing critique of the faculties, methods, and practices that one takes to be responsible for one's having the opinion. In other words, not only must the opinion be in accord with one's other reflective first-order opinions, it must also be in accord with one's reflective second-order opinions about the ways one can reliably acquire opinions.

Even opinions that are currently invulnerable to self-criticism are revisable over time, however. Additional evidence can undermine even the most confidently and deeply held opinions. Getting one's opinions to fit together so well that one is invulnerable to self-criticism does not provide one with a final intellectual resting place, which gives one immunity from the need for future revisions. Thus, it does not entitle one to be complacent, but it does at least achieve, in Robert Frost's memorable phrase, "a momentary stay against confusion."

Opinions are not the only phenomena that can be assessed for their rationality. Actions, decisions, intentions, strategies, methods, and plans can also be judged as rational or irrational. Moreover, there is a common way of understanding all these assessments; they are claims from a given perspective about how effectively the belief, action, decision, and so on promotes a goal or set of goals. More precisely, this is so for what might be called a 'strong' sense of rationality. In a weak sense, one is rational only if one's cognitive states are sufficiently rich and complex to warrant being assessed as either rational or irrational in the strong sense. To say that something is rational in this weak sense contrasts with saying that it is arational. Mountains, rivers, rocks, buildings, and acorns are neither rational nor irrational in the strong sense; they are arational. Only things which are not arational are capable of being rational or irrational in a strong sense. It is strong senses of rationality that are to be understood in terms of goals and perspectives.

A perspective is a set of beliefs, but a convenient way of identifying these beliefs is by reference to the individual whose beliefs they are. My perspective is constituted by my beliefs, your perspective by your beliefs, and so on for other individuals. Groups of individuals can also have perspectives. The perspective of my two brothers is constituted by their shared beliefs, and the perspective of a community is constituted by the beliefs widely shared by the individuals making up the community. By extension, we can also talk of the perspectives of hypothetical individuals. The perspective of an omniscient observer, for example, is constituted by the beliefs that a being with perfect knowledge would have. Likewise, we can speak of the perspective that an individual would have on reflection.

We assess each other's actions, beliefs, decisions, and so on from various perspectives, depending on our interests and the situation. For example, we sometimes evaluate decisions from the perspective of what a verific believer would have done in the decision maker's situation, where a verific believer is one who knows what the consequences would be of each of the alternatives open to the decision maker. We then use the language of rationality to express these evaluations. The decision was rational in this fully objective sense if it accords with the decision that a verific believer would have made in the situation in question. More precisely, a decision is rational in this sense if from the perspective of this hypothetical verific believer, its desirability is sufficiently high to make it a satisfactory option given the context, where desirability is a function of both the effectiveness of the decision in promoting the goals in question and the relative values of these goals,[2] and where the context is defined by the relative desirability of the alternatives and their relative accessibility to the decision maker. The fewer the alternatives there are

2 Compare with Richard Jeffrey, *The Logic of Decision*, 2nd ed. (Chicago: University of Chicago Press, 1983).

with greater desirability and the less readily accessible they are, the more likely it is that the decision in question is rational. It is rational not necessarily because it is the single best option, but rather because it is good enough given the context.

However, if from our external vantage point we are aware that no one could be reasonably expected to foresee what a verific believer would foresee about the consequences of a decision, we may be more interested in evaluating the decision from the perspective of what a reasonably knowledgeable, normal person would have done in the decision maker's situation. And again, often enough, in both legal and everyday contexts, we use the language of rationality to express this evaluation. The decision in question is reasonable only if it accords with what a normal, reasonable person could be expected to do in that kind of situation, where this hypothetical, normal individual is not to be thought of as someone who knows with certainty the consequences of each of the options available to the decision maker, but rather as a contemporary who is well informed and, as such, is in possession of widely available information about the probabilities of various options yielding various outcomes.

Sometimes, however, especially when the decision maker belongs to a time or culture that we judge to be less advanced than our own, it seems unfair to compare the decision with the one that would have been made either by a verific believer or by someone who is well informed by contemporary standards. It seems more appropriate and also more interesting to evaluate the individual's decision relative to the standards and level of knowledge that were in the air in her community, and once again we may give expression to this evaluation using the language of rationality and irrationality. Her decision was irrational, we may conclude, not so much because relatively well-informed contemporaries of ours would have judged it to be an ineffective way of promoting her goals, but rather because relatively well-informed people in her own community would have so regarded it.

On yet other occasions, we are interested in evaluating a decision not from the perspective of a verific believer or from the perspective of someone who is reasonably well informed by contemporary standards or from the perspective of the decision maker's community, but rather from the perspective of the very individual who is making the decision. We want to project ourselves to the extent possible into the decision maker's skin and see the decision from her personal viewpoint. One kind of situation in which we are especially likely to be interested in doing this is when the decision has turned out badly. In retrospect, it may even be obvious to us why it turned out badly and, accordingly, we are perplexed by it. Simply dismissing the decision as irrational does not remove our bewilderment. Besides, we may be inclined to be charitable, assuming that there may have been something in her situation, not immediately apparent to us, that resulted in her not recognizing what seems so apparent to us.

So, we try to enter into her situation and see the decision from her perspective. We bracket to the extent possible information that is now available to us but was not available to her, and we try to locate grounds for the decision that might have seemed appropriate to her, given her information and situation. The grounds might strike us as unacceptably risky or unreliable, and they might have struck even her contemporaries in the same way, but we might nonetheless grant that they were convincing and even natural for her. If we succeed in discovering grounds that identify the decision as a satisfactory one relative to her information, circumstances, and outlook, we can express this finding by saying that we have shown why, in at least one sense of "reason," she had reasons for her decision and hence, why, in at least one sense of "rational," the decision was a rational, albeit mistaken, one for her to have made. By contrast, if we judge that even given her limited information, she would have seen the decision's shortcomings had she been more reflective, we will conclude that we have shown in an especially convincing way why her decision was irrational. It was irrational not so much because it was at odds with what a knowledgeable observer by our standards would have regarded as a satisfactory way of achieving her goals, and not so much because it was at odds with what reasonably well-informed people in her own community would have regarded as a satisfactory way of achieving her goals, but rather because it was at odds with what she herself would have regarded as satisfactory had she been more careful, more reflective, and more vigilant.

This notion of rational (and irrational) decision is the practical counterpart of the notion of epistemically rational belief that is my principal concern, a notion that is to be understood in terms of a distinctively epistemic goal, that of now having an accurate and comprehensive belief system, and the individual's own perspective on reflection. An individual's belief is rational in this sense if on reflection she would think that her belief effectively promotes the goal of her now having accurate and comprehensive beliefs. On the other hand, if on reflection she herself would be critical of the belief, insofar as her goal is now to have accurate and comprehensive beliefs, her belief is irrational.

How lengthy are we to conceive this reflection as being? Is it enough that the individual would not be critical of her belief were she to reflect for a few moments, or is it necessary that she would not be critical of it even if she were to engage in lengthy reflection? The brief answer is that there must be a point of reflective stability. If one imagines a continuum from no reflection to increasingly lengthy reflection, there must be a point along this continuum that is such that she would endorse the belief, and that is also such that there is no point further along the continuum at which she would be critical of it (insofar as her goal is to have accurate and comprehensive beliefs). For some beliefs, the point of reflective stability is the current state. These beliefs are reflectively stable as they are; no amount of reflection would undermine them. Other beliefs are such that the point of reflective stability would be reached with brief reflection. With still others, it would be reached only with lengthy reflection, and with yet others, it would not be reached at all, in which case the beliefs are not epistemically rational.[3]

For an opinion to be rational in this sense, the individual need not actually deliberate in arriving at the opinion. It is enough that were she to be sufficiently reflective, she would endorse the opinion and further reflection would not prompt her to change her mind. Indeed, it may be unreasonable for her to spend time deliberating about the opinion. All of us have multiple goals, which place constraints on how much effort we should devote to intellectual pursuits. The amount of time and effort that it is reasonable for an individual to spend in investigating and reflecting on an topic is a function of the topic's importance, given the individual's total constellation of goals, both intellectual and practical. If a topic is insignificant, it is irrational to devote time or effort to it.

Considerations such as these illustrate that there is an important distinction between epistemically rational belief and what can be termed 'responsible belief'. Assume that a topic T has little intellectual or practical importance. Then it is not reasonable, given the total constellation of an individual's goals, for her to devote very much time to thinking about it. Nevertheless, suppose it is the case that were she to reflect thoroughly, she would be critical of her current beliefs about T, insofar as her goal is to have accurate and comprehensive beliefs. Under these

---

3   For more details, see Foley, *Working Without a Net*, 98–100.

conditions, her beliefs about T are not epistemically rational, because she herself on reflection would be critical of them, insofar as her goal is to have accurate and comprehensive beliefs, but they may nonetheless be responsible beliefs for her to have, given that it was reasonable, relative to all of her goals, for her not to engage in this reflection.[4]

In characterizing epistemic rationality in terms of a present-tense epistemic goal, that of now having an accurate and comprehensive belief system, I am assuming that goals can be concerned with current states of affairs as well as future states of affairs and, correspondingly, also assuming that there can be both constitutive and causally effective means to goals. If someone has the goal of being in good health and if good health is a state in which one not only lacks disease but also is not prone to disease, then not having high blood pressure is not so much a causal means to the goal of good health but rather part of what constitutes good health. Similarly, if being wise is incompatible with being rash, then not being rash is not a causal means to the goal of being wise but rather part of what constitutes being wise. Moreover, insofar as it is valuable for one not just to be wise and in good health in the future but also to be wise and in good health now, then now not being rash and now not having high blood pressure is part of what is involved in achieving the goal of now being wise and healthy. In an analogous manner, believing P can be a part of what is involved in achieving the goal of now having accurate and comprehensive beliefs.

Nevertheless, if anyone thinks that I am stretching the standard meanings of 'goal' and 'means' too far, it is easy enough to devise alternative terminology. 'Goal' can be replaced with 'desideratum' or 'value', and 'means' with a locution about what is appropriate or fitting given this desideratum. The overall schema for understanding the epistemic rationality of a belief P thus becomes: Insofar as it is a desideratum (that is, a valuable state of affairs) for one now to have accurate and comprehensive beliefs, it is appropriate (that is, fitting) for one now to believe P, if on reflection one would regard believing P as part of what is involved in one's now having accurate and comprehensive beliefs.

To understand the rationale for characterizing epistemic rationality in terms of a present-tense, intellectual goal, imagine that one's prospects

---

4 For a discussion of the distinction between epistemically rational belief and responsible belief, see Richard Foley, "The Foundational Role of Epistemology in a General Theory of Rationality," in L. Zagzebski and A. Fairweather, eds., *Virtue Epistemology* (Oxford: Oxford University Press, 2001).

for having accurate and comprehensive beliefs in a year's time would be enhanced by believing something for which one now lacks adequate evidence. For example, suppose a proposition P involves a more favorable assessment of my intellectual talents than my evidence warrants, but suppose also that believing P would make me more intellectually confident than I would be otherwise, which would make me a more dedicated inquirer, which in turn would enhance my long-term prospects of having an accurate and comprehensive belief system. Despite these long-term benefits, there is an important sense of rational belief, indeed the very sense that traditionally has been of the most interest to epistemologists, in which it is not rational for me to believe P. Moreover, the point of this example is not affected by shortening the time period in which the benefits are forthcoming. It would not be rational, in this sense, for me to believe P if we were instead to imagine that believing P would somehow improve my prospects for having accurate and comprehensive beliefs in the next few weeks, or in the next few hours, or even in the next few seconds. The precise way of making this point, in light of the above distinctions, is to say that in such a situation, it is not rational in a purely epistemic sense for me to believe P, where this purely epistemic sense is to be understood in terms of the present-tense goal of now having accurate and comprehensive beliefs.

This notion of epistemic rationality can be loosely characterized in terms of what one would continue to believe were one to be reflective, but it is more precise to say that a belief is rational in this sense if it is capable of standing up to one's own critical scrutiny. Beliefs that would survive reflection are usually also such that one would not be critical of them on reflection, and vice versa, but occasionally the distinction is important. Some beliefs are reflexive and, as such, tend to be unaffected by deliberation, for instance, beliefs about what one is directly perceiving. Suppose I believe that I see a red ball in front of me, but suppose also that if I were to reflect, I would recall that I have been taking a drug which often causes highly realistic hallucinations. Nevertheless, it might still be psychologically difficult for me not to believe that I am seeing a red ball. Even so, my belief need not be epistemically rational, because what makes a belief epistemically rational is not that it would survive reflection but rather that it would be immune to criticism on reflection, insofar as one's goal is to have accurate and comprehensive beliefs.

Automatic beliefs provide one illustration of the distinction between beliefs that would survive reflection and those that one would not criticize were one to be reflective, but there are other examples as well. Let P be the proposition that banana quits resemble goldfinches, and let P' be the proposition that I am currently thinking about P. Assume that I am in fact not thinking about banana quits or goldfinches, and as a result I do not believe P'. On the contrary, I disbelieve it, that is, believe that notP' is true. Like most of my beliefs at any moment, this belief is latent, since by hypothesis I am not thinking about banana quits or goldfinches. So far, there is nothing unusual about this case. It is simply an instance of the familiar distinction between activated and latent beliefs. Notice, however, that if I were to reflect on P', I would also be reflecting on P, since the proposition P' includes the proposition P. But then, I might very well come to believe P', and moreover it would be appropriate for me to do so, because I would now be thinking about banana quits and goldfinches. Nevertheless, this does not mean that my current opinion about P' is irrational. All it indicates is that the nature of the proposition P' is such that were I reflect upon it, the reflection itself would alter what it is reasonable for me to believe about P'. Reflecting on P' creates a reason, which currently does not exist, to believe P'. So, in this case, even though my opinion about P' on reflection would be different from my current opinion, and even though on reflection it would be appropriate for me to have this different opinion, these are not grounds for me to be critical of my current opinion.

I have said that if one's opinions are invulnerable to self-criticism, insofar as one's goal is to have accurate and comprehensive beliefs, they are rational in an important sense, but to accommodate such cases, as well as cases of automatic belief, invulnerability to intellectual self-criticism must be understood in terms of reflection on one's current doxastic attitudes, and not merely reflection on the propositional content of these attitudes. In particular, one current opinion about a proposition can be invulnerable to self-criticism in the relevant sense and, hence, be rational, even if one would appropriately have a different opinion about the proposition on reflection. The key issue is not whether on reflection one would believe what one currently believes but rather whether one's current attitude can withstand reflective scrutiny. Ordinarily these amount to the same thing, but as the above cases illustrate, this is not always so.[5]

5 Contrast this with the account of rational belief I defend in *Working Without a Net*. In that account, like the above account, I defend the idea that if one's opinions can withstand one's

A variety of other useful epistemological distinctions can be spelled out in terms of this general conception of epistemic rationality. According to the conception, a proposition P is epistemically rational for me if on reflection I would not be critical of my believing P, insofar as my goal is now to have accurate and comprehensive beliefs. If the proposition P is epistemically rational for me and I believe P, my belief is rational in one important sense, a propositional sense, but it need not be doxastically rational. For the belief to be doxastically rational, it must also be the case that I have acquired it, and am sustaining it, in an appropriate way. More precisely, the way I acquired and am sustaining the belief must not be such that on reflection I would be critical of it, insofar as my goal is to have accurate and comprehensive beliefs. For example, if I am in possession of information that on reflection I would regard as convincing evidence of Jones' guilt but, unbeknownst to me, it is my dislike of Jones rather than this evidence that causes me to believe that Jones is guilty, then my belief is propositionally rational but it need not be doxastically rational.[6]

Concepts of prima facie (epistemic) reason and prima facie (epistemic) rationality can also be developed out of the above conception. To say that a set of considerations constitutes a prima facie reason for me to believe P is to say that (1) I believe that this set of considerations obtains, (2) this belief is propositionally rational for me, and (3) on reflection I would think that when these considerations obtain, P is sufficiently likely to be true to make believing P appropriate, all else being equal, insofar as my goal is now to have accurate and comprehensive beliefs. My belief P is prima facie rational, then, just in case there is a prima facie reason for me to believe P.

In addition, the concept of one doxastic attitude being more reasonable than another can be explicated in terms of the above concepts. To say that in my current circumstances believing P is more reasonable for me than believing Q is to say that on reflection I would think that given

own critical scrutiny on reflection, they are rational in an important sense. However, in the *Working Without a Net* account, the target of reflection is on the proposition itself. The account thus implies that if on reflection one's opinion of a proposition would be different from one's current opinion, then one's current opinion is to that extent irrational. The above cases show that this is not always so. I am grateful to Marian David, Alvin Plantinga, Ernest Sosa, and Fritz Warfield for pointing out to me the relevance of these cases.

6 For a more detailed discussion of the distinction between propositionally rational beliefs and doxastically rational beliefs, see Richard Foley, *The Theory of Epistemic Rationality* (Cambridge, MA: Harvard University Press, 1987), 175–86.

such circumstances, believing P is more appropriate than believing Q, insofar as my goal is now to have accurate and comprehensive beliefs. Similarly, to say that in my current circumstances withholding on P is more reasonable than either believing or disbelieving P is to say that on reflection I would think that given such circumstances, withholding on P is more appropriate than either believing or disbelieving P, insofar as my goal is now to have accurate and comprehensive beliefs.

3. TWO THOUGHT EXPERIMENTS

Two kinds of thought experiments, each focusing on an extreme situation, place in sharp relief some of the most important features of the above notion of epistemic rationality. Consider, first, the familiar skeptical thought experiments, for instance, the brain-in-a-vat hypothesis, which imagines a world in which, unbeknownst to you, your brain is in a vat hooked up to equipment programmed to provide it with precisely the same visual, auditory, tactile, and other sensory inputs that you have in this world. As a result, your opinions about your immediate environment are the same as they are in this world. You have the same beliefs about your recent activities, your current physical appearance, your present job, and so on, but in fact you are a brain in a vat tucked away in a corner of a laboratory. Thus, in the brain-in-a-vat world, these beliefs are mistaken and mistaken not just in detail, but deeply mistaken. Even so, nothing in this scenario implies that you are irrational. On the contrary, in at least one important sense, your beliefs in the brain-in-a-vat world are as rational as they are in this world. After all, from your point of view, there is nothing to distinguish the two worlds.

The brain-in-a-vat scenario is an especially extreme example of a class of hypotheses that imagine our being extensively deceived by someone or something. Hypotheses of this general sort are possible even if one presupposes the adequacy of 'externalist' accounts of belief, which maintain that the contents of beliefs are shaped by external as well as internal factors. Thus, what one believes in two situations can be different even if from the skin inward one is identical in the two situations. Externalist accounts of belief are themselves controversial, but for purposes here, it is a narrower point that needs making, namely, hypotheses that imply that one's beliefs are extensively mistaken are compatible with all but the most extreme versions of belief externalism. All versions of belief externalism imply that the contents of one's beliefs are determined by external as well as internal factors, but only the most extreme versions allow the former to dominate the latter to such an extent that it becomes impossible for one's beliefs to be extensively mistaken. Indeed, a plausibility constraint on any proposed account of belief is that it not rule out, a priori, the possibility of extensive error.[7] Any account of belief that meets this plausibility constraint will be compatible with thought experiments that imagine two situations, indistinguishable from your viewpoint, in which you have very similar beliefs but in which these beliefs differ markedly in accuracy.

Being a brain-in-a-vat, or for that matter being in any situation in which you are thoroughly deceived, seriously disadvantages you. It deprives you of knowledge, but one of the lessons of such thought experiments is that being thoroughly deceived does not also automatically prevent you from being rational in one important sense, a sense that is closely associated with how things look from your perspective. Accuracy of opinion is the goal of this kind of rationality, but not an absolute prerequisite of it. Even in a bubbling vat, it is possible for you to have rational opinions. You may be a brain-in-a-vat, but you can nonetheless be a rational brain-in-a-vat.

A second thought experiment concerns intellectual rebels who consciously reject the prevailing opinions of their communities and the intellectual practices and assumptions of their traditions. The history of ideas is filled with examples of iconoclasts and mavericks. Indeed, according to one influential reading of the history of science, scientific progress is largely the result of those who foment scientific revolutions by replacing the prevailing paradigm with a new one. With respect to any specific instance of intellectual rebellion, there will always be questions about the extent to which the rebels were rejecting the opinions and practices of their contemporaries as opposed to making novel applications of opinions and practices that were already in the air; but these historical questions do not affect the key conceptual point of the thought experiment, which is that in one important sense, being rational is not a matter of adhering to the opinions, rules, practices, or presuppositions of one's community or tradition. Even if, historically, most intellectual revolutionaries draw heavily upon assumptions and standards implicit in their intellectual traditions, there are possible scenarios in which this is

---

7   See Peter Klein, "Radical Interpretation and Global Skepticism," in E. LePore, ed., *Truth and Interpretation* (Oxford: Basil Blackwell, 1986), 369–386; Colin McGinn, "Radical Interpretation and Epistemology," in LePore, op. cit., 356–368; and Richard Foley, *Working Without a Net*, 67–75.

not the case, that is, scenarios in which the revolutionaries reject in a wholesale manner the prevailing intellectual assumptions and practices. In these scenarios, the radical nature of their opinions does not necessarily preclude these opinions from being rational in at least one important sense.

These two thought experiments help mark off the boundaries of, and also dramatize the need for, a notion of rationality that cannot be understood in terms of reliability or in terms of social practices. Being rational in this sense is instead a matter of making oneself invulnerable to intellectual self-criticism to the extent possible, of living up to one's own deepest intellectual convictions and standards. It requires one to have opinions and to use faculties, methods, and practices that are capable of withstanding one's own, most severe critical scrutiny. Accordingly, one can be rational in this sense even if one is a brain-in-a-vat whose opinions are massively unreliable, and likewise one can be rational even if one's opinions, methods, and assumptions are massively at odds with those of one's community, era, and tradition.

These thought experiments also help illustrate other key characteristics of this notion of rational belief, as well as forestall some possible objections against it. For example, they help make clear various respects in which this notion of rational belief is internalist. It is internalist, first, because the conditions that make a belief rational in this sense are internal psychological conditions, which involve no significant, direct reference to conditions external to the individual. It is not a prerequisite, for example, that the faculties or procedures generating the belief be ones that are reliable in the individual's environment. Second, the notion is internalist in that it emphasizes the perspectives of individuals, as opposed to the perspective of an individual's community or some other perspective external to the individual. What any given individual believes is almost always deeply influenced by what other people believe. Nevertheless, the conditions that make an individual's beliefs rational in the above sense involve no significant, direct reference to the beliefs of other people. Third, when one's opinions are irrational, one is capable of generating one's own critique of those opinions. One need not rely on anything or anyone external to oneself to generate the criticism; all that is needed is thorough enough reflection. Thus, one has internal access in this sense to the conditions that make an opinion irrational.[8]

---

8 An opinion is rational, according to this account, only if one would not be critical of it on reflection, but because there is no transparent mark indicating when one has been suffi-

One can be rational in this sense despite having various intellectual flaws. Just as having opinions that are invulnerable to self-criticism does not inoculate one against the possibility of radical error, so too it does not inoculate one against other intellectual failings. The following joke, told by Peter Klein, illustrates this point. A psychiatrist was counseling a patient with a history of delusional beliefs. The patient was insisting that he was dead, and the psychiatrist was trying to persuade him out of his belief. The psychiatrist managed to get the patient to agree that the blood of dead people tends to coagulate rather than flow freely. The psychiatrist then proposed a test: "If I cut your finger and the blood flows, this will establish that you are not dead." The patient agreed to the test. The psychiatrist pricked the patient's finger, and blood flowed freely from the finger. The patient looked confused for a moment, but then confidently proclaimed, "I must have been wrong about the blood of dead people not flowing."

In reacting in this way, the patient was displaying an intellectual flaw, but he was not necessarily being irrational. It is conceivable that his opinions, albeit bizarre, were capable of standing up to his own toughest critical scrutiny. His first-order opinions and his second-order opinions about the faculties, methods, and practices used to generate and revise his first-order opinions may have fit together in a way that satisfied his own deepest intellectual dispositions. So, it is at least possible that he was being rational despite having opinions that were seriously mistaken, perhaps even delusional. Michel Foucault was fond of pointing out that the insane often reason impeccably from their delusionary premises. In a similar spirit, G. K. Chesterton once observed that madness is not always the absence of reason; sometimes it is the absence of everything else.[9]

ciently reflective (sufficient that additional reflection would not change one's mind), this notion of rational belief carries with it no commitment to the positive counterpart of access internalism. That is, it does not follow from the account that when one's belief is rational, one invariably has access to the conditions that make it rational. For a discussion of access internalism, see William Alston, "Internalism and Externalism in Epistemology," in Alston, *Epistemic Justification*, especially 211–23.

9 This is not to say, however, that there are no limits to irrationality. Various kinds of conditions may place constraints on irrationality. For example, the conditions that must be met for someone to have beliefs at all may constrain how irrational the beliefs of an individual can be. This is a point which Donald Davidson tries to exploit to great effect. Davidson argues that if we cannot from our point of view discern sufficient orderliness, logicality, and connectedness in the utterances and behavior of creatures we are trying to understand, we will not be able to ascribe beliefs to them at all. A fortiori, we will not be able to ascribe irrational beliefs to them. As discussed above, Davidson unsuccessfully tries

There is both a specific lesson and a more general lesson which the above story illustrates. The specific lesson is that being fixed on an opinion is not necessarily a mark of irrationality. This is so even in scientific contexts. As Duhem and Quine have both emphasized,[10] there are always ways of immunizing a favored scientific hypothesis against revision when faced with recalcitrant data. Background assumptions, auxiliary hypotheses, and even observational reports can be revised in order to shield the hypothesis against revision. To be sure, such protective maneuvers may result in theories that are needlessly complex and inelegant, and these are defects that are to be avoided, all else being equal. Be this as it may, one's opinions can display such defects but nonetheless be rational in one important sense.

The more general lesson is that not all intellectual flaws are marks of irrationality. Being fixed on an opinion is an intellectual failing but not necessarily a failure of rationality, and the same is true of many, other intellectual shortcomings. Imagine individuals who think that simple direct observation is a less reliable way of getting information about the environment than, say, relying on dreams. Most of us are convinced that perception generally provides us with reliable information about the world. Our beliefs typically extend well beyond what we can directly perceive, but direct observational beliefs, we think, provide a kind of tether even for these beliefs. They constrain our other beliefs and, we trust, prevent them from being utter fabrications. By contrast, the above individuals think, and we can stipulate that on reflection they would continue to think, that perception is a less reliable way of getting information about the world than relying on their dreams. If their opinions about the external world somehow manage to be in accord with these convictions, these opinions might conceivably pass the above test of epistemic rationality.

Because the convictions of such people strike most of us as seriously mistaken, it can be tempting to insist that an adequate account of epistemic rationality should include conditions that altogether preclude the possibility of these people being epistemically rational. Building such conditions into the account of epistemically rationality would have the effect of making it a necessary truth that people who regulate their

to convert this point into a refutation of skepticism. Nevertheless, his argument does suggest that there may be limits on irrationality, even if the limits are distant ones.

10   Pierre Duhem, *The Aims and Structure of Physical Theory*, trans. P. Wiener (Princeton, NJ: Princeton University Press, 1951); W. V. Quine, "Two Dogmas of Empiricism."

opinions in accordance with such convictions are being irrational. Tempting as this may be, especially to philosophers who sometimes seem prone to construing every intellectual defect as a mark of irrationality, it is a temptation to be avoided. Not every intellectual failing is a failing of rationality. For most of us, it would be seriously irrational to organize our opinions about the external world in accordance with our dreams as opposed to our observations, but not so much because doing so is intrinsically irrational, but rather because doing so is sharply inconsistent with our own deepest convictions about how to obtain information about the external world. Most of us are convinced that relying on perception is a more effective way of having accurate and comprehensive beliefs than relying on dreams. For example, I believe that when I seem to see a cat in front of me, then all else being equal it is reliable for me to believe that there is in fact a cat in front of me. Moreover, I have similar convictions about ostensible memories. I believe that when I seem to remember seeing to see a cat in front of me yesterday, then all else being equal it is reliable for me to believe that in fact I did seem to see a cat in front of me yesterday. By contrast, I do not think that relying on dreams is a straightforwardly reliable way to form opinions about the external world. I once dreamed that I had a conversation with my grandfather when I was an adult and he was a child, but I did not take the dream as indicating that such a conversation in fact ever took place.

It is convictions such as these that provide the epistemic principles of Roderick Chisholm with an aura of plausibility. Chisholm's principles collectively describe what he takes to be the principal sources of empirical justification – namely, introspection, perception, memory, and coherence of propositions with some antecedent positive epistemic status.[11] Many questions of details can be raised concerning these principles, but it is hard to deny that there is an intuitive pull to the suggestion that it is rational to regulate one's beliefs in accordance with them. However, Chisholm regards his principles as necessary truths. As such, he is committed to saying that they apply even to people whose reflective views about how to seek truth are quite different from those held by most of us. I disagree. I regard his principles as plausible generalities. They, or at least something like them, reflect the deep epistemic convictions of most people. Contrary to what Chisholm claims, the plausibility of his prin-

11 See Roderick M. Chisholm, *Theory of Knowledge*, editions in 1966, 1977, and 1989 (Englewood Cliffs, NJ: Prentice-Hall).

ciples is not the result of an a priori insight that allows us to recognize that his principles capture necessary truths about how to conduct inquiry. Rather, their plausibility is to be accounted for by the above notion of epistemic rationality and the contingent (although hard to avoid) fact that most of us believe, and on reflection would continue to believe, that introspection, perception, memory, and coherence are, in general, reliable ways of regulating opinion. Ultimately, it is this that makes it rational for most of us to have the kind of beliefs that the principles recommend.[12] On the other hand, were there to be people with very different, deep convictions about how to seek truth, Chisholm's principles would not describe what it is rational for them to believe. What it would be rational for them to believe would depend upon their deep epistemic standards and convictions, not ours. This is so even if, as we believe, their standards and convictions are deeply and irrevocably mistaken.

On the other hand, suppose that it is our standards, not theirs, that are irrevocably mistaken. For example, suppose that contrary to what we deeply believe, a demon had altered our world so that dreams are in general a more reliable way to get information about our environment than perception. Even so, this in no way implies that it is rational for us to rely on dreams as opposed to perception. It only shows that in these matters, as in other matters, we are fallible. The same fallibilistic lesson applies even to the logic we employ. It is at least possible that we are currently not even in a position to know the correct logic for dealing with vagueness and the semantical paradoxes. Suppose, then, that we are in fact employing an incorrect logic and that one hundred years from now we discover the correct logic. Nevertheless, this would not imply that we had been being irrational up until then.[13]

Just as the above sense of rational belief accounts for the underlying plausibility of Chisholm's epistemic principles, so too it accounts for the underlying plausibility of the method of reflective equilibrium, first proposed by Nelson Goodman for bringing into accord our judgments about particular inferences and our judgments about general principles

12   For a more detailed discussion of Chisholm's epistemic principles, see Richard Foley, "Chisholm's Epistemology," in L. Hahn ed., *The Philosophy of Roderick M. Chisholm* (Chicago: Open Court, 1997), 241–64.

13   See Hartry Field, "Disquotational Truth and Factually Defective Discourse," *Philosophical Review* 103 (1994), 405–52; and Field, "A Prioricity as an Evaluative Notion," draft.

of inference,[14] and later used by John Rawls for justifying moral principles and moral judgments.[15] What recommends the method of reflective equilibrium is that if all goes well, it results in judgments capable of withstanding one's own deepest critical scrutiny and, consequently, judgments that are rational in the above sense.

According to the above account, an individual's opinions are rational in an important sense if they are invulnerable to self-criticism, where this in turn is a function of the individual's deepest and firmest convictions, which are typically absorbed from one's social environment. Humans are social beings, intellectually as well as behaviorally, and as such their opinions and intellectual standards are typically shaped by the people, culture, and tradition surrounding them. Thus, social factors ordinarily play a major role in determining what it is epistemically rational for an individual to believe. However, they do so in an indirect and contingent way, through shaping the individual's deepest convictions and standards. Consequently, as the thought experiment involving intellectual iconoclasts illustrates, it is possible, given the above account, for one's opinions to be seriously at odds with one's contemporaries and tradition and yet still be capable of withstanding one's own most severe critical scrutiny and, hence, still be rational.

This conclusion is in tension with the views of thinkers as otherwise diverse as Peirce, Wittgenstein, Rorty, Latour, Vygotsky, and Foucault, all of whom conceive rationality as being constituted in some way by social practices.[16] On such accounts, there is a necessary connection between what is rational and what the community or tradition would approve or at least tolerate. Accounts of this sort have also been embraced, in stronger or weaker forms, by a number of sociologists and historians of science.[17] One of the characteristic drawbacks of such accounts is that they are inherently conservative. They risk canonizing the

---

14 Nelson Goodman, *Fact, Fiction and Forecast* (Indianapolis: Bobbs-Merrill, 1965).

15 John Rawls, *A Theory of Justice* (Cambridge, MA: Harvard University Press, 1971).

16 C. S. Peirce, *Collected Works* (Cambridge, MA: Harvard University Press, 1958); Ludwig Wittgenstein, *On Certainty*, trans. G. E. M. Anscombe and G. H. Von Wright (New York: Harper, 1969); Richard Rorty, *Philosophy and the Mirror of Nature* (Princeton, NJ: Princeton University Press, 1979); Bruno Latour, *Science in Action* (Cambridge, MA: Harvard University Press, 1987); L. S. Vygotsky, *Mind in Society*, eds. Michael Cole et al. (Cambridge, MA: Harvard University Press, 1978); Michel Foucault, *Discipline and Punish*, trans. A. Sheridan (New York: Vintage Books, 1978).

17 For example, see B. Barnes, *Scientific Knowledge and Sociological Theory* (London: Routledge, 1974); and D. Bloor, *Knowledge and Social Inquiry*, 2nd ed. (Chicago: University of Chicago Press, 1991).

intellectual status quo as intrinsically rational and, correspondingly, risk demonizing intellectual revolutions as intrinsically irrational. Even moderate social approaches to epistemic rationality run these risks. For example, Catherine Elgin proposes an account of epistemic rationality that in many ways resembles my account, but she inserts a strong social requirement. She maintains that "an acceptable cognitive system must answer not just to my initially tenable commitments but to ours."[18] Such a requirement flirts with definitionally precluding intellectual revolutionaries from being epistemically rational.

By contrast, my account, by emphasizing opinions that are invulnerable to criticism from one's own perspective, leaves room not only for the possibility of one's opinions being seriously unreliable and yet still being rational, but also for the possibility of their being seriously at odds with one's tradition or community and still being rational. It might be objected, however, that this same perspectival element makes it difficult to understand how one's opinions can be extensively irrational, given the above account. After all, how much divergence can there be between one's current opinions and one's own deep epistemic convictions?

The answer is that there can be sharp divergence. Nothing in the above account precludes the possibility that one would be radically dissatisfied with one's current opinions, given deep enough and thorough enough reflection. Moreover, this is so even though reflection on one's current opinions must begin with these very opinions. Consider an analogy with a reading of the history of science not as a history of successive revolutions but rather as one in which past theories are largely incorporated into successor theories. On this view of science, there are rarely wholesale rejections of immediately preceding theories, but nevertheless the changes over time made by successive theories can be momentous, with both deep and broad implications. An analogous point is true of the critiques one can mount on reflection against one's own current opinions. Given that the critiques must originate with one's current opinions, it may be relatively rare for them to result in a wholesale rejection of one's current opinions, but it nonetheless would be incorrect to say that what epistemic rationality requires on the above account is little more than a tidying up of one's belief system. This way of putting the matter underappreciates how extensive and significant self-critiques can be, and hence how extensive the current irrationality

18 Catherine Elgin, *Considered Judgement* (Princeton, NJ: Princeton University Press, 1996), especially 115–45.

can be. Any homeowner knows how a little light dusting can sometimes turn into an extensive spring cleaning and can occasionally even result in major renovations.

Moreover, it is all the more difficult to meet one's own deepest epistemic standards, given the "quick and dirty" ways we have to acquire most of our beliefs. Epistemic evaluations assess opinions against a single goal, that of having accurate and comprehensive opinions, but we have numerous other goals and needs, which impose constraints on how much time and effort it is reasonable to devote to intellectual concerns. It is not feasible, given the total set of our goals and needs, to devote all one's time and energy to having accurate and comprehensive opinions. Indeed, many topics are neither intellectually nor pragmatically important and, accordingly, it would be foolish to spend much time on them. What this means, in turn, is that the small amount of time I have devoted to investigating and reflecting on a topic may have been reasonable, given the relative unimportance of the topic and the pressing nature of many of my other goals and needs, and yet my resulting opinions may very well be ones that on deeper reflection I would not endorse as effectively satisfying the epistemic goal of having accurate and comprehensive beliefs. Thus, even if I have been a responsible believer with respect to a topic, devoting as much time and effort to it as is warranted, it need not be the case that my beliefs about the topic are epistemically rational, illustrating yet again why it is often not a simple or easy matter to be epistemically rational in the above sense.[19]

I have been arguing that one's opinions are epistemically rational if they can stand up to one's own, most severe critical scrutiny. This account presupposes that one has the ability to reflect back on one's opinions and to form second-order opinions about these opinions and the faculties, methods, and practices that produced them. Not coincidentally, this is the very ability that a creature must have in order for it to be appropriate to assess the rationality or irrationality of its opinions at all. Higher order animals other than humans may have beliefs, but insofar as they lack the capacities to deliberate extensively on these first-order beliefs, it strikes us as inappropriate to criticize their beliefs as irrational. If a dog, upon seeing its owner walk toward the front door, jumps up, wags its tail excitedly, and runs to the door, it is natural to conceive the dog as believing that the owner is about to take it for a

---

19 See Richard Foley, "The Foundational Role of Epistemology in a General Theory of Rationality."

walk. But even if the owner is walking to the front door only to lock it, as she does almost every night before going to bed, we are reluctant to criticize the dog's belief as irrational. One explanation for this reluctance is that whereas humans have the capacity to reflect back on their own opinions and to form extensive second-order opinions about them, we do not think that dogs have this capacity.

So, an implication of the above account is that only creatures with a certain level of cognitive sophistication are to be assessed as rational or irrational in an epistemic sense.[20] According to the account, the rationality (or irrationality) of a belief is a function of whether on reflection one would regard it as sufficiently likely to be true to make believing it appropriate, insofar as one's goal is to have accurate and comprehensive beliefs. Accordingly, in order for one's opinions to be characterized as either rational or irrational in this sense, one needs to have concepts (or proto-concepts) of what it is to have a belief (opinion), what it is for beliefs to be accurate (true) and comprehensive, and what it is for something to make likely the accuracy (truth) of a belief.[21]

4. SELF-TRUST AND INCONSISTENCY

The degree of intellectual self-trust it is appropriate to have in one's opinions and faculties is a function of how much epistemic confidence one has in them and how invulnerable to self-criticism this confidence is. The greater and the deeper one's confidence in the accuracy of an opinion, the more one is entitled to rely on it. Similarly, the greater and the deeper one's confidence in the reliability of an intellectual faculty, method, or practice, the more one is entitled to rely on that faculty, method, or practice.

These theses constitute the beginnings of an account of epistemically rational belief as well as the beginnings of an account of intellectual self-trust, but there are also important issues to be addressed about the limits of self-trust. In Chapter 3 I discuss how empirical studies documenting the tendency of people in general to make mistakes of reasoning and judgment can create internal intellectual tensions that raise questions

---

20 Keith Lehrer, in *Self-Trust: A Study of Reason, Knowledge, and Autonomy*, argues that 'metamental ascent', that is, the capacity to consider and evaluate first-order mental states, is centrally important for understanding a wide range of philosophical problems.

21 For a more extensive explication of this sense of epistemic rationality, see Richard Foley, *Working Without a Net*.

about how much trust it is appropriate to have in one's own opinions and faculties. I want first, however, to discuss a more explicit kind of internal tension, the presence of inconsistency among one's opinions. I will argue that not every inconsistency need be destructive of self-trust. One's opinions can accommodate certain kinds of internal inconsistencies without making one vulnerable to intellectual self-criticism and, hence, without generating irrationality.

The most extreme kind of internal inconsistency, and the one potentially most destructive of self-trust, would be to have explicitly contradictory beliefs. I say "would" because it is unclear, given the nature of belief, whether it is possible to have explicitly contradictory beliefs. It certainly is possible to believe of two sentences that each is true, without fully realizing that they express contradictory propositions. And, if there are such things as unconscious beliefs, it presumably is possible to believe a proposition consciously while believing its contradictory unconsciously. What is less clear is whether it is possible to understand fully both a proposition and its denial and in the same sense of belief to believe each.[22]

With respect to the epistemological issues that are my principal concern, however, it does not matter whether it is possible to have explicitly contradictory beliefs, for even if this is not possible, the threat of contradiction is itself enough to make one vulnerable to self-criticism. In argumentation there is no more powerful way of undermining the positions of others than demonstrating that their assumptions or ways of reasoning from these assumptions lead to contradictory conclusions. The same is true of self-argumentation. Nothing is more undermining of intellectual self-trust than becoming convinced that one's own opinions and reasonings commit one to a contradiction.

Not all inconsistencies involve explicit contradictions, however. A set of beliefs is inconsistent if it is impossible for all of them to be true. So, contradictory beliefs, if there are such things, are always inconsistent, but inconsistent beliefs are not always explicitly contradictory. Suppose I believe propositions P^1, P^2, P^3 ... P^{n-1}, P^n, which together, unbeknown to me, imply $notP^{n-1}$. If I do not believe $notP^{n-1}$, my beliefs are not explicitly contradictory, but they are nonetheless inconsistent. Similarly, if I believe a proposition that, unbeknown to me, is a necessary falsehood, my beliefs as a whole are inconsistent, but there need not be any

---

22   See Richard Foley, "Is It Possible to Have Contradictory Beliefs?" *Midwest Studies in Philosophy 1985*, 9, 327–57.

proposition P such that I believe both it and its negation. Hence, my beliefs need not be explicitly contradictory.

Beliefs can be inconsistent without being contradictory, but because inconsistency, like contradiction, is always a sign of inaccuracy, epistemologists have often found it easy to jump to the conclusion that consistency is a minimal requirement of epistemic rationality. Moreover, it becomes all the easier to jump to this conclusion if one assumes that the processes of belief fixation are holistic, but in fact, this assumption is mistaken. Many mechanisms of belief fixation turn out to be modular, that is, they operate in such a way that they do not have ready access to, and hence do not utilize, all the information that the agent has stored.[23] A consequence of this informational encapsulation is that inconsistency can easily emerge in an individual's overall belief system even when the local processes of belief fixation are largely reliable. Individually reliable processes can easily lead to inconsistencies across different domains of beliefs.[24] By contrast, a genuinely holistic system of belief acquisition could monitor and eliminate inconsistencies by making appropriate adjustments throughout the entire system of beliefs. So, if one assumes that belief acquisition is holistic, it can seem a relatively easy step to the conclusion that it is a requirement of rationality that all inconsistencies be eliminated. On the other hand, a more realistic, and less holistic, view of belief fixation makes this idea much less tempting.

In any event, whatever the motivations are for stipulating that consistency is a prerequisite of epistemic rationality, it is far too strong a requirement. It unrealistically requires us, in the name of rationality, to be able always to detect and hence avoid inconsistencies. Sometimes, however, we lack the cognitive powers to do so. Even if we do well enough at detecting inconsistencies on most occasions, some logical connections among propositions are so complex that it is beyond our capacities to recognize them. Accordingly, it is possible for even seemingly unproblematic propositions to imply the negations of other seemingly unproblematic propositions but to do so in such a complicated way that we are incapable (at least currently) of discerning this. If so, we have inconsistent beliefs even though there is nothing we could have done to spot the inconsistency.

Similarly, consider Goldbach's conjecture, which states that every

---

23 For the classic discussion of modularity, see Jerry Fodor, *The Modularity of Mind* (Cambridge, MA: MIT Press, 1983).

24 Hilary Kornblith, "Some Social Features of Cognition," *Synthese*, 73 (1987), 27–41.

even number greater than two is the sum of two primes. The conjecture is either necessarily true or necessarily false, but it has never been proved or disproved. Still, because no one has ever succeeded in finding an even number greater than two that is not the sum of two primes, despite repeated efforts by generations of mathematicians to do so, most investigators reasonably believe the conjecture to be true, However, suppose that at some future time, much to everyone's surprise, someone manages to prove that the conjecture is in fact false, using techniques that are unknown today. Then, future investigators, from their position, will be aware that current investigators believed a proposition that is necessarily false, and, hence, their beliefs as a whole were inconsistent. Nevertheless, this would in no way show that it was not rational for current investigators, given their situation, to believe the conjecture. But if so, inconsistency of beliefs can coexist with their rationality.

Some inconsistencies are beyond our ken, and hence it is unrealistic to make it a condition of rationality that we avoid them, but perhaps it is a prerequisite of rationality that we search our belief systems for inconsistencies and eliminate them to the extent possible. However, even if we ignore the obstacles posed by modularity, this proposal is also too strong. As Christopher Cherniak points out, testing for inconsistency becomes exponentially more complicated as a belief set increases in size, and hence eliminating inconsistencies to the extent possible would swallow up all of our time.[25] Epistemic rationality is a matter of having appropriate beliefs insofar as one's goal is to have beliefs that are both accurate and comprehensive. It thus involves a balancing of the value of accuracy against the value of comprehensiveness, whereas devoting all one's energies to the elimination of inconsistencies would be to emphasize the first of these aspects to the exclusion of the second.

A more modest proposal is that epistemic rationality requires that we not be knowingly inconsistent. The suggestion, in other words, is not that we seek to eliminate all inconsistencies among our beliefs but rather that we eliminate any inconsistency of which we become aware. However, even this condition is too strong. In general, it is epistemically desirable to eliminate inconsistencies when we become aware of them, but sometimes the costs are too high, as the lottery and preface cases illustrate.

Imagine a lottery of a million tickets, and suppose you are justified in believing that the lottery is fair and that as such it has only one winning

---

25   See Christopher Cherniak, *Minimal Rationality* (Cambridge, MA: MIT Press, 1983).

ticket. Suppose also you have no reason to distinguish among the tickets concerning their chances of winning. Thus, the probability of ticket #1 losing is .999999, the probability of ticket #2 losing is .999999, and similarly for each of the other tickets. Accordingly, you have extraordinarily strong reasons to believe that ticket #1 will not win. If we deny that it is rational for you to believe this proposition, we will be hard-pressed to avoid the skeptical conclusion that not very many of your other beliefs are rational either, since the chances of their being in error are at least as great. However, your position with respect to ticket #2, ticket #3, ticket #4 . . . and ticket #1,000,000 is the same as your position with respect to ticket #1. Like cases are to be treated alike; equiprobable propositions deserve equal credence.[26] So, if it is rational for you to believe that #1 will lose, it is also rational for you to believe this of each of the other individual tickets. But then, since by hypothesis it is rational for you to believe that exactly one ticket (you know not which) will win, you have rational but inconsistent beliefs. Thus, it is not an absolutely necessary condition of rationality that one eliminate inconsistencies in one's opinions whenever one becomes aware of them.

The preface case can also be used to illustrate this conclusion. Suppose you have written a book about, say, ornithology. In it you have made an enormous number of claims about the names, habits, songs, and other features of a variety of birds. You have meticulously researched each claim, and thus each is a reasonable claim for you to make. However, you have made such a large number of claims that it is also reasonable for you to believe that somewhere in the book, you know not where, you have said something false. You acknowledge this in the preface of the book. But then, the total set of claims you are making is inconsistent, and yet once again, each claim is reasonable for you.[27]

5. RATIONALITY AND LESS THAN IDEAL OUTCOMES

If you know that your beliefs are inconsistent, you know that they are less than ideally accurate. In particular, you know that at least one is false. Thus, in having such beliefs, you are knowingly forgoing the opportunity of having only true beliefs. Still, it is a mistake to think that this is always and everywhere irrational. In general, it is important to

---

26 See Catherine Elgin, *Considered Judgement*, 37.

27 For more detailed discussions of the lottery and the preface, see Foley, *Working Without a Net*, §4.5.

avoid inconsistency, but it is a mistake to try to turn this general rule into an utterly categorical requirement of epistemic rationality.

In other domains, it is not always irrational to adopt strategies that we know to be less than ideal. On the contrary, strategies that deliberately court error are common. For example, investment strategies that seek a balance of investments are often of this sort. Some of the recommended investments hold out the prospects of high returns but also involve high risks. Some are secure but will generate at best only modest returns. Some will do well if inflation is high. Others will do well if inflation is low. Indeed, an increasingly common investment strategy makes use of both indexed funds, which are designed to rise or fall with a stock index (e.g., the Dow Jones average), and contrarian funds, which are designed to move in the opposite direction of the market. A portfolio of investments that includes both index funds and contrarian funds may as a whole be reasonable, despite the fact that the portfolio is designed so that not all of the investments will do well simultaneously.

Similarly, there can be betting games in which the optimal strategy is to make a series of bets that one knows is less than ideal, in the sense that one knows in advance that not each individual bet in the series will win. For example, suppose I am given an opportunity to play a game in which I know that exactly three of the four cups on the table have a pea under it. Without looking underneath the cups, I am allowed to place a bet at 1:1 odds on each cup, declaring whether or not it has a pea under it. The strategy that maximizes my estimated return is to bet "pea" on each of the four cups. Doing so will result in my winning three of the bets and losing one, for a net profit of two dollars. By contrast, if I bet pea on three cups and "not-pea" on one, I have to guess which of the cups does not have a pea under it. I have a .25 chance of guessing correctly, in which case I will win all four bets, and my profit will be four dollars. On the other hand, I have a .75 chance of guessing incorrectly, in which case I will win two bets and lose two, and my profit will be zero. So, my estimated return is .25($4) + .75($0) = $1. Thus, in this game, betting pea on each of the four cups is preferable to betting pea on three of the cups and not-pea on the fourth, despite the fact that the latter strategy holds out the possibility of an ideal outcome (winning each of my bets) whereas the former strategy does not.

Our epistemologies must acknowledge that it is no different with intellectual strategies. They must acknowledge that it can be rational to adopt strategies that deliberately court error. Epistemic rationality, I have been arguing, is to be understood in terms of the goal of now having accurate and comprehensive beliefs. Strategies that deliberately court error are sometimes defensible means to this goal, because small sacrifices in accuracy can sometimes allow great benefits in comprehensiveness. The lottery and preface cases are illustrations of this point. You know that not all of your beliefs about the lottery are true, since you believe of each of the tickets that it will lose and believe also that one of the tickets will win. On the other hand, you are also enormously confident that almost all of these beliefs are true. Indeed, assuming that the lottery is fair and that exactly one ticket will win, you can be confident that 999,999 of your beliefs about the individual tickets are true and that only a single belief is false.

The key issue here, however, is not about counting beliefs but rather about recognizing that confidence in the overall accuracy of one's opinions and methods can reasonably coexist with inconsistency. This is not to say that the discovery of inconsistency is ever unimportant. Inconsistency is a sign of inaccuracy and, hence, is always a sign to be on one's guard. Nevertheless, sometimes it is reasonable to tolerate some inaccuracy. The critical question for epistemology is not whether inconsistency is ever to be tolerated, but rather when it is to be tolerated.

My answer to this question, briefly stated,[28] is that inconsistency is not to be tolerated in the premises of arguments. An argument is credible only to the degree that the conjunction of its premises is credible, but if one knows that a set of propositions is inconsistent, one knows that their conjunction is false. So, one should never knowingly allow inconsistency in the premises of arguments. Nor is inconsistency to be tolerated in a small or theoretically tight set of propositions, where by 'theoretically tight' I mean propositions that are so theoretically intertwined with one another that they tend to stand or fall together. However, inconsistency can sometimes be permitted in large and theoretically loose sets of propositions, as long as one does not utilize the propositions together to argue or deliberate about the truth of other propositions. The set of propositions at issue in the lottery is an example of a very large and theoretically loose set of propositions.[29]

The most important point for my purposes here, however, is not whether this answer is exactly right but rather that intellectual self-trust can reasonably coexist with certain kinds of internal intellectual conflicts

28 For more details, see Foley, *Working Without a Net*, §4.5.
29 For a similar treatment of the lottery and preface, see Robert Nozick, *The Nature of Rationality* (Princeton, NJ: Princeton University Press, 1993), especially 89–92.

or tensions. Rationality, in one important sense, is a matter of one's opinions fitting together sufficiently well as to make oneself invulnerable to self-criticism, insofar as one's goal is to have accurate and comprehensive beliefs. Nevertheless, one's opinions can contain certain kinds of internal conflicts – indeed, they can even be inconsistent – without providing grounds for intellectual self-criticism and, hence, without generating irrationality. This result will be important in Chapter 3, which focuses on an especially common kind of internal tension that need not rise to the level of inconsistency.

3

Empirical Challenges to Self-Trust

1. STUDIES DOCUMENTING OUR TENDENCIES TO MAKE ERRORS

In the context of an epistemological inquiry into our role as inquirers, worries about the reliability of our faculties and opinions arise naturally. We wonder whether our cognitive equipment and our ways of employing this equipment are sufficiently well suited for our environment as to be reliable. The most extreme version of these worries can be illustrated by skeptical thought experiments, which entertain the possibility that an evil demon is deceiving us perceptually, or that we are in fact dreaming when we take ourselves to be awake, or that we are brains-in-a-vat.

These thought experiments, which have been widely discussed by epistemologists, raise questions about the degree of trust it is appropriate to place in our faculties and opinions. It is less frequently noted but no less true that empirical studies also have the capacity to raise such questions. Data about the way we make judgments and inferences can reveal that we are less than ideally reliable in certain kinds of situations and, thus, may provide grounds for not placing much confidence in the opinions we form in those situations.

Consider an example. In a wide range of studies, short personal interviews, typically one hour, have been proven unhelpful in improving the accuracy of predictions about the future accomplishments or behavior of the interviewees. One of the studies involves medical school admission committees that conducted personal interviews of applicants to supplement statistical and other impersonally gathered data about the applicants (MCAT scores, grade point average, class rank, quality of undergraduate institution, etc.). The task for the committees was to

55

predict future success in medical school as measured by the grades the students would receive. Another study focused on committees that interviewed candidates for teaching posts and then made assessments of the candidates' likely success in teaching as measured by ratings on teaching evaluation forms. Still another study involved parole boards making predictions of recidivism among convicted criminals as measured by future criminal convictions.

The conclusion of these studies is that personal interviews do not improve predictions of future accomplishments or behavior. They did not help the interviewers identify who would become successful in medical school (as measured by grades), nor who would become good teachers (as measured by students' ratings), nor who would lead crime-free lives (as measured by an absence of convictions). Indeed, far from improving predictive performance, the interviews actually worsened the accuracy of the predictions made. For example, medical school committees using only impersonally gathered data (MCAT scores, grade point average, etc.) did better at predicting future success in medical school than committees using these data plus interviews. Other studies have produced the same pattern of results.[1]

These are remarkable findings, which if taken seriously would have enormous social implications. Millions of hours and billions of dollars are expended on personal interviews in the United States alone. The prevailing assumption is that such interviews help employers, schools, and agencies make more accurate predictions about future job performance and behavior, but the studies seem to suggest that they in fact lead to less accurate predictions.

The most obvious explanation of the worsened predictive performance is that in conducting interviews, interviewers are exposed to irrelevant information, such as the appearance and mannerisms of the interviewees, and this irrelevant but salient information swamps out relevant information. Moreover, even if appearance, mannerisms, and the like turn out to be not completely irrelevant in predicting future performance − that is, even if such characteristics do to some extent affect teaching evaluations, grades in medical school, criminal convictions, and so on − this information, because of its salience, gets weighted more heavily than it should. A second, complementary explanation is that one-hour interviews are simply too short to be useful. The kinds of

---

1 For a summary of some of the findings, see Robyn Dawes, *House of Cards* (New York: The Free Press, 1994).

accomplishments being predicted, for example, success in the classroom or in medical school, require a broad range of abilities and skills, but the interviewers see an interviewee for only one hour and usually only in one setting. So, the interviewers simply do not have a large enough sample of the interviewee's total range of behaviors to make reliable predictions about future accomplishments.

To be sure, there are ways of challenging the above studies. For instance, questions can be raised about the exact content of the predictions. Although the interviewers are instructed to predict as best they can who will become successful in medical school as measured by grades or who will become good teachers as measured by students' ratings, they may in fact not be doing this, especially if they have doubts about grades and student evaluations as adequate measures of success. Such doubts might prompt the interviewers, consciously or unconsciously, to rely on their own preferred criteria to identify who will become the best doctors or the best teachers. But if this is what the interviewers are doing, the grades or student evaluations that the interviewees eventually receive cannot be used to establish that the interviewers' predictions were unreliable, since, according to this hypothesis, the actual content of the predictions was about who would be successful as measured by some criterion other than grades or student evaluations.

Nevertheless, I am going to ignore this concern and others like it, because nothing hinges on this particular example or even on the particular set of studies about interviewing on which the example is based. If one has reservations about the example or the studies lying behind it, it is not difficult to come up with other examples and other studies. There is now an extensive literature describing the tendencies of people to make mistakes of judgment and reasoning in a variety of everyday situations.

For example, studies of "overconfidence bias" document that subjects consistently overestimate their own abilities. In an enormous survey of one million high school seniors, students were asked to evaluate themselves as average, below average, or above average in leadership ability. Accurate self-assessments would be expected to result in roughly equal percentages of students in the highest and lowest categories, but the actual self-assessments were strikingly different. A full 70 percent of the students viewed themselves as being above average in leadership ability, whereas only 2 percent regarded themselves as being below average. Even more remarkably, when asked to rate their ability to get along with others, virtually all the students thought they were above average, with 60 percent evaluating themselves in the top 10 percent and 25 percent evaluating themselves in the top 1 percent. Similar studies have been conducted on adults with similar results. For example, a hugely disproportionate percentage of adult drivers rate themselves as better than average drivers. Yet another survey, with special relevance to academia, revealed than a stunning 94% of university professors assessed themselves as better at their jobs than their average colleagues.[2]

So, if one has reservations about the interviewing studies, one can construct one's favorite analogous problem case, using studies of over-confidence bias or some other study in the literature, whether it has to do with neglect of base rates, probability blindness, anchoring effects, availability bias, framing effects, or fabrication and revision of personal histories by memory.[3]

I am focusing on the first-person epistemological questions that such studies prompt. On the assumption that it is reasonable for me to accept at least some of these studies at face value, the question is what effect the studies should have on me when I am the one making the judgments. If people in general are unreliable when they make certain kinds of judgments, should this undermine my trust in my own ability to make such judgments reliably? If so, to what extent?

Suppose I have interviewed Smith and on the basis of this interview, supplemented by what I have learned from Smith's resume and my background opinions about teaching, I now have opinion X about Smith's likely success in the classroom, as measured by teaching evaluations. I then recall the above studies, which for the sake of the discussion we can assume make it reasonable for me to believe that after conducting personal interviews, most interviewers tend to make less reliable predictions about the future job performance and behavior of interviewees. These studies may well give me a good reason to avoid conducting personal interviews at all, but suppose I have had no choice in the matter. My job required me to interview Smith. Now that I have done so, the question is whether I should trust my postinterview assessment.

2   Thomas Gilovich, *How We Know What Isn't So* (New York: Macmillan, 1991), 75–87. For a summary of research that has been conducted on illusions about one's self, and an argument that these illusions are often psychologically useful, see S. E. Taylor, *Positive Illusions: Creative Self-Deception and the Healthy Mind* (New York: Basic Books, 1989).

3   See, for example, D. Kahneman, P. Slovic, and A. Tversky, eds., *Judgement under Uncertainty: Heuristics and Biases* (Cambridge: Cambridge University Press, 1982); and R. E. Nisbett and L. Ross, *Human Inference: Strategies and Shortcomings of Social Judgement* (Englewood Cliffs, NJ: Prentice-Hall, 1980).

When I directly consider the issue of whether Smith is likely to be a successful teacher, I have opinion X. However, when I go up a level and consider that people in general are unreliable in their postinterview assessments, my opinion looks less credible. Perhaps I should instead rely on my preinterview opinion of Smith, or if I had no preinterview opinion, perhaps I should altogether withhold judgment on Smith's likely success in the classroom.

Vigorous debates have built up around the literature that describes people's tendencies to make mistakes of judgment and reasoning. However, the debates have generally not focused on the first-person issues I am raising. They have instead centered on more impersonal questions, for example, what do these studies tell us about the rationality of humans in general? Do they suggest widespread irrationality?

I am going to describe a small portion of these debates in order to contrast the issues typically raised in them with the first-person issues I will be discussing. In addition, I have a second motivation for discussing these debates, namely, there is a way of framing them such that they naturally lead back to a consideration of the first-person issues that are my primary concern.

The most circumspect and least controversial interpretation of the studies is that they show we are less than ideally accurate cognizers. In itself, this conclusion is hardly surprising. No one should be startled to learn that humans make intellectual mistakes. When we are tired, we are often sloppy in our reasonings; when we are emotionally distressed, we have a tendency to jump to conclusions we would resist in calmer moments; and when we have consumed too much alcohol, we tend to make overly simplistic judgments. What is noteworthy, however, is that the studies in question establish that we regularly make mistakes of reasoning and judgment even when we are not tired, emotionally distressed, inebriated, or in any other obvious way disadvantaged. Moreover, the kinds of errors we make are predictable, not in the sense that we can say in advance whether a particular individual will make the mistakes in question, but rather in the sense that we can be confident that a large percentage of randomly selected individuals will make them.

The extensiveness and predictability of the errors documented in the studies have made it easy to slide from the noncontroversial conclusion that people are less than ideal cognizers to the more controversial and pessimistic conclusion that people in general are deeply irrational. It is especially easy for the charge of irrationality to arise if it is assumed that less-than-ideal accuracy is always a mark of less-than-ideal rationality.

With this assumption in hand, it then seems but a small additional step to the position that the irrationality revealed is deep, because the ease with which the errors have been reproduced in a variety of studies suggests that relatively fundamental cognitive structures are at work.

In Chapter 1, I argue against the assumption that if our opinions are rational, we can be assured they are also for the most part accurate, and I also argue against the assumption that if our opinions are generally inaccurate, they cannot be rational. I won't dwell on these points again here, because even granting them, it might nonetheless be true that the studies in question reveal deep-seated irrationality. It is just that they do so in some way that is more complicated than by simply revealing inaccuracy. Besides, in the literature, challenges to the pessimistic interpretation of these studies have generally taken a different turn.

An especially provocative challenge denies that the subjects of the studies are guilty of any irrationality, or at least any deep systematic irrationality. The appearance of irrationality disappears, it is argued, once we broaden the context by looking at the evolutionary advantages of the cognitive structures that are responsible for the mistakes of reasoning and judgment documented in the studies. The underlying assumption of this argument is that our most fundamental cognitive structures have been selected for usefulness and, hence, they are, if not optimal, at least much better than random with respect to promoting survival. These structures evolved in the late Pleistocene, because they were useful to our hunter-gatherer ancestors in that epoch of the Quaternary period, but if they and the kinds of reasoning they encourage are useful for promoting survival, then, according to this argument, they are also rational, or at least not irrational.[4]

Some potential objections to arguments of this sort are listed in §1.4, but the most telling complaint for purposes here is that the argument is not so much mistaken as not fully to the point. Suppose we grant that the cognitive structures that dispose us to make the kinds of mistakes documented in the studies were well designed for hunter-gatherers in the late Pleistocene. Suppose we also grant that this is enough to show that these structures were rational, at least in a broad pragmatic sense, for our ancestors. Nevertheless, we are not hunter-gatherers in the late

---

4   For a good critical summary of the issues involved in this literature, see R. Samuels, S. Stich, and P. Tremoulet, "Rethinking Rationality: From Bleak Implications to Darwinian Modules," in E. LePore and Z. Pylyshyn, eds., *Rutgers University Invitation to Cognitive Science* (London: Basil Blackwell, 1999).

Pleistocene and, thus, these points have no immediate implications for our rationality. In contrast to our hunter-gatherer ancestors, we are not preoccupied, or at least not so directly and constantly preoccupied, with issues of sheer day-to-day survival. Hence, the structures in question may not be well designed for us in our current environment. A fortiori, they may not be well designed for the conduct of our intellectual projects.

Projects in the basic sciences, philosophy, mathematics, and many other fields are not principally motivated by practical concerns, much less by concerns of survival. This is not to say that there may not be pragmatic payoffs of these intellectual inquiries, but it is to say that their primary end is intellectual. The goal is to get things right, that is, to have accurate and comprehensive beliefs about the domain at issue. Accordingly, if in the midst of deciding, debating, and pursuing these intellectual projects, investigators discover that they have made mistakes of the sort documented in recent studies, for example, if they discover they have ignored base rates, they should and presumably would correct these mistakes. It would be a failing not to do so. Moreover, it does not matter if it can be shown that the mistakes are the products of cognitive structures that in some broad sense serve the investigators well. Nor, a fortiori, is it relevant that the structures served our ancestors well hundreds of thousands of years ago. It would be beside the point for these investigators to say, "Yes, we know that we ignored base rates in reaching our conclusions, but the cognitive structures responsible for our doing so were useful for our Pleistocene ancestors." In doing basic science, mathematics, or philosophy, such considerations are irrelevant. The goal is, or at least should be, to have accurate and comprehensive beliefs about the issues in question and, hence, the relevant kind of rationality to aspire to is epistemic.

In some contexts, nonepistemic considerations may generate reasons to believe a claim. Pascal's reasons for believing in God are the most notorious example, but there are also less extreme and less direct non-epistemic reasons for belief. Some beliefs may comfort me. If so, I have reasons, if only weak ones, related to my psychological well-being to have such beliefs. Other beliefs may serve me well economically and professionally, for example, the belief that hard work is likely to pay off. If so, I have economic and professional reasons, again perhaps only weak ones, to have such beliefs. Still other beliefs may promote my health. If I am beset with a serious illness, the belief that I am going to recover may increase my chances for recovery and, thus, once again I have reasons to have such beliefs. Similarly, nonepistemic considerations can generate indirect reasons for a belief, by providing a reason to employ some method which, if followed, would yield the belief in question. For example, in an environment where most poisonous fruits are red, a method that classifies all red fruits as poisonous may enhance prospects for survival, even if most red fruits in the environment are not poisonous. Thus, people in that environment may have reasons to adopt this method even though in general it is an unreliable way to identify poisonous and nonpoisonous fruits.

However, insofar as the context is one in which the goal is to have accurate and comprehensive beliefs and, hence, insofar as the kind of rationality at issue is epistemic, none of these considerations is at all relevant. It does not matter whether a belief will comfort me or serve me well economically. Nor does it matter that the belief would be generated by a method which, if used, would enhance my chances for survival. What does matter is whether there are considerations indicating that the belief or method is defensible insofar as the goal is for my current belief system to be accurate and comprehensive. What matters, in other words, is whether there are considerations indicating that the belief is likely to be true and the method likely to be reliable.

Cognitive structures that dispose us to make mistakes in reasoning may serve us well in many contexts, and it may even be that at a remote time they were critical for our survival as a species. If so, then in these contexts there is (or was) no strong reason for us to guard against our tendency to make mistakes of the sort documented in the studies. However, in other contexts, in particular contexts in which our goals are predominantly intellectual, the situation is markedly different. In such contexts, it is irrational not to guard against our tendency to make the mistakes in question, because the goal is to get things right.

This conclusion pushes into the foreground once again the first-person, epistemic questions that are my principal concern. Studies documenting our tendencies to make mistakes of reasoning and judgment have inspired a literature that focuses for the most part on intriguing questions about the rationality of humans in general, and about whether some of our cognitive structures might be important to us for nonepistemic reasons. From a first-person epistemic point of view, however, a more immediate question is how am I to react to these studies in arranging my own intellectual life, insofar as my goal is to have accurate and comprehensive beliefs?

2. FIRST-PERSON EPISTEMOLOGICAL ISSUES RAISED BY THE STUDIES

One way for me to react to studies documenting the tendency of people to make errors of judgment and reasoning is to assert that I am different from most people. Whereas others have a tendency to make mistakes of the sort documented, I do not. For example, with respect to the studies indicating that personal interviews worsen rather than improve predictive performance, I can try telling myself that although other people are poor interviewers, letting irrelevant factors influence their judgments, I am not. Thus, unlike others, I need not be especially wary of my postinterview assessments.

Unfortunately, this response is mere bluster unless there is evidence indicating that I really am different. Occasionally, there may be such evidence. For instance, studies indicate that in a variety of circumstances, individuals are susceptible to committing "sunk costs" fallacies. Their reluctance to abandon a course of action is more a function of past investments of time, effort, and resources than of estimated future costs and benefits. However, there are also studies that suggest that economists as a group are less likely than the general population to commit sunk costs fallacies. They constitute a kind of protected class, as it were, with respect to these errors.[5] Accordingly, if I have had training in economics, I may have good reason to think I am indeed different from most other people when it comes to these mistakes.

Moreover, even if I am not a member of a protected class, there may be strategies I can adopt to guard against the mistakes in question. For example, certain kinds of errors of statistical reasoning largely disappear if information is presented and processed in an appropriate format. In particular, mistakes are far less common if subjects are given the information in the form of relative frequencies rather than in the form of single event probabilities. Thus, insofar as I am careful not to make quick judgments on the basis of information presented in the form of single event probabilities and instead take the time to translate the information into relative frequencies, I may not need to worry as much about making these kinds of errors.

---

5   See R. Larrick, J. Morgan, and R. Nisbett, "Teaching the Use of Cost-Benefit Reasoning in Everyday Life," in R. Nisbett, ed., *Rules for Reasoning* (Hillsdale, NJ: Lawrence Erlbaum, 1993), 259–78.

Consider an example. When subjects are asked to respond to the following problem, which is framed in terms of single case probabilities, they tend to perform very poorly.

Suppose that 1% of the population has colon cancer. Suppose also that when an individual with colon cancer is given the standard diagnostic test, there is an 80% probability of the test being positive. On the other hand, when an individual without colon cancer is tested, there is a 10% probability of the test being positive. John Smith has tested positive. On the basis of this evidence, what are the chances that Smith has colon cancer?

Most subjects say that the probability is greater than 50%. An especially common answer is slightly less than 80%. However, the correct answer is approximately 7.5%. The calculation can be done using a version of Bayes Theorem:

$$p(e/h) \times p(h)/p(e/h) \times p(h) + p(e/-h) \times p(-h) = .8 \times .01/.8 \times .01 + .1 \times .99 = .008/.008 + .099 = .008/.107 = .0748.$$

By contrast, performance soars when essentially the same problem is recast in a frequency format:

Suppose that in a population of 1000 people, 990 do not have colon cancer whereas 10 do have the cancer. Of the 990 who do not have cancer, 99 have tested positive for the cancer and 891 have tested negative. Of the 10 who have the cancer, 8 have tested positive and 2 have tested negative. John Smith has tested positive. On the basis of this evidence, what are the chances that Smith has colon cancer?

When the problem is formulated in this way, most people correctly answer that the probability of Smith having cancer is low, in particular, less than 10%.

A hypothesis that purports to explain the difference in performance in the two kinds of cases is that the best formats for humans to process information have been shaped by natural selection. In particular, if information is presented in a format that resembles how important information was presented to our Pleistocene ancestors, performance can be expected to improve, the assumption being that our current cognitive structures were selected for usefulness during the Pleistocene and that, hence, the structures that evolved then must have been capable of reliably processing information crucial for survival in that environment. The above studies, which show that performance improves when information in presented in the form of relative frequencies, are read by some as providing some encouragement for this hypothesis:

What was available in the environment in which we evolved was the encountered frequencies of actual events – for example, that we were successful 5 times out of the last 20 times we hunted in the north canyon. Our hominid ancestors were immersed in a rich flow of observable frequencies that could be used to improve decision making, given procedures that could take advantage of them. So, if we have adaptations for inductive reasoning, they should take frequency information as input.[6]

Other kinds of mistakes also tend to disappear if information is presented in a suitable format. For instance, performance on "selection tasks" improves markedly when these tasks are presented in a way that emphasizes social rules and prohibitions. The original and now classic formulation of selection task problems, by contrast, is relatively abstract:

There are four cards on the table. Each card has a number on one side and a letter on the other. Two cards on the table are displayed with the letter side up and two with the number side up. Your task to assess whether the following claim is true of all the cards on the table: if a card has a vowel on one side, then it has an odd number on the other side. To determine whether this claim is true, which of the below cards do you have to turn over?

A	K	3	6

Numerous studies have shown that subjects tend to perform poorly on this kind of selection task. Most subjects correctly note that the A card must be turned over, but they incorrectly say that the 3 card must also be turned over, when in fact the 3 card will not falsify the claim at issue regardless of whether a vowel or consonant is on the other side. Most subjects also incorrectly say that the 6 card need not be turned over, even though without turning it over, there is no way of knowing whether there the claim in question is falsified by there being a vowel on the other side.

6   L. Cosmides and J. Tooby, "Are Humans Good Intuitive Statisticians After All? Rethinking Some Conclusions from the Literature on Judgement under Uncertainty," *Cognition* 58 (1996), 1–73. Also see G. Gigerenzer, "How to Make Cognitive Illusions Disappear: Beyond 'Heuristics and Biases,'" *European Review of Social Psychology*, 2 (1994), 83–115; and G. Gigerenzer and U. Hoffrage, "How to Improve Bayesian Reasoning without Instruction: Frequency Formats," *Psychological Review*, 102 (1995), 684–704.

On the other hand, when a selection task is presented in a format emphasizing social rules and prohibitions, subjects do much better. For example, consider the following selection task:

The legal drinking age in the state is 21. Four people are sitting at a table in a bar with drinks. The four cards below represent the four people. Each card provides information about the person it represents. One side of the card gives the person's age, and the other side tells what the person is drinking. To determine whether any of the four people are breaking the law, which of the cards do you have to turn over?

BEER	WATER	AGE: 23	AGE: 19

When a selection task is embedded in this kind of story, performance by subjects improves greatly, despite the fact that the logical form of the task is no different from the more abstractly formatted ones. Subjects correctly say that the BEER card and the AGE:19 card must be turned over, whereas the other two cards need not be turned over.

Once again, some commentators have proposed an evolutionary hypothesis to explain this enhanced performance. The hypothesis is that natural selection has led to our having cognitive mechanisms whose job it is to detect those who accept the benefits of reciprocal exchange arrangements but do not pay the costs. Reciprocal exchange arrangements create the possibility of exchanges among individuals that are "non–zero–sum," meaning that the overall benefits to the recipients can be greater than the overall costs to the donors. The sharing of food by animals is an example. Well-fed and successful hunters who share food with their hungry and unlucky fellow hunters provide significant benefits to the hungry animals, but such altruism involves costs, if only modest ones, to the successful hunters. Even if they are satiated, eating the extra meat would produce a little extra body fat, which might be useful later. Despite these costs, it may be in the overall interest of successful hunters to share food with starving hunters if this behavior is a part of a stable, reciprocal exchange system of behavior, under which all (or almost all) animals in the group are prepared to share food with those in the group who have been unsuccessful. All parties are likely to be better off under such arrangements, because each individual animal can count on others in time of need.

The downside of such arrangements is that they are vulnerable to cheating. Individual animals will do best by taking food when it is offered in times of need but not reciprocating when it is they who have an abundance of food. On the other hand, cheating tends to undermine systems of reciprocal behavior, and if cheating becomes sufficiently widespread, reciprocity may break down entirely, which in turn will leave all the individual animals worse off. Thus, if there are to be stable, mutually beneficial, reciprocal exchange arrangements, which are precisely the kind of arrangements essential for social living, individuals must be able reliably to detect and then discourage cheating. This suggests that a species' prospects for survival are enhanced if it evolves cheater-detecting mechanisms. The hypothesis, then, is that natural selection has indeed resulted in humans having cognitive structures that are highly sensitive to cheating. The further hypothesis is that it is these structures that account for improved performance on selection tasks when the tasks are formulated within a framework of social rules, permissions, and prohibitions.[7]

With respect to the first-person epistemic issues that are my main concern, however, the data indicating improved reliability in the above cases are more important than the evolutionary hypotheses proposed to explain the enhanced reliability. Whatever the explanation for the improved performance, the data potentially provide a way of countering worries about one's own reliability. The original studies indicate that subjects tend to make certain kinds of statistical errors with regularity and tend to do poorly on selection tasks, but the additional studies indicate that these mistakes tend to disappear when subjects approach statistical problems in terms of frequencies and approach selection tasks in terms of a social framework. Thus, if one is presented a statistical problem formulated in terms of frequencies or a selection task formulated in terms of a social framework, or if one goes to the trouble of recasting problems into these forms, one may not need to worry as

---

7   See L. Cosmides, "The Logic of Social Exchange: Has Natural Selection Shaped How Humans Reason? Studies with Wason Selection Task," *Cognition*, 31 (1989), 187–276; and R. Cummins, "Evidence for the Innateness of Deontic Reasoning," *Mind and Language*, 11 (1996), 160–90.

much about making mistakes of the sort documented in the original studies. Proper formulation of the information or problem provides one with an escape route from these worries.

Examples such as these illustrate in a concrete way how empirical studies of reasoning and judgment can help improve intellectual performance. Such studies document the kinds of errors we are prone to make, thus putting us on guard about these errors, and they also can be helpful in identifying salutary strategies for avoiding the errors. Correspondingly, the studies can have either a negative or positive affect on self-trust. Insofar as the studies identify errors that people in general are prone to make in certain situations, they raise questions about how much I should trust my own opinions in those situations, but insofar as further empirical studies help identify strategies for avoiding these same errors, they potentially provide grounds for restoring confidence in my opinions.

3. SELF-MONITORING

I have been discussing some ways of escaping the first-person epistemic worries raised by studies documenting our tendencies to make mistakes of reasoning and judgment. For example, I may be a member of a protected class, that is, a group of people who are not prone to making such errors. Alternatively, I may be able to formulate information or problems in such a way that the mistakes in question largely disappear.

Unfortunately, the literature on interviewing to this date has unearthed no such potential escape routes. There is no well-defined group whose predictions have been found to be unharmed by one-hour interviews, and there is no specific technique, analogous to formatting statistical problems in terms of relative frequencies, for neutralizing the harmful effects of short interviews. Besides, even if future studies do identify a protected group, there are no assurances that I will belong to it. Similarly, even if some technique or set of circumstances is found to eliminate most of the harmful effects of personal interviews, there are no assurances that the technique will be feasible for me or the circumstances applicable to me.

Thus, there is no obvious way to neutralize the first-person epistemic worries raised by the interviewing studies. Nor is it acceptable for me simply to assert without evidence that I am different from most people and that, hence, I need not concern myself with the effects of personal interviews. Such a stance is blindly optimistic. How, then, am I to react to the studies?

A pessimistic answer is that I must entirely discount personal interviews. By hypothesis, I have evidence to think that in general personal interviews make interviewers less reliable. Thus, on the assumption that there is no evidence to indicate that I am different from most people, it might seem as if my only reasonable option is to revert to (or hold onto) my preinterview opinions, or if this is not possible, since I may not have had any preinterview opinions, to have no opinion at all. The appropriate reaction, in other words, is the intellectual analogue of shielding my eyes. I must try to prevent personal interviews from having any bearing on my opinions about the future performance of the interviewees.

I may not have to do so forever. The harmful cognitive effects of an interview may fade with time. The memory of the interviewee's personality or manner may become less vivid, permitting me to weigh more judiciously the evidence that bears most directly on future performance. If so, I eventually may have the ability to think about the interview and to factor it into my deliberations without being unduly swayed by its irrelevant features. But in the meantime, according to the above response, the only reasonable strategy is for me to disregard the interview to the extent possible and either to rely on my preinterview opinion or to withhold judgment altogether.

However, I will be arguing that sometimes there may be another way of reacting to such studies, a way which steers a course between blind optimism and complete pessimism. By hypothesis, I have evidence indicating that most people have a tendency to be unreliable in their postinterview predictions. This evidence constitutes a warning about my own postinterview predictions, a warning that I cannot reasonably ignore. On the other hand, even if I do not have specific evidence that I am in a protected class, and even if I do not have a specific technique for neutralizing worries about my reliability, analogous to reformulating statistical problems in terms of frequencies, I do not necessarily have to discount entirely personal interviews. Nor do I necessarily have to wait for their harmful effects to fade. Further self-monitoring may sometimes also be an option.

Careful introspection is a place to begin. I can reflect on my personal reactions to the interviewees and try to identify any tendency on my part to give greater weight to my subjective impressions than to more objective information about the interviewees. For example, I can make special efforts to identify introspectively any tendency on my part to be unduly swayed by the mannerisms or the appearance of the interviewee. Effective self-monitoring is usually more than a matter of careful introspection, however. It also involves noting and interpreting my outward behavior as well other people's reactions to this behavior. Observing oneself from the outside, as it were, is as important for self-monitoring as peering inward. Indeed, sometimes there is no substitute for it.

Consider an analogy with color blindness. Some people do not discover for decades that they are color blind. Because the defect is not detectable by introspection alone, one needs to rely on public evidence to detect it. There is, for instance, a widely available and easily administered test for color blindness. Likewise, everyday life is full of occasions that potentially draw attention to the impairment. The color of objects is a frequent topic of conversation and, thus, ordinarily there are numerous occasions for individuals to compare their own assessments of color with those of others. As a result, most people who are color blind come to realize this about themselves in a relatively early age. However, a few do not. They are not given the standard test; other kinds of public evidence are not sufficiently conspicuous; and introspection alone is not capable of revealing the problem.[8]

In an analogous way, it is difficult to detect by introspection alone whether one's predictions about the future performance of interviewees have been unduly swayed by their manner or other irrelevant aspects of the interviews. Effective self-monitoring usually requires attention to public evidence as well as introspective evidence. For instance, I can note my behavior toward the interviewees as well as their reactions to my behavior and then provide an interpretation of this behavior. As I think back on an interview, perhaps I remember not returning the interviewee's overly ingratiating smile or I recollect myself staring out the window during the interview. These are warning signs that I may have been put off by the interviewee in some way and, as a result, may have been overly critical in my assessment. In addition, if there were other interviewers present, I can compare their impressions of the interviewees with mine. To the degree that their impressions conflict with mine, I have an occasion to seek the source of the differences, which in turn may lead to the discovery of idiosyncracies or biases in my assess-

---

8   The example is from Hilary Kornblith, "What Is It Like to Be Me?" *Australasian Journal of Philosophy* 76 (1998), 48–60. For a summary of the incidence of color blindness and its detection, see Leo Hurvich, *Color Vision* (Sunderland, MA: Sinauer Associates, 1981).

ments. I can also ask the other interviewers what they thought of my questions and behavior during the interviews, as an external check on whether I have been as impartial as introspection would lead me to think. If the other interviewers regard my questions as having been unusually difficult or my manner especially cool, this again should put me on guard.

The most thorough processes of self-monitoring thus typically involve public evidence as well as introspective evidence. Using both kinds of evidence, I can construct an interpretation of myself, my motivations, and my tendencies, much as I use various sources of information to construct interpretations of others. The aim is to mobilize all relevant sources of information in an effort to recognize and then avoid the kind of errors that the studies on interviewing warn me against.

Alternatively, if I cannot altogether avoid these tendencies, I can try to adjust for them and recalibrate my opinion. We often find it useful to engage in recalibrations. Suppose I am marking a student paper that argues for a position that I regard as untenable. Because I regard the conclusion as so implausible, I monitor myself against bias as I mark the paper. However, I realize there is a part of me that cannot help but regard as weak any arguments for the position in question. Thus, after completing the paper, I try to correct for my own bias by assigning a slightly higher grade than I would otherwise have been inclined to assign. Similarly, if I know my right eye is somewhat stronger than my left, with the result that objects at a distance are displaced a little to the right, then when aiming at a distant target, I can try to aim slightly to the left of what would otherwise seem appropriate. Recalibration is always a delicate business, in part because one has to guard against overcompensation. Nevertheless, when used judiciously, it sometimes is a useful way to compensate for a defect.

Neither self-monitoring nor recalibration are realistic options in the interviewing case, however, unless I have some idea, if only vague, about the causes of unreliability. In this respect, the interviewing situation is no different from other kinds of potentially risky situations. For example, I regard cigarette smoking as irrationally dangerous given what is known about the links between smoking and lung cancer, but not everyone who smokes gets cancer. So, if I knew which factors caused some smokers to contract cancer and knew also that I was free of these factors, I might not have to worry about the threat of lung cancer. I lack such knowledge, however, and hence I regard smoking as too risky. Analogously, if I have no sense of what it is about personal interviews that causes interviewers to be unreliable in their postinterview assessments of interviewees, I will have no clear idea about how to monitor myself for the error-producing factors or how to recalibrate my opinion in light of them.

Fortunately, I do have some sense of the main sources of unreliability in one-hour personal interviews. Only a tiny sample of the interviewee's total range of behaviors is witnessed in one hour; the interviewee is typically seen in only one setting; and irrelevant information from the interview, such as the mannerisms and appearance of the interviewee, is so salient that it tends to dilute more relevant information. Because I am aware of these potential sources of unreliability, self-monitoring and recalibration may sometimes be a possibility. I can try to correct for the flattering (or brusque) manner and the appealing (or unappealing) appearance of the interviewee, and I can also make adjustments for the fact that I have witnessed only a small sample of behavior and in only one setting. Moreover, if I perform the self-monitoring (or recalibration) carefully enough, the resulting opinion may be such that it is capable of withstanding my own deepest critical scrutiny, despite the fact that, by hypothesis, I am convinced that in general personal interviews tend to make such opinions unreliable. If so, that is, if the opinion and the efforts of self-monitoring (or recalibration) are indeed such that further reflection would not prompt me to be critical of them, insofar as my goal is to have accurate and comprehensive beliefs, then it is appropriate for me to have trust in the opinion and, according to the account of epistemic rationality defended in Chapter 2, the opinion is an epistemically rational one for me to have.

4. THE LIMITS OF SELF-MONITORING

I have been arguing that self-monitoring can sometimes be a reasonable response to studies documenting our tendencies to make mistakes of reasoning and judgment. This is a modest enough conclusion, which cautions against both glib optimism and reflexive pessimism. It acknowledges that individuals must come to grips with the first-person epistemic problems raised by the data. Unless there is evidence indicating that one is relevantly different from the subjects of the studies, one cannot simply dismiss the studies as being irrelevant to one's own epistemic situation. Nevertheless, even when such evidence is lacking, one is not necessarily forced, on threat of irrationality, to be skeptical about one's ability to avoid the mistakes in question. Sometimes it can be reasonable to rely on careful self-monitoring to guard against the errors in question.

This is a relatively modest conclusion, but it may still seem in principle misguided, given that self-monitoring will often involve the very cognitive faculties, abilities, and practices the reliability of which the studies are questioning. However, it is really this objection that is misguided, because it fails to recognize that in addressing basic epistemological issues, it is not inherently inappropriate to utilize faculties and procedures that are themselves under scrutiny.

Recall the worries that Descartes faced with respect to his method of doubt, the ones that led to his struggles with the Cartesian circle. Descartes recommended that we believe only that which is impossible to doubt, and he asserted that if we follow his recommendation, we can be assured of not falling into error. However, he also wondered whether that which is psychologically impossible for us to doubt might nonetheless be false. When we consider a proposition P directly, it may be impossible for us to doubt its truth, but when we consider ourselves and our opinions in a more general way, we cannot altogether dismiss the possibility that a proposition might be false despite its being indubitable for us.

Descartes's strategy for dealing with this worry was to use the method of doubt to argue that God exists and then to argue that God would not allow us to be deceived about propositions that are impossible for us to doubt. In other words, he appealed to what he regarded as indubitable propositions to argue that indubitability assures us of truth, hence the circle that worries so many commentators. Descartes's arguments, I have already said, are not capable of providing the guarantees of truth he sought, and to make matters worse, the arguments do not satisfy even Descartes's own requirements. His proof of God's existence is not indubitable, and his proof that a good God would not allow falsehoods to be indubitable is not indubitable either. On the other hand, there was nothing inherently inappropriate about his resorting to the method of doubt in trying to reply to worries about the reliability of the method. The method was proposed by him as the fundamental method of inquiry and, thus, if he was going to respond to the worries about it at all, he had better use the method. Some questions have to be answered circularly if they are to be answered at all. First and foremost among such questions are ones about the reliability of our most fundamental intellectual faculties and procedures. In trying to answer such questions, it is appropriate to rely on these same faculties and procedures.

The usual objection to circular defenses is that if they are permitted, anything at all can be defended, but this objection fails to make distinctions among kinds and degrees of circularity. The most blatant kind of circularity occurs when P is itself used as a premise in an argument for P. Because any proposition entails itself, this kind of circularity, if permitted, would allow one to defend any proposition whatsoever. However, it is a decidedly different kind of circularity to make use of one's own faculties and procedures in trying to defend the reliability of those same faculties and procedures, and the surest sign of the difference is that it is not always possible to mount this kind of defense. On the contrary, one's faculties and procedures, if employed consistently and rigorously, may well generate evidence that undermines their own pretensions of reliability. As discussed in §1.2, a coherent and potentially powerful strategy of would-be skeptics tries to exploit this very possibility.

So not only is it not improper to employ one's most fundamental faculties and procedures in addressing worries about the reliability of those faculties and procedures, it is a shortcoming of these faculties and procedures if they cannot be so used. The least that should be expected of a set of faculties and procedures is that, when used in their own defense, they generate data that is consistent with the assumption of their own reliability. Thus, it is far too simplistic to dismiss attempts to use our fundamental faculties and procedures to address worries about the reliability of these same faculties and procedures on the grounds that such attempts are unacceptably circular. This is overly simplistic whether the worries are generated by thought experiments about evil demons, brains in a vat, and the like, or whether they are generated by empirical studies.

As a way of underscoring this point, consider a hypothetical extension of the interviewing studies. Assume that we have in hand not just studies indicating that interviews worsen predictive performance but in addition studies indicating that performance is not improved even when interviewers are warned in advance about the inaccuracies created by personal interviews and are explicitly asked to guard against them.

I know of no empirical study of this sort. Moreover, contrary to what I am assuming, it would be surprising if advance instruction and warnings did not lessen the negative effects of interviewing. With respect to many of the mistakes of reasoning and judgment described in the literature, there have been studies of this sort, and, for the most part, they indicate that to be forewarned is to be forearmed. Base rate errors are significantly reduced with the right sort of prior warnings and instruction, and the same is true of a wide range of other errors.[9]

Nevertheless, for the sake of pushing issues of self-trust to their limits, let us assume that we have evidence showing that forewarning does not significantly decrease the harmful effects of personal interviews on predictions of future performance. It might then seem as if we really do have no reasonable option but to discount entirely personal interviews, because the ability to self-monitor has itself been shown to be futile or of only limited benefit. So, reverting to previous opinion or altogether withholding judgment might seem to be the only reasonable alternatives.

But even here, in this most extreme of cases, this is too simplistic a response. The fact that I have to rely on challenged abilities to reach an opinion, if I am to have an opinion at all, does not entirely eliminate the possibility of my reasonably having an opinion. To be sure, I cannot reasonably ignore the warnings posed by the (hypothetical) study and simply assume that unlike most others, I have the ability, when forewarned about the harmful affects of the one-hour personal interview, to self-monitor. Quite the reverse. This itself is one of the issues about which I must deliberate and on which I must take a stand.

What stand it is reasonable for me to take will depend on the nature of the (hypothetical) studies indicating that, in general, predictions are not improved even when interviewers are forewarned and asked to guard themselves against the problems created by personal interviews. If the studies provide no clues as to why self-monitoring is not effective for most people, I will have nothing to guide me in my efforts to guard myself against unreliable self-monitoring. (Recall the smoking analogy.) On the other hand, the studies themselves may well provide clues about what it is that typically goes wrong in these attempts to self-monitor. If so, I may be able to conduct my self-monitoring in such a way as to try to protect myself against the problems that most people encounter when they try to self-monitor. Moreover, if the resulting opinion is both confidently and deeply held, such that no further reflection – not even further reflection on the studies that inform me of the general unrelia-

9 Many of the essays in Richard Nisbett, ed., *Rules of Reasoning* (Hillsdale, NJ: Lawrence Erlbaum, 1993) document how training and education can reduce mistakes of reasoning and judgments. See especially Nisbett's introductory essay "Reasoning, Abstraction, and the Prejudices of Twentieth-Century Psychology" and the essays by various authors in Part 2 ("Teaching Statistical Rules"), Part 5 ("Rules for Choice"), and Part 6 ("Implications for Education").

bility of self-monitoring – would make me critical of the opinion, I am entitled to this opinion and am entitled also to rely on it in further deliberations, despite the fact that in forming the opinion I have employed the very procedures and abilities that are being challenged.

Having said this, however, self-monitoring may not be much more than a theoretical possibility here. Self-trust is being stretched to the limit in these cases, precisely because it is so difficult to mobilize my faculties and procedures in their own defense. Indeed, just the opposite is occurring. By hypothesis, my faculties and procedures can find no fault with the studies indicating that faculties and procedures similar to mine generally are not to be trusted when one is asked to predict the future behavior or accomplishments of interviewees after a personal interview. I can find no fault, moreover, with the studies indicating that reliability is not improved even when one is forewarned about this problem. Thus, this hypothetical case is exactly the kind of scenario that is potentially the most damaging to self-trust. Under such conditions, it will ordinarily be too risky to allow personal interviews to have any effect on my opinions. All I have been claiming is that this need not always and everywhere be the case. There are possible exceptions. It is not, in other words, an epistemic categorical imperative that, given the above described conditions, I refrain from forming postinterview opinions about the future performance of interviewees. Even when I know of studies indicating that reliability is generally not improved when interviewers are forewarned about the harmful effects of personal interviews, I can try to protect myself against these effects, provided that I have some notion of what it is that typically goes astray in attempts to identify and correct for these harmful effects. So, even under these extreme conditions, self-monitoring is at least theoretically an option, if only a remote one.

5. THE LACK OF GUARANTEES

I have been pointing out that in addressing epistemic worries raised by empirical studies, it can sometimes be appropriate to use faculties and procedures the reliability of which the studies throw into question, much as Descartes used his method of doubt to address worries about the method's reliability. Recall, however, that although there is nothing inherently inappropriate in resorting to the method of doubt in order to defend the reliability of the method, Descartes's strategy was not capable of producing the guarantees of reliability that he sought. Because he was using the indubitable to defend the indubitable, he could not possibly succeed in altogether extinguishing skeptical worries. He would not have succeeded even if he had somehow found an indubitable proof that God exists and an indubitable proof that God would now allow false-hoods to be indubitable.

In Chapter 1, I argue that the problem of the Cartesian circle is generalizable into a problem of the epistemological circle, which con-fronts every epistemology and potentially every inquirer. Like Descartes, we want to be able to defend our most fundamental faculties and methods, but the only way to do so is by using these faculties and methods, which means that we will never succeed in altogether ruling out the possibility that our opinions are widely mistaken. On the other hand, one of the lessons to be learned from Descartes's failed enterprise is that it is not a condition of our being rational that we be able to escape this circle and obtain such guarantees.

The same lesson applies to the empirically based worries I have been discussing. There can be no assurances that in trying to monitor myself against the kinds of errors documented in the studies, I will be able to do so successfully. Having opinions and using methods that are invulner-able to self-criticism, insofar as the goal is to have accurate and compre-hensive beliefs, involves noting and correcting, to my own deep satisfac-tion, any intellectual bias or any other shortcoming that is likely to interfere with this goal.[10] Even with the most diligent deliberation and self-monitoring, however, there are no foolproof signs to indicate that I have actually succeeded in eliminating biases and correcting shortcom-ings.

Consider, for example, the difficulties of distinguishing genuinely good reasons for belief from mere rationalizations. Even the most intel-ligent people are confronted with this problem. Indeed, in some respects, the threat of rationalizations is all the greater for intelligent people. Because they are adept at providing reasons for their beliefs, intelligent individuals are also well-equipped, by virtue of that very ability, to provide rationalizations for their beliefs, rationalizations that may possess many of the marks of good reasoning.[11]

The difficulty of distinguishing rationalizations from genuine reasons makes it important to check one's own opinions and reasonings against

10 "[I]t is part of rationality to be intent on noticing biases, including its own, and controlling and correcting these." Nozick, *The Nature of Rationality*, xii.
11 See Hilary Kornblith, "Distrusting Reason," *Midwest Studies in Philosophy*, 22 (1998).

the opinions and reasonings of others, because doing so can be an effective way to detect rationalizations and biases, especially if the factors distorting opinions are diverse and spread throughout the community in no particular order. Under these conditions, the public exchange of ideas is likely to be useful in canceling out individual biases and correcting for individual perspectives. On the other hand, if the sources of distortion are widely and uniformly distributed throughout the entire community, public debate and exchange of ideas will themselves be shaped by bias and, hence, may serve to reinforce biases rather than correct for them. Marxists view class interests as shaping political debate in just this way.[12]

Such dangers are real, and insofar as our goal is to have accurate and comprehensive beliefs, rationality requires that we monitor ourselves and our social environment against these dangers. There can be no assurances, however, that such monitoring will succeed and, hence, there can be no assurances of the reliability of our methods or the accuracy of our opinions. On the other hand, I have been arguing that assurances of reliability and accuracy are not prerequisites of epistemic rationality. The analogous point concerning practical rationality is widely acknowledged and readily appreciated. Prisoner's dilemma and other game theory cases illustrate that there are situations in which things can turn out badly, even disastrously, for everyone despite the fact that everyone is acting rationally. It is no different with epistemic rationality. Having rational opinions no more guarantees that one will achieve one's epistemic ends than making rational decisions guarantees that one will achieve one's practical ends.

What this illustrates, yet again, is that a significant dose of intellectual trust in ourselves, which cannot be defended in a non–question-begging way, is an inevitable part of our intellectual lives. If we had guarantees of the sort that classical foundationalists such as Descartes sought, such self-trust would not be so necessary, but we do not, and so it is.

6. INTERNAL CONFLICT AND CONFLICT WITH OTHERS

There is a final analogy worth pursuing briefly, since it anticipates some of the issues to be discussed in Part Two. It is an analogy between the first-person epistemic issues raised by the empirical studies I have been discussing and the issues raised by cases of intellectual conflict with others.

12 Again, see Kornblith, "Distrusting Reason."

The basic analogy is that in thinking about the relevance of these empirical studies for me and my opinions, I am looking at myself from the outside. I am taking an external stance with respect to myself, at least to the extent possible. The warnings I give myself, based on empirical data about the kinds of mistakes people in general make, are in effect warnings from an external vantage point to the effect that I am to be wary of having too much confidence in how things look from my perspective. The first-person epistemic question I have been addressing is, what am I to make of such warnings?

Framing the issue in this way makes it easy to appreciate analogies between these cases and cases involving intellectual conflicts with other people. The opinions of others often present challenges for some of my specific opinions, but they can also raise more general challenges, as when someone (or some group) tells me that my whole way of approaching a set of issues is fundamentally flawed. It is inappropriate for me simply to ignore or discount such challenges, but on the other hand, when the challenge is broad enough, it can be appropriate for me to try to address it using the very faculties, procedures, and opinions that are being challenged. I can employ my faculties, procedures, and opinions to reexamine as best I can my way of thinking about the issues and to monitor myself in light of the challenge. This may sometimes prompt me to reverse my previous opinions and defer to others. Other times I may conclude that withholding judgment is the best option, at least until further investigation establishes which, if either, party is right. At least sometimes, however, the best option may be to retain my previous opinions, with at most only minor adjustments.

This might seem an unacceptably partisan way to proceed, in that it allows one of the parties to the conflict to arbitrate it. However, it is deeply misleading to think about such conflicts in terms of a model of neutral arbitration between conflicting parties, especially insofar as the concern is with the first-person question, what am I to believe in the face of this conflict? In addressing this question, I am entitled to make what I can of the conflict using the faculties, procedures, and opinions I have confidence in, even if these faculties, procedures, and opinions are the very ones being challenged by others.

Precisely the same set of points holds with respect to conflicts or tensions produced by the empirical studies I have been discussing. As with the challenges arising out of interpersonal intellectual conflicts, I cannot simply dismiss these challenges by assuming that I am reliable and to leave the matter at that. I must instead reexamine as best I can my way of thinking about the issues and monitor myself in light of the warnings raised by the studies. However, I am entitled to do this from my own perspective, using the faculties, procedures, and opinions I have confidence in, even if the reliability of these very same faculties, procedures, and opinions are at issue in the studies.

Two

*Intellectual Trust in Others and in
One's Own Future and Past Self*

4

Self-Trust and the Authority of Others

When you tell me that something is the case, there are two kinds of questions for me to face. First, there are questions about your sincerity. Do you really believe what you are telling me, or are you trying to mislead me, and how can I tell the difference? Second, there are questions that presuppose that I can reliably determine whether or not you actually believe what you are telling me and that then go on to ask how, if at all, your opinion should affect my opinion.

Questions of the first sort are concerned with the sincerity or character of those providing the testimony rather than their reliability as inquirers. Politicians, salespersons, and lovers sometimes deny what they know to be true or assert what they know to be false, and virtually everyone stretches the truth from time to time. Given the extent to which we rely on others for information, it is important that we be able to determine reliably whether or not someone is sincerely trying to convey information.

Nevertheless, I will be principally concerned with questions of the second sort, which strip worries about sincerity from the problem of testimony and thereby focus attention on the intellectual authority of other people. Questions about the intellectual authority of others are, in turn, entangled with questions of self-trust. Whenever the opinions of others conflict with mine, there is a question as to whether I should defer to them or trust myself, and even when I have no opinion about a claim, there is a question as to whether to rely on the other person's opinion or to refuse to take any stand until I am in a position to form my own opinion.

Moreover, the central claim I defend in Part Two is that intellectual trust in others and trust in oneself are interrelated not just in specific cases but also in a more general, theoretical way. In Part One, I sketch the beginnings of an account of intellectual self-trust. In Part Two, I argue that grounds for trusting the opinions of others can be found in the intellectual trust one has in oneself.

A convenient way of fixing upon these issues is to suppose that I have found a partial inventory of what some other person believes. Call this person Anonymous. Although the inventory is extensive, many of Anonymous's beliefs are not listed, and suppose that among the omitted ones are those from which I could extract information about who Anonymous is. As a result, I know little or nothing about his or her background, training, abilities, and circumstances. Moreover, I have no knowledge about Anonymous from any other source. Under these conditions, how, if at all, should I adjust my opinions in the light of Anonymous's opinions?

Let's also stipulate that I can safely assume that the opinions on the list are deeply held by Anonymous. Stipulating this helps avoid some needless complications, since even in my own case mere opinion counts for little when issues of epistemic rationality are at stake. Some of my opinions are the doxastic counterparts of whims, in that I would not be prepared to stand by them on reflection, whereas others are less superficially held. These more stable and more deeply held opinions are the ones most determinative of what else I have reasons to believe.[1] An analogous point holds with respect to the opinions of others. If the opinions of others are to have an effect on my opinions, it is the deeply held ones rather than the superficial ones that ought to be taken most seriously by me.

There are variations of the above scenario that are also worth exploring. In the original scenario, I know nothing about Anonymous other than what the entries on the list allow me to infer, and they provide only minimal information. However, we can imagine scenarios in which the list provides me with additional information about Anonymous, and we can then ask whether this information should make a difference in how I regard the listed opinions. For example, would it make a difference if I knew that Anonymous is a contemporary of mine, as opposed to someone who lived in a different age? Would it matter if I knew

---

1   See the discussion in Chapter 2, especially §2.1.

Anonymous is from a very different culture? Does it matter whether Anonymous is male or female, old or young, or rich or poor?

I later consider several scenarios of these sorts, but for the moment I want to concentrate on the original scenario, because it is the one that raises most starkly the issue of whether it is reasonable to grant authority universally to the opinions of others. If this is reasonable, then even the opinions of complete strangers can be prima facie credible for me. Universal authority is to be contrasted both with specialized authority and with what Alan Gibbard has aptly called 'Socratic influence.'[2]

Suppose you get me to believe a claim through a series of well thought-out questions and instructions. Afterwards, I understand what you understand and, hence, believe what you believe. Because I now understand on my own why the claim is true, my believing it is not dependent upon your believing it. As I use the terms, you have exercised *influence* over me but not *authority*. There is not always a sharp line dividing the two. In many cases, they are hard to distinguish. Still, there is a difference, and epistemologically it is a significant one. Crudely put, it is the difference between my taking your word for something and my not doing so.

Even when I am prepared to take your word about something, however, I may be doing so only because I have special information about you, for example, information to the effect that your evidence, abilities, or circumstances put you in an especially good position to evaluate the claim in question. If so, I am granting you specialized authority. On the other hand, if the opinions of others universally have authority for me, I can reasonably take your word about a claim even if I know little or nothing about you.

Authority, whether specialized or universal, can be exercised either directly or indirectly. If you say "P" and I trust you and thereby come to believe P myself, your authority over me has been direct. On the other hand, if you recommend method M to me and if as a result I adopt M which then leads me to believe P, your authority over me with respect to M has been direct but with respect to P it has been indirect. For the sake of simplicity, I will be discussing only direct authority, although the theses I will be defending apply, mutatis mutandis, to indirect authority as well.

One of these theses is that it is reasonable, at least for most of us, to

2   Alan Gibbard, *Wise Choices, Apt Feelings* (Cambridge, MA: Harvard University Press, 1990), 174–5.

grant authority universally to the opinions of others. Thus, even when we have little or no information about someone, and in particular no information about the person's history of reliability, it can be reasonable to regard the person's opinions as credible. The contrary position is that universal authority is bogus and that every instance of rational authority is an instance of specialized authority. I will be calling this position 'epistemic egoism' and will in turn be distinguishing it from a more extreme position which I shall be calling 'epistemic egotism'.

Epistemic egotists maintain that it is never reasonable to grant authority to the opinions of others. The only legitimate way for someone else to affect my opinions is through Socratic influence. If you are able to instruct me about a topic so that I come to understand what you understand, I can reasonably believe what you believe; but according to egotists, it is never reasonable for me to borrow opinions from you, that is, to believe what you believe on the basis of your authority.

By contrast, epistemic egoists maintain that it sometimes can be reasonable for me to grant authority to others, but only if I have special information about them that gives me reasons to think that they are reliable with respect to the claim in question. The most straightforward way for me to have such reasons is by being acquainted with their track record. If by my lights their past record on the issues is a good one, I have reasons, all else being equal, to count their current opinions as credible. For example, if you tell me that P is true and I am familiar with your long history of reliability with respect to issues of this sort and I do not yet have my own opinion about P, I should be inclined to take your word about P. In a nice phrase, Philip Kitcher has called this 'earned authority'.[3]

Not all specialized authority is earned authority, however. Even if I have no knowledge of your track record, I can still have reasons to trust your opinions. You may have had training that gives you expertise, or you may have had access to relevant information, or you may have deliberated at great length about the issue. These kinds of considerations, and others like them, can make it reasonable for me to grant you authority, albeit not authority that is earned on the basis of your having a good record of reliability. Earned authority derives from your past

3 Philip Kitcher, "Authority, Deference and the Role of Individual Reason," in E. Mc-Mullin, ed., *The Social Dimension of Scientific Knowledge* (Notre Dame, IN: University of Notre Dame Press, 1992).

opinions being calibrated with the truth as I see it. Unearned but specialized authority derives from some other kind of information that attests to your reliability.

Since by hypothesis I have little or no information about Anonymous's background, training, abilities, or circumstances, I have little or no reason to grant specialized authority to Anonymous. More precisely, I have no such reason unless the list of propositions that Anonymous believes is extensive enough that it itself provides evidence of a reliable track record or special expertise. For simplicity's sake, however, let's assume that the entries on the list are too sparse or randomly scattered to provide such evidence. If so, the opinions of Anonymous have no specialized authority for me. Because egoists insist that the only legitimate authority is specialized authority, they will conclude that I have no reason to believe what Anonymous believes. Egotists take the more extreme position that it is never reasonable to grant any kind of authority to others. So, they too will say that I have no reason to believe what Anonymous believes. Thus, despite their other differences, egoists and egotists agree that unless Anonymous's opinions manage to exercise Socratic influence over me, they should not affect what I believe. Epistemic universalists, by contrast, say that it can be reasonable to grant authority universally to the opinions of others, and hence, according to them, even the beliefs of Anonymous, about whom I know little, can have authority for me.

The above positions – epistemic universalism, epistemic egoism, and epistemic egotism – have counterparts in ethics. According to ethical universalists, the goals, desires, and needs of other people should always count for something in one's deliberations about how to act. Ethical egoists and egotists both deny this. According to egoists, when the interests of other people are the objects of one's own goals, those interests can give one a reason to do something. Thus, if my doing X would promote your interest Y, this gives me a reason to do X if I have it as one of my goals that your interest Y be satisfied. Egoists insist, however, that I am under no compulsion to care about your interests. I can lack altruistic goals without being inconsistent or irrational. Ethical egotists go a step further. They say that it is irrational to have altruistic goals. Not only am I not required to have anyone else's interests as one of my goals, I am not permitted to do so. This is not to say that I cannot reasonably act in a way that promotes the interests of other people, but it is to say that it is never their interests that provide me with reasons for acting in this way. I can have a reason to do X, where X will promote your interests Y, but only if X would satisfy some nonaltruistic goal of mine.

It is not a simple matter to identify ethical egoists or egotists from their public behavior, especially because they may judge it prudent to appear as if they were universalists. It is no easier to identify epistemic egoists and egotists from their intellectual demeanor. They need not appear intellectually arrogant. They can even be publicly deferential. What distinguishes ethical egoists and egotists from ethical universalists is not their public behavior but rather their views about whether, or under what conditions, the goals, desires, and needs of others give one a reason to do something. Correspondingly, epistemic egoists and egotists are distinguished from epistemic universalists by their views about whether, or under what conditions, the opinions of others give one a reason to believe something. Universalists regard the opinions of other people as prima facie credible. They universally grant authority to others, even those about whom they know little or nothing. Both egoists and egotists refuse to grant universal authority. The former are willing to grant specialized authority to those whom they have reason to regard as reliable, whereas egotists are not willing to grant even specialized authority. According to egotists, it is never reasonable to believe something on the authority of another person and, hence, the only appropriate way for others to affect one's opinions is through Socratic influence. More exactly, this is so for the most extreme egotists. For convenience, I have been talking as if epistemic egoism, epistemic egotism, and epistemic universalism are sharply distinct positions, but for most purposes the differences among them are better viewed as being matters of degree.

In particular, the degree of universality or egoism in an account of intellectual trust is a function of the quantity and specificity of information that the account says I need about someone in order for his or her opinions to be prima facie credible for me. The less information I need and the more general this information can be, the easier it is for others to have intellectual authority for me and, hence, the more universalist the account is. Just the reverse is true of the degree of egoism in an account. The more information I need and the more specific this information must be (about the person's background, circumstances, and education, or about the particular faculties, methods, and procedures the person used in coming to the opinion in question), the more difficult it is for others to have intellectual authority for me and hence, the more egoistical the account is. As the requirements for special information become more demanding and, hence, as it becomes increasingly difficult for someone else's opinion to be prima facie credible for me, the account begins to shade into egotism. In the limiting case of pure egotism, no one has intellectual authority for me, and the only appropriate way for others to affect my opinions is through Socratic influence.

2. LOCKE ON THE AUTHORITY OF OTHERS

Among the major figures in the history of epistemology, David Hume developed what is perhaps the most sustained account of the role that the opinions of others should play in forming one's own opinions. I will have more to say about his views shortly, but the views of John Locke are a more interesting point of departure, because they are more extreme than Hume's. Locke expresses sympathies for epistemic egoism, and even for epistemic egotism. These leanings are most apparent in Books One and Four of *An Essay Concerning Human Understanding*, where he discusses the regulation of opinion. His central claim is that all of us have an obligation to make our opinions as accurate as possible and the way to meet this obligation is to gather evidence and then proportion our degrees of confidence in propositions to this evidence. Moreover, he repeatedly insists that in the process of regulating opinion, appeals to the intellectual authority of others are to be avoided.

In asserting that we have an obligation to make our opinions as accurate as possible, Locke was not denying that opinions can have desirable features in addition to that of being accurate, but he had little tolerance for the idea that we should pursue any of these other desiderata. Our obligations, as they apply to our beliefs, pertain only to their accuracy. In governing beliefs, we are to practice "indifference" to all other merits and demerits of beliefs. We have a duty to try to get things right and the way to do this is to follow what Nicholas Wolterstorff calls "Locke's principles of evidence and proportionality":[4]

(i) Principle of evidence: One has an obligation to base one's opinions on one's evidence, where one's evidence is what one knows with certainty.
(ii) Principle of appraisal: One has an obligation to appraise the probability of propositions on one's evidence.

4 Nicholas Wolterstorff, *John Locke and the Ethics of Belief* (Cambridge: Cambridge University Press, 1996).

(iii)   Principle of proportionality: One has an obligation to adopt degrees of confidence in propositions that are proportionate to their probabilities on one's evidence.

Underlying these principles is a set of presuppositions which Locke takes almost entirely for granted. First, there is his optimism: if individuals use their intellectual equipment well, following the above principles of evidence and proportionality, they can expect to have accurate opinions. Second, there is his individualism: his principles require individuals to exercise their own judgment about how strongly their evidence supports other propositions. Finally, there is his egalitarianism: his principles are intended for everyone, not just the intellectually elite.

This combination of optimism, individualism, and egalitarianism makes Locke a good candidate for being the first unqualifiedly modern epistemologist. Descartes, whose work is often cited as the beginning of modern epistemology, shared Locke's individualism and optimism but not his egalitarianism. The method of doubt that Descartes advocated was intended for philosopher-scientists, not ordinary people.[5]

These three Lockean presuppositions have been hugely influential, but in the twentieth century each presupposition has been widely and effectively attacked. As a result, it is no longer credible to hold any of them in the strong forms in which Locke held them. Nevertheless, I will be suggesting that there is something worth preserving in each.

This is getting ahead of the story, however. For now, it will do to point out that Locke is not naïve or simple-minded about any of the above presuppositions. For example, he qualifies his optimism in important ways, discussing at length what he calls "wrong measures of probability," that is, sources of inaccuracies in our opinions. Locke lists four such wrong measures of probability:

(i)   False propositions are inculcated in us from youth as self-evident.
(ii)   We become attached to familiar explanations and do not consider alternatives.
(iii)   We allow our emotions rather than a disinterested concern for truth to shape our opinions.
(iv)   We give allegiance to authority.

Locke adds that this last "wrong measure" is especially destructive:

The fourth and last wrong measure of probability I shall take notice of, and which keeps in ignorance, or errour, more people than all the others together,

5   Wolterstorff, op. cit.

is that which I have mentioned in the fore-going chapter, I mean, the giving up our assent to the common received opinions, either of our friends, or party; neighborhood, or country. How many men have no other ground of their tenets, than the supposed honesty, or learning, or number of those of the same profession? As if honest, or bookish men could not err; or truth were to be established by the vote of the multitude: yet this with most men serves the turn. The tenet has had the attestation of revered antiquity, it comes to me with the passport of former ages, and therefore I am secure in the reception I give it: other men have been, and are of the same opinion, for that is all is said, and therefore it is reasonable for me to embrace it. A man may more justifiably throw up cross and pile for his opinions, than take them up by such measure.[6]

Locke repeatedly stresses the dangers of using the opinions of others as a source of one's own opinions. The following is an especially sharply worded remark:

For, I think, we may as rationally hope to see with other Mens Eyes, as to know by other Mens Understandings. So much as we our selves consider and compre-hend of Truth and Reason, so much we possess of real and true Knowledge. The floating of other Mens Opinions in our brains makes us not one jot the more knowing, though they happen to be true. What in them was science, is in us but Opiniatretry, whilst we give up our Assent only to reverend names, and do not, as they did, employ our own Reason to *understand* those *Truths*, which gave them reputation. . . . In the Sciences, every one has so much, as he really knows and comprehends: What he believes only, and takes upon trust, are but shreds; which however well in the whole piece, make no considerable addition to his stock, who gathers them. Such borrowed Wealth, like Fairy-money, though it were Gold in the hand from he who received it, will be but Leaves and Dust when it comes to use.[7]

In these passages and many others like them, Locke's individualism, optimism, and egalitarianism are all at work to make him utterly distrust-ful of granting intellectual authority to others. Indeed, as the second of the above passages illustrates, he so emphasized the importance of intel-lectual self-reliance that he seems to be expressing doubts even about granting specialized authority to the opinions of others. He regards deference as an excuse for not bringing one's own intelligence to bear on the issues at hand. It is a recipe for error and for what would later come to be called "group think." Locke's view is that there is always

6   John Locke, *An Essay Concerning Human Understanding*, ed. Peter Nidditch (Oxford: Clar-endon Press, 1975), IV, xx, 17.
7   Locke, *An Essay Concerning Human Understanding*, I, iv, 23.

something substandard in taking someone else's word for the truth of a claim. He has no objection to being open to Socratic influence, because in such cases we come to understand for ourselves why the claim in question is true, but when we rely on the intellectual authority of others, the resulting belief is no more than "the floating of other Mens Opinions in our brains."

The alternative to trusting the opinions of others is for everyone, even ordinary people (Locke's egalitarianism), to rely on their own judgment and reason (his individualism), and if they are careful to conform to their opinions to the evidence, the result will be "real and true knowledge" (his optimism).

Few twentieth-century epistemologists are prepared to defend epistemic egotism, but there are those who are at least sympathetic to egoism. For example, both J. L. Mackie and Robert Audi emphasize the necessity of having information about the person providing testimony if one is to revise one's opinions in light of the testimony. Thus, Mackie argues that "authoritative knowledge" requires information about the credibility of the witnesses:

Knowledge that one acquires through testimony, that is, by being told by other people, by reading, and so on, can indeed be brought under the heading of this authoritative knowledge, but only if the knower somehow checks, for himself, the credibility of the witnesses. And since, if it is a fact that a certain witness is credible, it is an external fact, checking this in turn will need to be based on observations that the knower makes himself – or else on further testimony, but, if an infinite regress is to be avoided, we must come back at some stage to what the knower observes for himself.[8]

Audi makes a similar claim regarding epistemic justification:

I cannot acquire justification for believing something on the basis of testimony unless I have some degree of justification for believing that the attester is credible, as well as for certain other propositions, such as that I heard the testimony correctly. This justification cannot come entirely from testimony.[9]

3. THE SOCIAL CONSTRUCTION OF OPINION

One of Locke's earliest critics, Thomas Reid, offered what is still one of the most powerful critiques of Locke's epistemology. He insisted upon

8 J. L. Mackie, "The Possibility of Innate Knowledge," *Proceedings of the Aristotelian Society*, 70 (1969–70), 254.
9 Robert Audi, "The Place of Testimony in the Fabric of Knowledge and Justification," *American Philosophical Quarterly*, 34(1997), 405–22.

the reasonableness of our natural attitudes of trust both in our own intellectual faculties and those of others. According to Reid, it is reasonable, all else being equal, for us to rely on the testimony of other people, even if we know little or nothing about their reliability. He regarded it as a first principle of epistemology that testimony-based beliefs, as well as perceptual beliefs, are by their very nature prima facie justified. Like other first principles, this principle cannot be proved but it can be supported by such factors as common assent, naturalness, and practical necessity. Indeed, Reid thought that if our natural attitudes of trust, in ourselves and in others, were not reasonable, the inevitable result would be skepticism. There would be little that we could reasonably believe:

I believe by instinct whatever [my parents and teachers] told me, long before I had the idea of a lie, or a thought of the possibility of their deceiving me. Afterwards, upon reflection, I found that they had acted like fair and honest people, who wished me well. I found that, if I had not believed what they told me, before I could give a reason for my belief, I had to this day been little better than a changeling. And although this natural credulity hath sometimes occasioned my being imposed upon by deceivers, yet it hath been of infinite advantage to me upon the whole; therefore, I consider it as another good gift of Nature.[10]

The wise and beneficent Author of Nature, who intended that we be social creatures, and that we should perceive the greatest and most important part of our knowledge by the information of others, hath, for these purposes, implanted in our natures two principles that tally with each other. The first of these principles is, a propensity to speak the truth, and to use the signs of language so as to convey our real sentiments. . . . Another original principle implanted in us by the Supreme Being, is a disposition to confide in the veracity of others, and to believe what they tell us. This is the counterpart of the former; and, as that may be called the principle of veracity, we shall, for want of a more proper name, call this the principle of credulity. . . . It is evident that, in the matter of testimony, the balance of human judgement is by nature inclined to the side of belief; and turns to that side of itself, when there is nothing put into the opposite scale. If it was not so, no proposition that is uttered in discourse would be believed, until it was examined and tried by reasons, and most men would be unable to find reasons for believing the thousandth part of what is told them.[11]

These passages indicate that Reid is an epistemic universalist and, moreover, a universalist of an especially strong sort. According to Reid,

10   Thomas Reid, *Essays on the Intellectual Powers of Man*, in *Thomas Reid's Inquiry and Essays*, eds. R. Beanblossom and K. Lehrer (Indianapolis: Hackett, 1983), VI, 5, 281–2.
11   Reid, op. cit., 93–5.

it is a first principle of epistemology to trust, all else being equal, the opinions of others. Testimony is necessarily prima facie credible and testimony-based beliefs necessarily prima facie reasonable.

Like Reid, David Hume readily acknowledges the need to rely on the testimony of other people, but he argues that one should rely on testimony only to the degree that one has independent evidence of its general reliability:

> [T]here is no species of reasoning more common, more useful, and even necessary for human life, than that which is derived from the testimony of men, and the reports of eye-witnesses and spectators. This species of reasoning, perhaps, one may deny to be founded on the relation of cause and effect. I shall not dispute a word. It will be sufficient to observe that our assurance in any argument of this kind is derived from no other principle than our observation of the veracity of human testimony, and of the usual conformity of facts to reports of witnesses. It being a general maxim, that no objects have any discoverable connexion together, and that all the inferences, which we draw from one to another, are founded merely on our experience of their constant and regular conjunction; it is evident that we ought not to make an exception to this maxim in favour of human testimony, whose connexion with any other event seems, in itself, as little necessary as any other.[12]

> The reason we place any credit in witnesses and historians, is not derived from any connexion, which we perceive *a priori*, between testimony and reality, but because we are accustomed to find a conformity between them.[13]

Hume rejects any notion that there is an a priori reason to think testimony is reliable, and he correspondingly rejects the idea that testimony is a basic source of justification. Even so, this does not preclude him from being an epistemic universalist, as I use the term here. Like Reid, he thinks that it can be reasonable to trust the opinions of someone about whom one knows little or nothing, for example, Anonymous. However, unlike Reid, he thinks that this is so only because each of us has, or can potentially construct, an inductive argument to the effect that testimony in general is by and large reliable. Thus, Hume speaks of "our observation of the veracity of human testimony" and of our being "accustomed" to find a "conformity" between testimony and reality.[14]

---

12   David Hume, *An Enquiry Concerning Human Understanding*, ed. P. H. Nidditch and L. A. Selby-Bigge (Oxford: Oxford University Press, 1975), 111.

13   Hume, *An Enquiry Concerning Human Understanding*, 113.

14   In a similar spirit, F. H. Bradley argues that testimony can never be an independent source of information, analogous to first-person observation, since "it must by its nature involve

Reid and Hume both sought to develop an account of testimony that was sensitive to the fact that we are social beings in intellectual matters as much as in other matters. They were right to do so. An adequate account of intellectual authority and testimony must do justice to the extent to which our opinions are formed out of the opinions and concepts of others. In early childhood we acquire an enormous number of beliefs from our immediate family, and we do so with little or no deliberation. The range of people directly influencing us soon widens to include friends, teachers, and other acquaintances. As we continue to develop, it widens still further to include authors, journalists, lecturers, and countless others whom we do not know personally. Moreover, the most pervasive and powerful influences on us come not from identifiable individuals but from our culture and tradition. Our most fundamental concepts and our deepest assumptions, the material out of which most of our opinions are formed, are not self-generated. They are passed down to us from previous generations as part of our intellectual inheritance. We are thus thoroughly indebted to others for our beliefs.

Moreover, many of these beliefs are ones that we are not in a position to justify personally. I believe, and take myself to believe reasonably, that the phlogiston account of fire has been proven false, that Henry James wrote *The Golden Bowl*, that the Romans occupied part of what is now Great Britain, that the sun is much larger than the earth's moon, and that Lincoln was assassinated by John Wilkes Booth. However, there is little that I can personally mount in the way of a defense of any of these beliefs. I do not have first-hand knowledge of any of these claims. So, in coming to have these beliefs, I must have relied on the opinions of others, but I cannot recall the exact source for any of them. I do not know whether it was one of my parents, or a friend, or a teacher, or a book, or something else that convinced me of them.

Nor does it seem feasible, despite Hume's suggestion to the contrary, for me to use my own personal experiences and observations of the reliability of witnesses to construct an inductive defense of the reliability of testimony in general (from whatever source). The range of cases in which I have observed first-hand "the veracity of human testimony" is too narrow. I can personally confirm the reliability of only a tiny per-

an inference, and that inference must be founded on our direct knowledge. It is an extension of our personal experience, but an extension that proceeds from and rests on that basis." Bradley, "The Evidence of Spiritualism," in *Collected Essays*, vol. 2 (Oxford: Oxford University Press, 1935), Essay 29.

centage of the total set of human testimony. I am not even in a position to confirm personally more than a small portion of the testimony that I as an individual have relied upon. The extent to which I rely on testimony is so great that, realistically, I have the time and resources to check out the accuracy of only an insignificantly small fraction of it. Accordingly, my own observations and experiences are far too meager and narrow in scope to constitute a sufficient inductive base for the conclusion that the testimony that I personally have relied on is reliable, much less for the conclusion that testimony in general is reliable. Ernest Sosa succinctly makes the point as follows:

If we are largely justified in accepting testimony, how so? We might appeal to a principle like this: (T) Testimony is correct more often than not. But how to justify acceptance of T? There is so much testimony, past, present, and future! There are so many cultures, and cultures so diverse. How can one be sure about anything so strong as T?[15]

C. A. J. Coady makes a similar criticism, arguing that Hume's attempt to defend the general reliability of testimony by appealing to "our observation of the veracity of human testimony" is either insufficient or circular. Coady observes that "our reliance on testimony rightly goes beyond anything that could be justified by personal observations." Thus, Hume's defense is insufficient if by "our observation" he means to be referring to the personal observations made by each of us as individuals. On the other hand, if by "our observation" Hume means to include the collective experience of human beings, it is conceivable that this collective experience might constitute an appropriately broad base for an inductive defense of the general reliability of testimony. Unfortunately, the collective experience of human beings is available to me to use in an inductive defense of testimony only if it is reasonable for me to trust testimony in the first place, hence the circle.[16]

Problems of this sort with the Humean account of testimony, in combination with an increasing appreciation for the extent to which our opinions are formed by others, have convinced many of the most influential contemporary epistemologists to follow Reid in claiming that

15   Ernest Sosa, "Testimony and Coherence," in Sosa, *Knowledge in Perspective*, 215–24.
16   See C. A. J. Coady, *Testimony* (Oxford: Oxford University Press, 1992). For arguments similar to Sosa's and Coady's, see Alvin Plantinga, *Warrant and Proper Function*, especially p. 79; and Frederick Schmitt, "Socializing Epistemology: An Introduction through Two Sample Issues," in F. Schmitt, ed., *Socializing Epistemology* (Rowman and Littlefield: London, 1994), 1–28.

testimony is necessarily prima facie credible. For example, Coady argues that the existence of a common language carries with it a commitment to some degree of unmediated acceptance of testimony. According to Coady, necessarily, in any public language a very high proportion of the statements made by the community are testimonial statements, and in addition, necessarily, a very high proportion of these statements are true. Coady concludes that necessarily any particular instance of testimony is prima facie justified.[17] Tyler Burge, as a part of a larger rationalist account of knowledge, argues that we have a priori justification for relying on "rational sources, or resources for reason," including memory, perception, and other people's testimony. Indeed, Burge argues that not only is there an a priori justification for Reid's principle of credulity, but in addition the individual beliefs formed on the basis of testimony are themselves properly regarded as a priori.[18] Richard Swinburne makes a similar claim about testimony, arguing that testimony is necessarily prima facie evidence for the truth of what it testified.[19] Other epistemologists argue that trust in the opinions of others is part of the fabric of our intellectual practices and as such must be regarded a prima facie credible. For instance, Edward Craig proposes that the concept of knowledge derives from the notion of a good informant and that, thus, reliance on testimony is built into the concept of knowledge.[20] William Alston makes an analogous claim with respect to justification, arguing that key features of our concept of justification are parasitic on the practice of justifying propositions in dialogue with one another, a practice that presupposes that testimony has at least some initial credibility.[21]

Each of these philosophers correctly recognizes that an adequate epistemology must be sensitive to the fact that virtually everything we think and believe has been shaped, directly or indirectly, by others. On the other hand, it is not hard to detect a hint of desperation in some of these accounts. The working assumption seems to be that there is no choice but to try to resurrect a Reidian account of testimony. If epistemic egotists are unacceptably dismissive of all intellectual authority, and if epistemic egotists are unacceptably skeptical about our relying on the

17 C. A. J. Coady, *Testimony*.

18 Tyler Burge, "Content Preservation," *Philosophical Review*, 102 (1993), 457–88.

19 Richard Swinburne, *The Existence of God* (Oxford: Oxford University Press, 1979), 260, 272.

20 Edward Craig, *Knowledge and the State of Nature* (Oxford: Clarendon Press, 1990).

21 William Alston, "Internalism and Externalism in Epistemology," in *Epistemic Justification* (Ithaca, NY: Cornell University Press, 1989).

opinions of people about whom we know little or nothing, and if Humeans are unacceptably optimistic about the project of constructing an inductive defense of the general reliability of testimony, it may seem as if the only alternative is to side with Reid and to assert precisely what Hume was at such pains to deny, namely, that there is some property of testimony that makes testimony necessarily prima facie credible and testimony-based beliefs necessarily prima facie reasonable. According to Reid, God implanted in humans a propensity to speak the truth and a corresponding propensity to believe what others tell us, and it is this that explains why testimony is necessarily reliable in general and why testimony-based beliefs are necessarily prima facie reasonable. Most contemporary epistemologists, by contrast, are reluctant to resort to a theistic defense of testimony[22] and, thus, they feel pressured to search for some nontheological property of testimony that would explain why testimony-based beliefs are necessarily prima facie reasonable. Witness, for example, Coady's contention that the very notion of a public language carries with it a commitment to some degree of unmediated acceptance of testimony.

I argue in the coming pages that there is a better approach to the problem of intellectual authority and testimony, one that rejects Locke's egoism and that does not depend upon a Humean induction to support the general reliability of testimony but that also does not take the desperate Reidian route of stipulating that testimony is necessarily prima facie credible. Moreover, it is an approach that steers its way between two dangers that are to be avoided in fashioning an account of intellectual authority.

One of these dangers is that of not sufficiently emphasizing the extent to which we are social beings, intellectually as well as otherwise. No account of intellectual authority can afford to ignore the degree to which our opinions are shaped by the opinions of others. However, as discussed in Chapter 2, neither should an account of intellectual authority ignore the importance of intellectual independence, which was at the heart of Locke's epistemology. This is the second of the dangers to be avoided, that of becoming so fixated on the social construction of opinion that respect for intellectual self-reliance and tolerance of intellectual rebellion is eroded. The greater the emphasis on the inescapability of one's own opinions being shaped by the opinions of others, and the more this emphasis is built into the conditions of rational belief, the less room

22 An exception is Alvin Plantinga; see Plantinga, *Warrant and Proper Function*, 80.

there is apt to be for individuals to engage in radical but rational critiques of the prevailing opinions and assumptions of their community. In Locke, we may see the dangers of an apotheosis of the individual and his or her reason, but there are equally real dangers of an apotheosis of the social.

An adequate account of intellectual authority must find a way of steering a course between both of these dangers. It must acknowledge that in intellectual matters, as in other matters, we are thoroughly social beings and, more specifically, it must explain how it can be reasonable for us to rely on the expertise and information of people about whom we know little. However, it must also acknowledge the importance of intellectual self-reliance and, more specifically, it must leave room for the possibility of rational iconoclasm, that is, for the possibility of individuals rejecting the most cherished opinions of their contemporaries or the most deeply held assumptions of their traditions and yet still being rational.

For the moment, however, I am going to set aside this problem and instead return to the issue of intellectual trust in oneself, because the materials for constructing an adequate account of the intellectual authority of other people are to be found there.

4. THE INCOHERENCE OF EPISTEMIC EGOTISM AND EGOISM

In Chapter 1, I argued that trust in one's own intellectual faculties, procedures, and opinions is a part of any nonskeptical intellectual life. Any defense of our most fundamental faculties, procedures, and opinions will make use of those same faculties, procedures, and opinions. Thus, there are no non–question-begging guarantees of our reliability, and all our intellectual projects require that we have intellectual faith in ourselves.

Those who cannot accommodate themselves to this reality and who refuse to be satisfied with anything short of a non–question-begging defense of their own reliability are forced to be skeptics. Although there is nothing inherently incoherent about skepticism, the fact of the matter is that most of us are not skeptics. By and large, we are prepared to trust our own intellectual faculties and the opinions they generate even if we lack airtight assurances of their reliability. Moreover, it can be reasonable for us to have such trust. Rationality does not require us to have non–question-begging defenses of our own reliability.

But if we have basic trust in our own opinions and intellectual faculties, can we coherently withhold trust from others? Both epistemic egotists and egoists say "yes." They deny that it is reasonable to grant authority universally to the opinions of others. The question is whether this is a coherent position for those who have basic intellectual trust in themselves.

In thinking about this question, it is important to resist the view that some version or another of epistemic egoism is inevitable, because we have no choice but to make up our own minds about who is reliable; no one can do this for us. It might then seem a manageably small step to the conclusion that whenever we rely on the opinions of others, we are in effect granting, or refusing to grant, specialized authority to them. The conclusion, in other words, is that once we probe deeply enough, all instances of authority can be seen as instances of specialized authority.

Suppose I rely upon your opinion about some issue. Then, according to this way of thinking, I must have decided that you are more reliable than I, or if I had no prior opinion about the issue, I have at least decided that you are not unreliable. In either case, I am responsible for granting you authority. The notion that one cannot escape responsibility for one's life and conduct is a familiar preoccupation of both existentialists and management experts, the former with their talk of our being condemned to be free and the latter with their aphorism, "one can delegate authority but not responsibility." The claim here is analogous, namely, granting intellectual authority to others cannot excuse me from responsibility for my own opinions, because it is I who bestows authority, if only by omission.

But even if all of this is correct, it misses the interesting epistemological question. Grant for the sake of argument that insofar as I rely on the opinions of others, there has been an implicit decision on my part to do so and that I am thus responsible for having granted them authority. Nevertheless, this leaves unanswered the question of whether I am compelled, on pains of irrationality, to grant this authority, given that I trust my own intellectual faculties. What makes epistemic egoism an interesting position is that it answers "no" to this question. Egoists (and of course, egotists as well) are prepared to assert that there is nothing incoherent in my having a basic trust in my own intellectual faculties while not having such trust in those of others.

Attempts to trivialize epistemic egoism are similar to attempts to trivialize ethical egoism. In the ethical case, the strategy is to try to show that those who appear to be altruistically motivated – parents, lovers, friends, even the Albert Schweitzers of the world – are really egoistically motivated. Schweitzer desired to relieve the suffering of others. So, to the extent that he succeeded in reducing the suffering of others, he satisfied one of his desires. Thus, if happiness is essentially a matter of having one's desires satisfied, Schweitzer acted in a way that made him happy. The conclusion that is supposed to follow from these observations is that his motivation was not different in kind from that of, say, a used-car dealer who pretends to be concerned for the well-being of a customer in trying to make a sale. Both are motivated by the achievement of an end that would make them personally happy.

There is much to be said, and much that has been said, about arguments of this sort, but for purposes here the important point is that they fail to address the central ethical question, which is whether, and under what conditions, the desires and goals of others should influence our decisions about what to do. Even if it is true that we are motivated to act benevolently only when we desire that the desires, goals, and needs of others be satisfied – a desire whose satisfaction, like any other, brings us a kind of contentment – this leaves unanswered the question of whether it would be wrong or incoherent or irrational for us not to have such a desire, especially insofar as we take our own desires and goals seriously in making decisions.

Similarly, even if it is granted that when we rely on the opinions of others, we are implicitly making a decision to grant them authority, this leaves unanswered the interesting epistemic question, which is whether it would be incoherent for us not to grant some such authority to others, given that we trust our own intellectual faculties. Most of us have prima facie trust in our own faculties even though we cannot give a non-question-begging defense of their reliability. But if so, might not we be rationally compelled to have prima facie trust in others as well? I argue that the answer to this question is "yes" and, thus, I will be defending a version of epistemic universalism. Epistemic egoists and egotists, by contrast, are committed to answering "no" to the question.

Whatever their other differences, however, egoists and universalists can and should agree that intellectual authority, whether universal or specialized, has a role to play in influencing opinion only to the extent that one can reasonably infer what it is that the person with authority believes. Even if your opinions about P are prima facie credible for me, your belief P does not give me a reason to my alter my opinion about P unless it is rational for me to believe that you in fact believe P. Mere belief is not enough. It must be rational for me to believe this. This point is important for the discussions in Chapters 5 and 6, where I extend the account of intellectual authority sketched here to other domains. But for the moment, the task is to explain why it is incoherent for us not to grant authority to others if we are not skeptical about our own intellectual abilities and opinions.

Our belief systems are saturated with the opinions of others. In our childhoods, we acquire beliefs from parents, siblings, and teachers without much thought. These constitute the backdrop against which we form yet other beliefs, and, often enough, these latter beliefs are also the products of other people's beliefs. We hear testimony from those we meet, read books and articles, listen to television and radio reports, and then form opinions on the basis of these sources of information. Moreover, our most fundamental concepts and assumptions, the material out of which our opinions are built, are not self-generated but rather are passed down to us from previous generations as part of our intellectual inheritance. We are not intellectual atoms, unaffected by one another. Our views are continuously and thoroughly shaped by others. But then, if we have intellectual trust in ourselves, we are pressured also to have prima facie intellectual trust in others. For, insofar as the opinions of others have shaped our opinions, we would not be reliable unless they were.

Of course, not everyone affects the opinions of everyone else. I live in one place, and you in another, and we may not have had any contact with one another. So, you have probably not influenced my opinions in any significant way. On the other hand, unless one of us has had an extraordinary upbringing, your opinions have been shaped by an intellectual and physical environment that is broadly similar to the one that has shaped my opinions. Moreover, your cognitive equipment is broadly similar to mine. So, once again, if I trust myself, I am pressured on the threat of inconsistency also to trust you.

This is not to deny the obvious truth that there are significant intellectual differences among people. Cognitive diversity is an undeniable fact. The increasing ease of global communications has made our differences more apparent than ever, while cultural anthropology and cognitive sociology has made the study of diversity into a staple of academic literature. As a result, there is now impressive documentation of differences in the belief systems of North Americans and East Asians, Arabs and Europeans, Germans and Italians, Christians and Buddhists, rural peoples and urban peoples, blue collar workers and professional workers, college graduates and high school dropouts, and of course, men and women. Striking as these differences sometimes are, they should not be allowed to obscure the fact that there are also broad cognitive commonalities among humans. Indeed, the differences among humans look insignificant when compared to the differences between us and other intelligent creatures, for example, ants, whales, and bats. Because we tend to take our similarities for granted, it is easy to overlook how similar we are to one another in intellectual faculties and backgrounds. It is our differences that fascinate us. A sign of this is that we make far finer distinctions about one another than we do about anything else, and among the most intricate distinctions we make are those concerning our respective capacities, personalities, and backgrounds.

The availability of so many distinctions, and the zeal with which we employ them, may sometimes make it appear as if we are radically different from one another, but any careful look will reveal that this is an exaggeration. The intellectual capacities and the intellectual environments of all people with whom we are familiar have broad commonalities. As a consequence, their beliefs also have broad commonalities. This is true even of those who are distant from one another in time and place. For example, they all believe that there are other human beings, that there are living things other than human beings, that some things are larger than others, that some things are heavier than others, that some events occurred before other events, that some things are dangerous and others are not, that some things are edible and others are not, and so on.

Ignoring the enormous backdrop of shared beliefs and narrowly fixing upon the undeniable differences in beliefs across cultures can create an impression that people in cultures far removed from one another in time or place have beliefs utterly different from one another. This impression can be further encouraged, and even acquire an aura of inevitability, by holistic theories of concepts and beliefs, the most extreme of which assert that beliefs and concepts are so intertwined with one another that it is impossible to understand any specific belief without understanding the system in which it is embedded in its entirety. Such accounts might seem to lend support to the claim that there is no large, shared backdrop of beliefs across peoples and cultures. According to these accounts, differences in beliefs and concepts among cultures have endless rippling effects. There is no such thing as a narrowly contained difference. Given the interconnectedness of concepts and beliefs, even seemingly small differences across cultures permeate everything that people within those respective cultures think. As a result, concepts are incommensurable and beliefs massively different across cultures. It is not even safe to infer that very basic beliefs, for example, that some things are heavier than others, are shared across cultures. Indeed, given the incommensurability of concepts, people in one culture cannot even really understand what it is that people in a distinct culture believe.

Extreme holism is itself an immensely controversial position,[23] and as such cannot provide an unproblematic, theoretical justification of radical cognitive diversity. For the discussion here, however, the most interesting point is that extreme holism can also be marshaled, indeed has been marshaled, to argue for exactly the opposite position, namely, the impossibility of radical cognitive diversity. Donald Davidson maintains that precisely because the concepts and beliefs making up a belief system are inevitably so intertwined with one another, one cannot make good sense of the idea of there being beliefs and concepts massively different from one's own.[24]

Davidson's conclusion is stronger than I want or need to make, but a number of his preliminary discussions and penultimate conclusions are both right and important. In mounting his arguments, Davidson focuses on instances of radical interpretation, where it is an open question whether the creatures being interpreted have beliefs at all. He observes that it is only by assuming broad agreement on basics with those whom we are interpreting that we can get the interpretation process started. Unless we can assume that the creatures have perceptual faculties that provide them with extensive information about their immediate environment and that this information influences their bodily movements, and unless we can also assume that the information being provided to them about their environment has broad similarities with what we take their immediate environment to be, we will not be in a position to establish the kind of correlations between their environment and their bodily movements that would give us reasons to infer that they have beliefs at all, much less be able to infer what those beliefs are. Davidson attempts to move from this epistemological point to the metaphysical conclusion that it is altogether impossible for there to be belief systems massively different from one another. This is an inference that many philosophers find implausible,[25] but the epistemological point is an im-

23 For a detailed, critical assessment of holism, see Jerry Fodor and Ernest LePore, *Holism: A Shopper's Guide* (Oxford: Basil Blackwell, 1992).

24 Donald Davidson, "A Coherence Theory of Knowledge and Belief," in E. LePore, ed., *The Philosophy of Donald Davidson: Perspectives on Truth and Interpretation* (London: Basil Blackwell, 1986), 307–19.

25 For example, see Peter Klein, "Radical Interpretation and Global Skepticism," and Colin

portant one on its own. It is an effective antidote to the idea that it is both easy and common for one to have convincing evidence that the beliefs of people in other cultures have few if any commonalities with one's own beliefs.

Given the broad commonalities in the intellectual equipment and environment of peoples across times and cultures, it is not surprising that there are correspondingly broad commonalities in the concepts and beliefs of these peoples. Nor should it be surprising that these commonalities pressure us, on threat of inconsistency, to trust one another. Admittedly, the pressures need not be uniform. The greater the differences between peoples and cultures, the less the pressure there is for them to trust one another intellectually. Still, because the abilities and circumstances of even distant peoples have broad commonalities with one's own, one has at least some reason, if only a weak one, to trust even them intellectually.

So, insofar as it is rational for me to believe that someone else believes P, I automatically have at least a weak reason to believe P myself. I do not need to know anything special about the person. In particular, I do not need to have information about the person's talents or training or track record with respect to the kind of issues in question, as egoists suggest. All else being equal, it is incoherent for me not to trust the other person, given that I trust myself.

F. H. Bradley argued that I can trust what others tell me only if I legitimately view them as observing on my behalf. I need to be able to regard them as "extending" my own personal experiences. He also argued that I can legitimately view others as extending my personal experiences only if I am justified in thinking that they have essentially the same outlook as I. The phrase Bradley uses is "identification of consciousness."[26] The above argument requires nothing so strong. The argument does presuppose that there are broad commonalities between the person giving and the person receiving testimony, but there being these broad commonalities is compatible with the familiar observation that often part of the value of testimony is that it comes from someone with a different outlook.

At the heart of the above argument is a consistency claim. Given that

McGinn, "Radical Interpretation and Epistemology," both in E. LePore, ed., *Truth and Interpretation: Perspectives on the Philosophy of Donald Davidson*.

26   See F. H. Bradley, "The Presuppositions of Critical History," in *Collected Essays* (Oxford: Oxford University Press, 1969), 1–76.

it is reasonable for me to think that my opinions have been thoroughly influenced by others and that my intellectual faculties and my intellectual environment have broad commonalities with theirs, I risk inconsistency if I have intellectual trust in myself and do not have intellectual trust in others. The prima facie intellectual trust I have in myself pressures me also to have prima facie intellectual trust in others. Trust in myself radiates outwards toward others.

The argument I am making here is an epistemic, not a pragmatic, argument. H. H. Price, in the spirit of Reid, advocated a policy of trusting testimony, but he offered an explicitly pragmatic defense of the policy: we would forfeit a large supply of information that serves us well if we did not follow such a policy.[27] By contrast, the grounds offered above for trusting the opinions of others are epistemic. Insofar as it is epistemically rational for me to have prima facie trust in the general reliability of my own faculties and opinions, so too it is rational for me, insofar as my goal is to have accurate and comprehensive beliefs, to have prima facie trust in the general reliability of other people's faculties and opinions.

There are various ways of trying to block the above argument's force, but none of these ways is especially plausible. One strategy is for me to deny that my intellectual faculties have broad commonalities with those of others. Another is to deny that the intellectual and physical environment that helped shape my beliefs have broad commonalities with the environments that have shaped the beliefs of others. Still another is to deny that my environment has affected me in the way that the environments of others has affected them, because I have somehow managed to rise above my environment.

Most of us at one time or another are tempted to think of ourselves as distinctive in thought as well as behavior. We want to believe that what we think and perhaps even how we think is out of the ordinary. Nevertheless, in its most extreme form, this is not a view that many of us would be willing to endorse. At least in our most thoughtful moments, we think of ourselves as not being fundamentally different from others.

Even so, there is nothing inherently incoherent in my thinking that I was born with radically different abilities from others or that I was raised in a radically different way from others or that unlike almost everyone else I have managed to rise entirely above the influences of my intellec-

27 H. H. Price, *Belief* (New York: Humanities Press, 1969), especially 111–12.

tual environment. Accordingly, there is nothing inherently incoherent in my refusing to grant intellectual authority to others. Thus, it is not an utterly necessary condition of rationality that I grant such authority. The conclusion of the above argument is weaker than this. It is that intellectual self-trust creates a pressure to grant authority to others that is extremely difficult to avoid. Most of us would be willing to admit, at least on reflection, that our intellectual faculties have broad commonalities with those of others and that a large portion of our opinions have been influenced by the same kinds of factors that have influenced others and that we have not cast off these influences. But then, insofar as we have intellectual trust in ourselves, that is, insofar as we are not skeptics, it is reasonable, all else being equal, for us to trust the opinions of others as well.

To accept this conclusion is to accept a modest form of epistemic universalism, "modest" because in its strongest form, universalism implies that the opinions of others are necessarily prima facie credible. Nothing in the above arguments, which are based on considerations of influence and similarity, are capable of supporting anything stronger than a contingent claim. The conclusion is not that the opinions of others are necessarily prima facie credible, or that the pressures to trust their opinions are completely and utterly inescapable. The conclusion, rather, is the more cautious one that these pressures are extremely difficult to avoid.[28] There are broad features of our intellectual situation that threaten us with inconsistency if we do not generally trust the opinions of others.[29]

---

28 Compare the conclusion here with Jonathan Adler, "Testimony, Trust, Knowing," *Journal of Philosophy*, 91 (1994), 264–75. Adler argues that testimony is trustworthy until shown otherwise and that it gets this status from extensive background information which in normal circumstances is rarely noticed.

29 For other important approaches to the problem of testimony, see Jonathan Adler, "Testimony, Trust, Knowing"; Robert Audi, "The Place of Testimony"; Tyler Burge, "Content Preservation"; David Christenson and Hilary Kornblith, "Testimony, Memory and the Limits of the A Priori," *Philosophical Studies*, 5 (1996), 1–20; C. A. J. Coady, *Testimony*; Elizabeth Fricker, "The Epistemology of Testimony," *Proceedings of Aristotelian Society Supplement*, 61 (1987), 57–83; Alvin Goldman, *Knowledge in a Social World* (Oxford: Clarendon Press, 1999), 103–130; John Hardwig, "Epistemic Dependence," *Journal of Philosophy*, 82 (1985), 335–49, and Hardwig, "The Role of Trust in Knowledge," *Journal of Philosophy*, 88 (1991), 693–708; Richard Holton, "Deciding to Trust, Coming to Believe," *Australasian Journal of Philosophy* 72 (1994), 63–76; Alvin Plantinga, *Warrant and Proper Function*, especially 77–88; Michael Root, "How to Teach a Wise Man," in *Pragmatism, Reason, and Norms*, ed. K. Westphal (New York: Fordham University Press, 1998), 89–110; Frederick Schmitt, "Justification, Sociality, and Autonomy," *Synthese* 73

The presumption of trust in others is generated out of self-trust. My opinions have been shaped by faculties and circumstances that have broad commonalities with the faculties and circumstances that shape the opinions of others. Thus, insofar I trust my own opinions and faculties, I am pressured to trust the opinions and faculties of others as well, even when I know little or nothing about their track records of reliability or their specific circumstances and backgrounds.

The trust is only presumptive, however, not absolute. The credibility that attaches to an individual's opinion can be defeated if I have information about their having a history of errors with respect to issues of the sort in question. Or, I can have information about their lacking a critical piece of evidence or their not having had the training necessary to assess the evidence. And in some unfortunate cases, I can have information about their suffering from a cognitive impairment that interferes with their ability to assess adequately the issues in question.

In addition, there is an important and common way in which the prima facie credibility of someone else's opinion can be defeated even when I have no specific knowledge of the individual's track record, capacities, training, evidence, or background. It is defeated when our opinions conflict, because, by my lights, the person has been unreliable. Whatever credibility would have attached to the person's opinion as a result of my general attitude of trust toward the opinions of others is defeated by the trust I have in myself. It is trust in myself that creates for me a presumption in favor of other people's opinions, even if I know little about them. Insofar as I trust myself and insofar as this trust is reasonable, I risk inconsistency if I do not trust others, given that their faculties and environment are broadly similar to mine. But by the same token, when my opinions conflict with a person about whom I know little, the pressure to trust that person is dissipated and, as a result, the presumption of trust is defeated. It is defeated because, with respect to the issue in question, the conflict itself constitutes a relevant dissimilarity between us, thereby undermining the consistency argument that generates the presumption of trust in favor of the person's opinions about the issue. To be sure, if I have other information indicating that the person

(1987), 43–85; Ernest Sosa, "Testimony and Coherence," in Sosa, *Knowledge in Perspective;* Leslie Stevenson, "Why Believe What People Say?" *Synthese,* 94 (1993), 429–51.

is a reliable evaluator of the issue, it might still be rational for me to defer, but in cases of conflict I need special reasons to do so.

By "conflict," I mean an explicit conflict. If someone else believes a proposition and I have no opinion at all about it, then as I am using the phrase, there is no conflict between us. This is a noteworthy point, because there are many propositions about which I have no opinion. Often I am not in a position to have one. Suppose the issue concerns a technical field about which I have only passing familiarity. I could try to assess the issue, but even if I did, my assessment would be more akin to a hunch than a genuine opinion. I can also fail to have opinions about nontechnical issues. Indeed, sometimes I do not even have an opinion about how to assign a probability to a proposition. If asked how probable it is that there is a man somewhere in Manhattan now standing on his head on a sidewalk, I would respond that I have no idea. If forced, I might be willing venture a guess, but the guess should not be taken to represent my current opinion, and certainly not one that I would be willing to stand behind. If my opinion is to be represented by probabilities at all, it is some very large segment of the interval 0 to 1 that best represents it. But insofar as this interval represents anything, it represents a refusal to take a stand. By contrast, when I assess the probability of a fair coin coming up heads to be approximately 0.5, I am taking a definite, albeit probabilistic, position about the chances of the coin coming up heads.

None of this is to say that when I have no prior opinion, I am rationally required to take the word of others at face value. It is merely to say that one kind of defeater of the prima facie trust that it is reasonable for me to have in the opinions in others is not available. Their authority is not defeated by the fact that I have a conflicting opinion, but I still can have reasons to distrust their opinions. Perhaps their track record on such issues is not very good, or perhaps they lack the relevant training, or perhaps their circumstances are not favorable for reliably assessing these issues.

Nevertheless, in general, the fewer opinions I have about a set of issues, the more likely it is that I have reasons to defer to the opinions of others. If I am unfamiliar with a field of inquiry, I am unlikely to have very many opinions about it and, hence, there won't be many opportunities for conflicts between my opinions and those of others. As a result, there is plenty of room for others to exercise intellectual authority over me. On the other hand, the more opinions I have about a set of issues, the less likely it is that it will be reasonable for me to rely on others. If I am an expert in a field, for example, I am likely to have opinions about most issues in the field. Hence, there are more opportunities for conflicts between my opinions and those of others, and correspondingly less room for deference.

More completely stated, the position I am defending is this: if someone else's opinion is to give me a reason to alter my opinion, it must be rational for me to believe that the person has this opinion; if this is rational for me, I have at least a prima facie reason to believe what the other person believes; like all prima facie reasons, this prima facie reason can be defeated by other information, for example, information indicating that the person is not in a good position to have reliable opinions about the matter in question; however, even in the absence of such information, this prima facie reason can be defeated; it is defeated if I have a conflicting opinion; on the other hand, even when the prima facie reason I have to trust the other person is defeated by my having a conflicting opinion, it nonetheless may still be epistemically rational for me to defer to the person, but only if I have special reasons indicating that he or she is better positioned than I to assess the claim in question.

For example, even if it is rational for me to believe that I have the faculties, training, and information needed to make relatively reliable judgments about the issue in dispute, it may be reasonable for me to believe that you have skills or information that put you in an even better position than I to evaluate the issue. If so, it is reasonable for me to defer to you. Despite the fact that my conflicting opinion defeats the prima facie authority of your opinion, you still have specialized authority for me.

Suppose it is reasonable for me to believe that you are no more and no less skilled than I and that we have the same information. Even so, if our opinions conflict, I may still have reason to defer to you, because you have devoted more time than I to thinking about this information. Your more extensive study of the issue may give me a reason to believe that I would have reached the same conclusion had I taken sufficient time to examine and deliberate about the information in hand.

On the other hand, suppose it is rational for me to believe that we are equally well positioned to evaluate the issue and equally skilled and equally well informed and that we have also devoted an equal amount of time and effort to thinking about the issue. If we still disagree, there is room only for Socratic influence. You need to convince me, to show me where I have gone wrong. I have no reason simply to defer to your authority. On the other hand, neither is it permissible for me simply to go on believing what I had been believing. Insofar as it is reasonable for me to regard us as exact epistemic peers with respect to the issue, it is reasonable for me to withhold judgment until I better understand how one or both of us have gone wrong.

Thus, I cannot simply ignore the opinions of others when they disagree with me. Even when the prima facie trust that it is reasonable for me to grant universally to others is defeated by my having a conflicting opinion, I may still have reasons to grant others some degree of specialized authority, and if their authority is sufficiently strong, it can be reasonable for me to defer to them, as when I have evidence that they are in a better position than I to evaluate the claim in question. Other times, their authority will be at least strong enough to make it reasonable for me to withhold judgment, as when I have evidence that they are in no better and no worse position than I. Moreover, even a conflict with others does not provide me with sufficient grounds for immediately revising my opinion, it may nevertheless provide me with grounds for investigating the issue further, which in turn might eventually uncover grounds sufficient for revision. Intellectual conflicts inevitably raise the question of how well positioned I am to make a reliable assessment of the issue. A conflict thus puts me on guard and, if the issue is important enough, gives me reasons to gather additional information or to consult with others whom I might have stronger reasons to trust.

So, to repeat, when I have reasons to believe that someone else believes P, this gives me at least a weak prima facie reason to believe P myself. I need not know anything special about the person. However, this prima facie reason is defeated if I have a conflicting opinion. Even so, it may still be epistemically rational for me to defer, if I have reasons to think that the other person is in a better position than I to evaluate P.

This account rejects both epistemic egoism and egotism, asserting that an attitude of credulity toward the opinions of others is reasonable even if I know little or nothing about them. If it is rational for me to believe that someone else believes P, I have a prima facie reason to believe P myself. Just as it is reasonable for me to have an attitude of trust in my own cognitive faculties and the opinions they generate, so too it is reasonable for me to have an attitude of trust in the faculties and opinions of other people. The account thus explains how it can be rational for me to rely so extensively on the opinions of others. The range of people influencing me includes family, friends, teachers, authors, journalists, lecturers, and countless others. All these people have prima facie

111

credibility for me, and, hence, it can be reasonable to rely on them even if I know little or nothing about them. By extension, it can also be reasonable, all else being equal, to rely on assumptions and concepts that are not the products of identifiable individuals but rather are the products of an amorphous group. One of the most powerful influences on our opinions is culture and tradition. Our most fundamental concepts and our deepest assumptions, which are the materials out of which our opinions are formed, are part of our intellectual inheritance. This inheritance is the collective product of people whom it is reasonable to trust, all else being equal, even if I do not know exactly who they are. Similarly, I confidently use information devices, such as barometers, maps, gas gauges, thermometers, and compasses, despite the fact that I would be hard pressed to provide a general defense of their reliability. Even if I am inexperienced with such devices and thus lack inductive evidence of their reliability, it can be reasonable for me to rely on them for my opinions, because they are the products of people who have prima facie credibility for me, albeit I do not know who these people are.

Although this account rejects epistemic egoism, it nonetheless does manage to preserve some of its spirit. It does so, because according to the account, when my opinions conflict with the opinions of someone else, the presumption of trust in the other person is defeated. So, with respect to cases of conflict, which of course is an important and extensive set of cases, egoists are basically right. In these cases, if it is to be rational for me to alter my opinion as a result of the opinions of others, I need to have special reasons to trust them.

The dangers of two extreme positions are thus avoided by the above account of intellectual authority. The skeptical dangers associated with egoism are avoided, because I do not need special information about the reliability of someone else's opinions in order to trust those opinions. It can be reasonable for me to grant authority even to strangers. On the other hand, the account also avoids the dangers associated with positions that so emphasize the social construction of opinion that little or no room is left for intellectual independence. When my opinions conflict with the opinions of others, the prima facie reason I have to believe what others believe is defeated, and I thus have reasons to defer to these others only if I have special reasons to think that they are in a better position than I to assess the issues in question. This in turn leaves plenty of space for the possibility of rational dissent from the prevailing opinions of my community and tradition.

112

I have been gliding over a number of complications for the sake of simplicity. One of these complications is that I have been talking in an all-or-nothing fashion about several issues that are more accurately regarded as matters of degree. For instance, even when I have a special reason to defer to you, it won't always be clear how strong a reason your opinion gives me to change my opinion. I may be less than fully sure how much more skilled you are than I or how much more time and effort you have devoted to the issue than I. I may even be less than fully sure what exactly it is that you believe. As a result, it may not be clear to how strong a reason I have to alter my opinion in light of your opinion.

Similarly, I can have, or come to acquire, information that undermines or overrides to a greater or lesser degree your credibility for me. For example, your credibility about P for me is undermined to the degree that I have reasons to think that you lack critical evidence about P or lack the expertise necessary to evaluate the evidence. The stronger such reasons are, the more they undermine your credibility. Analogously, if I have information about P itself that runs counter to what you believe, such information tends to override your credibility about P for me and does so in proportion to the strength of the reasons it gives me.[30]

Likewise, belief itself is sometimes appropriately treated as a matter of degree rather than an all-or-nothing phenomenon.[31] If issues of authority are approached in terms of degrees of beliefs, rather than beliefs simpliciter, the basic structure of the above account need not be altered, but the notion of conflict of opinion does have to be clarified. Degrees of belief are in general best represented not by precise subjective probabilities but rather a range of subjective probabilities. Thus, my degree of belief in P might be best represented by the range .7 to .9. If your degree of belief in P lies entirely outside this range, for example, in the range .4

---

30 As I use the terms, something undermines a prima facie reason for P if it defeats the reason by virtue of defeating the connection between it and the truth of P, whereas something overrides a prima facie reason for P if it defeats the reason by virtue of providing reasons for the truth of notP. Undermining defeaters attack the connection between the reason and P; overriding defeaters attack P directly, by providing evidence for notP. Compare with John Pollock's discussion of Type I and Type II defeaters, Pollock, *Knowledge and Justification* (Princeton, NJ: Princeton University Press, 1974), especially 42–3. See also William Alston, "Justification and Knowledge," in *Epistemic Justification* (Ithaca, NY: Cornell University Press, 1989), 172–82; and Ernest Sosa, "Knowledge and Intellectual Virtue," in *Knowledge in Perspective*, 225–41, especially 241.

31 However, see Richard Foley, *Working Without a Net*, especially 170–73, on the importance, for many purposes, of treating belief as an all-or-nothing phenomenon.

to .6, we have conflicting degrees of belief. Your opinion also conflicts with mine if part of its range lies outside the range of my opinion, for example, if your degree of belief in P is in the range .6 to .8. In both kinds of cases, the prima facie reason I have to trust your opinion is defeated, and hence I have no reason to move my opinion in the direction of your opinion unless I have special reasons for thinking that you are in an especially good position to assess P. A more difficult issue is what to say when your range of belief is different than mine but lies entirely within my range, for example, when your degree of belief in P is in the range .7 to .8. One possible answer invokes an asymmetrical notion of conflicting opinions. Namely, your belief does not conflict (in the relevant sense) with mine and, hence, your prima facie credibility for me is not defeated, because your degree of belief lies entirely within the range of my degree of belief; however, my belief does conflict (in the relevant sense) with yours and, hence, my prima facie credibility for you is defeated, because part of the range of my degree of belief lies outside the range of your degree of belief.

Another issue is how questions of authority are to be treated when there are disagreements among others. If I have no opinion about a topic and others do, I have a prima facie reason to defer to them, but others often disagree among themselves, in which case the prima facie credibility of their opinions tend to cancel each other out. Thus, if I have no information about the relative reliability of the disputants, I should withhold judgment on the issue. On the other hand, when I do have information about their relative reliability, I can try to conform my opinion to the opinions of those whom I have reasons to regard as most reliable, but assessing who among the disputants is most reliable is almost always difficult and almost always also a matter of degree.

Yet another issue is whether, and under what conditions, the prima facie trust it is reasonable for me to have in the opinions of others gives me an additional reason to believe what I already believe. If I have no opinion at all about P and discover that you believe P, this gives me at least a weak reason, all else being equal, to believe P myself. On the other hand, if I already believe P and discover that you also believe it, does this strengthen whatever reasons I previously had to believe P? The quick answer is that it does so only to the degree that your belief is independent of my belief. At one extreme are situations in which you believe P only because of my testimony, in which case your believing P adds nothing to my reasons for P. At the other extreme are situations in which the considerations that led you to believe P are largely independent of those that led me to believe, in which case your believing P may very well strengthen my reasons for P.[32]

Opinions involving matters of value raise different kinds of complications. A major issue, for instance, is whether it is appropriate to conceive such opinions as having truth values. According to one school of thought, the answer is "no." Only opinions that aspire to be representational are capable of being true or false (or more or less accurate), but opinions involving matters of value are best thought of as being, at least in part, expressions of attitudes or prescriptions. On this construal of value judgments, the above account of intellectual authority is not applicable to them. According to the account, the pressures to trust the opinions of others arise out of trust in one's own reliability, but if opinions involving matters of value are neither true nor false, reliability is not the appropriate standard for assessing such judgments. Hence, the argument that trust in the reliability in one's own opinions pressures one to have trust in the reliability of the opinion of others cannot even get started.

This result is based on a controversial construal of value judgments, but it does, if acceptable, help provide a defense for the view that we should be more reluctant to rely on others for our moral and aesthetic opinions than for other kinds of opinions. With respect to many matters, most people have no qualms about borrowing opinions from even complete strangers, but in general people are less comfortable about borrowing moral or aesthetic opinions from those they do not know. Similarly, on many issues, people readily defer to the experts, but they tend to be more wary of the suggestion that there are moral experts to whom they ought to defer. The idea of there being aesthetic experts is perhaps more familiar, but even on aesthetic issues, most people are reluctant simply to borrow their opinions from the experts, as opposed to being open to Socratic influence by them. They look to the experts to instruct them so that they come to appreciate what the experts

---

32 "Suppose a mathematician has made a discovery in that science, which he thinks important; that he has put his demonstration in just order; and, after examining it with an attentive eye, has found no flaw in it. . . . He commits his demonstration to the examination of a mathematical friend, whom he esteems a competent judge, and waits with impatience the issue of his judgement. Here I would ask again, Whether the verdict of his friend, according as it has been favorable or unfavorable, will not greatly increase or diminish his confidence in his own judgement? Most certain it will and it ought." Thomas Reid, *Essays on the Intellectual Powers of Man*, in *Thomas Reid's Inquiry and Essays*, ed. R. Beanblosson and K. Lehrer, 6, 4, 262–3.

appreciate, which may well result in their making evaluations similar to the experts, but not simply out of deference to their authority. The above account of intellectual authority, in conjunction with a construal of value judgments as not being representational, potentially helps justify these differences between our attitudes about value judgments and our attitudes about other kinds of judgments. With respect to the kinds of judgments that have truth values, trust in the reliability of our own judgments creates a pressure for us to trust in the reliability of the judgments of others as well, but for judgments lacking truth values, such pressures are absent.

A final complication is how to react to empirical studies of testimony. In Chapter 3, I discuss studies that document our tendencies to make various mistakes of reasoning and judgment. When we make predictions about the future job performance of the applicants after having interviewed them in person, we tend to be overly swayed by the mannerisms and appearance of interviewees; when we assess causal influences on the basis of statistical data, we tend to ignore base rates; when we make self-assessments, we tend to be overly confident of our talents; and so on. Similarly, empirical studies of testimony can raise troubling epistemic issues about testimony-based beliefs.

For example, numerous studies have corroborated our tendency to process testimony so as to avoid conflict. In many contexts, we tend to seek out testimony that reinforces our own beliefs and attitudes, and ignore testimony that does not (by selective exposure, perception, or retention).[33] In yet other contexts, we avoid conflict not so much by seeking out testimony that is consistent with our own opinions (or avoiding testimony that is not), as by discounting our own ability to make independent judgments. For example, in Solomon Asch's classic studies of suggestibility, subjects were asked which of three lines is closest in length to a target line. The target subjects first observed a number of other individuals, apparently also subjects, respond to the question. These other individuals, who were actually confederates of the experimenter, picked out a line that was obviously incorrect. Even so, by the time the actual subjects were asked for their own opinions, they

33 W. J. McGuire, "The Nature of Attitudes and Attitudinal Change," in G. Lindzey and E. Aronson, *Handbook of Social Psychology*, 3rd ed. (Reading, MA: Addison-Wesley, 1969); M. I. Alpert and W. T. Anderson, "Optimal Heterophily and Communication Effectiveness – Some Empirical Findings," *Journal of Communication* 23 (1973), 328–43; E. W. Rogers, *Diffusion of Innovation* (New York: Free Press, 1983).

came, in a majority of cases, to agree with the others.[34] The standard interpretation of these studies is that they provide evidence of the difficulty of making an independent judgment about an issue when one's peers are unanimous in their opinions.

Like the studies discussed in Chapter 3, such studies raise difficult first-person epistemological questions. On the assumption that it is reasonable for me to accept at least some of these studies at face value, what effect should the studies have on me when I am the one making the judgments? If people in general are unreliable processors of testimony, should this undermine my trust in my own ability to process testimony reliably? If so, to what extent?

A complete account of intellectual authority would do justice to these and other complexities, which for the most part I am ignoring so that the overall structure of the account of intellectual authority is not lost. The most important features of this structure are, first, that we are pressured, at risk of inconsistency, to regard the opinions of others as prima facie credible and, second, that the prima facie credibility of these opinions is defeated when we have conflicting opinions. This constitutes at least the beginnings of an account of intellectual authority.

6. ANONYMOUS RECONSIDERED

Recall the case of Anonymous. I have discovered a list of Anonymous's opinions, but I have no special information about who Anonymous is. Even so, according to the account sketched above, I have a prima facie reason to believe the propositions listed. By hypothesis, I know that Anonymous believes them, and this gives me a reason to believe them as well. On the other hand, if a proposition on the list conflicts with what I believe, my prima facie reason to trust Anonymous on this issue is defeated. Moreover, since by hypothesis the list contains no other information that gives me grounds for granting specialized authority to Anonymous, I have no reason to alter my opinion in the face of Anonymous's conflicting opinion.

Let's now vary the basic scenario. Suppose I have information that Anonymous was a contemporary of Chaucer. Should this information alter my reaction to the opinions listed? It depends. Suppose one of the

34   Solomon Asch, *Social Psychology* (Englewood Cliffs, NJ: Prentice-Hall, 1952); and Asch, "Studies of Independence and Conformity: A Minority of One against a Unanimous Majority," *Psychological Monographs* 70, no. 9 (1956).

listed propositions is about everyday life in the fourteenth century. The fact that Anonymous believes this proposition gives me a prima facie reason to believe it as well. Moreover, I am unlikely to have a conflicting opinion, because I do not know many details of daily life in the fourteenth century. In addition, there is no reason to think that Anonymous was not in a good position to have reliable beliefs about these kinds of matters. On the other hand, if the list includes propositions about the motions of the planets, the causes of pneumonia, and the nature of fire, it is not reasonable for me to adopt Anonymous's beliefs on these matters, even if I have no firm opinions about them myself. If I lack opinions about these matters, there is no conflict that defeats the prima facie credibility of Anonymous's opinions, but their credibility is defeated by other considerations. In particular, given the general state of knowledge in the fourteenth century, I have reasons to think that Anonymous was not in a good position to have reliable beliefs about these kinds of issues.

Now change the scenario so that I know that Anonymous is my contemporary, and suppose that at least some of the listed propositions concern technical matters about which I have no opinion and no expertise. Although I have no information indicating that Anonymous is an expert, I still have a prima facie reason to believe what Anonymous believes about these matters. Even the opinions of strangers are prima facie credible for me, and what this means, among other things, is that it is reasonable for me to assume that in general they do not form their opinions in unreliable ways. So, if the list of Anonymous's opinions includes an opinion on a technical matter, I can assume, all else being equal, that Anonymous either is an expert or has relied on experts. The difference between this case involving a contemporary Anonymous and the previous case involving the opinion of a medieval Anonymous on, say, the causes of pneumonia is that I am aware that in the middle ages not even medical experts knew anything about viruses. So, even if medieval Anonymous had relied on the opinions of experts, the resulting opinion would still not be credible.

Let's now vary the information about me rather than Anonymous. Suppose I am an expert on matters about which Anonymous has opinions. Even as an expert, I should be open to Socratic influence, and Anonymous's beliefs might contain enough information and ideas to persuade me to change my mind. However, as an expert, I am unlikely to have reasons simply to rely on Anonymous's authority. There are two kinds of considerations that make experts in general less open to authority than nonexperts. First, experts tend to have extensive opinions about their areas of expertise. Part of their role as experts is to make up their own minds on questions within their specialty.[35] So, when they encounter the opinions of another person on issues within their specialty, it is likely that they themselves will already have opinions on these issues, and if the opinions are conflicting ones, they defeat the prima facie reason the experts have to trust the other person. By contrast, nonexperts usually have fewer opinions about the subject, and there is thus more room for intellectual authority. Second, experts are unlikely to have reasons to think that others are in a better position than they to evaluate issues within their specialty. Hence, experts are unlikely to have special reasons to defer to others, not even when the other people are themselves experts. With nonexperts, just the reverse is the case. They ordinarily have reasons to think that experts are in a better position than they to evaluate the issues in question and, accordingly, they ordinarily have special reasons to defer when confronted with a conflicting expert opinion. Indeed, because nonexperts are often not competent to assess the evidence, they can have reasons to defer even if, after having been provided access to all of the data and deliberations of the experts, the latter's conclusions continue to strike them as counterintuitive. On the other hand, if one is an expert on the issues in question and has access to the data and deliberations of the other experts and has taken the time to study this information, it is unlikely to be reasonable to defer; one is in a position to make up one's own mind.[36]

To be sure, because of the division of intellectual labor, there are still numerous opportunities for experts to defer to one another. In most technical fields, experts rely extensively on the conclusions of other experts without taking the time to verify these conclusions on their own. In addition, one implication of the increasing specialization of intellectual work is that expertise tends to be defined more and more narrowly, which in turn creates additional opportunities for experts in the same general field to defer to one another. One's expertise is not so much in physics per se as in theoretical physics and not so much in theoretical physics per se as in string theory, and so on. Nevertheless, neither of these observations affects the overall point, which is that insofar as one is an expert on a set of issues, however narrowly the set is

35   F. Schmitt, "Consensus, Respect, and Weighted Averaging," *Synthese* 62 (1986), 25–46.
36   Contrast with K. Lehrer and C. Wagner, *Rational Consensus in Science and Society* (Dordrecht: D. Reidel, 1981).

defined, and insofar as one has taken the time to acquire and assess the available data, there is less room for intellectual deference.

Change the scenario concerning Anonymous once again. Suppose I have assurances that the list of propositions represents not the opinions of a single individual but rather the settled opinions of most of my contemporaries. Does this give me a stronger reason to accept these propositions than if the list represented the opinions of just one person? The quick answer is that consensus across a large group of individuals does ordinarily provide me with a stronger reason to believe a claim than does the belief of a single individual. The central thesis of the account of intellectual trust I have been developing is that intellectual trust in myself radiates outward toward other people, pressuring me to trust them as well. The trust radiates in all directions, providing me with at least a weak prima facie reason to trust every individual. Thus, insofar as I know that a wide range of individuals, each of whom is prima facie credible, believes P, I have a stronger reason, all else being equal, to believe P myself than I would have if I knew of a single individual who was convinced of the truth of P. For example, suppose P is the proposition that the hit-and-run driver in a recent accident had blond hair. If I am aware that there are numerous witnesses and all of them believe P, I have a stronger reasons to believe P myself than I would have if I knew that one of the witnesses believed P but was ignorant of what the other witnesses believed.

Indeed, the above account helps explain why consensus is epistemically significant. Consider a group of individuals $I_1, I_2, I_3 \ldots I_n$. If the opinions of $I_1, I_2, I_3 \ldots$ and I_n as individuals lacked even prima facie credibility for me, it would be difficult to explain why their agreeing with one another should matter to me. Credibility is not created ex nihilo. If none of the witnesses of the hit-and-run accident had any degree of credibility on their own, the fact that they agree with another would not matter, but because each of the witnesses does have a degree of credibility as an individual, consensus among them is epistemically significant. The point here is reminiscent of one of the standard complaints against pure coherence theories of epistemic justification. If there is nothing at all to recommend a set of beliefs $B_1, B_2, B_3 \ldots B_n$ other than the fact that they cohere with one another, it is hard to understand why the set as a whole should be regarded as credible. By contrast, if there is something other than coherence to recommend each of the individual beliefs $B_1, B_2, B_3 \ldots B_n$, then it is not hard to understand why their cohering with one another enhances their collective credibility.

Consensus across a wide range of individuals is especially likely to be a decisive factor in determining what it is rational to believe when there is not much room for expertise, as is the case in eyewitness reports of accidents. Admittedly, some of us have better eyesight than others, some of us are more observant than others, and some of us may even have special training to be observant in cases of accidents. Still, for the most part, those who are in roughly comparable positions to observe an event will have roughly comparable standing when it comes to making eyewitness reports about it. Accordingly, if the reports of the observers are independent of one another and in agreement, it won't be easy for me to dismiss them on the grounds that they lack the requisite expertise. Indeed, I may very well have a reason to defer to the consensus opinion even if I too have witnessed the accident and have a conflicting opinion. For example, suppose I remember the driver as having dark hair. Then the prima facie credibility of the other eyewitnesses is defeated by my conflicting opinion, but I will still need to explain why they all disagree with me, and it may not be easy to come up with an explanation. After all, in general I do not have reasons for thinking I am in an especially privileged position with respect to making such observations, and there need not be any obvious nonevidential consideration that is shaping the beliefs of the other witnesses.

Although consensus, all else being equal, gives me a stronger reason than otherwise to believe a claim, there are numerous situations in which all else is not equal. Indeed, in some contexts, the presence of consensus may itself be an indication that unreliable factors are at work in shaping opinions. For example, recent surveys have indicated that almost 90 percent of people in the United States believe that there is intelligent life elsewhere in the universe. Given the complexity of evaluating the various kinds of evidence for this claim, it is probably reasonable to assume that something other than the evidence is influencing people's opinions to create the consensus. Perhaps they want it to be true that there is intelligent life elsewhere, because the thought is comforting to them; or perhaps repeated, vivid depictions of alien life in popular culture have made the idea so commonplace that most people uncritically accept it. Whatever the explanation, the fact that there may be something approaching consensus on this proposition need not give me a strong reason to believe it as well.

John Locke was one of the first egalitarian epistemologists. He claimed that all of us have an obligation to think carefully about matters of importance and to come to our own opinions about them. Of the three Lockean presuppositions listed in §4.2 – optimism, individualism, and egalitarianism – it is the last that survived best over the centuries. We tend to side with Locke in abhorring the idea of there being an intellectual elite to whom ordinary people ought to defer for their opinions. However, these egalitarian sentiments fit uneasily with the deference given to experts in technical fields, a deference that the above account of intellectual authority allows and even encourages. We often lack opinions about highly technical issues, and according to the above account, when we have no opinion about an issue, we have at least a prima facie reason to defer to those who do have opinions. In technical fields this usually means deferring to the experts. Moreover, even when we do have an opinion about a technical issue, if it conflicts with what the experts believe, we ordinarily still have a reason to defer, because the experts, we grant, are in a better position than we to evaluate the issue.

The increasing division of intellectual labor, and the specialization it has engendered, has made deference to expert opinion an ever more common occurrence. Our societies have become more complex, and so inevitably have our ways of gathering, pursuing, and organizing intellectual pursuits. Moreover, we have witnessed, especially in the last hundred years, what a powerful tool the division of intellectual labor can be. Enormous progress on important intellectual questions has been made by breaking up complex problems into smaller, more manageable ones and then encouraging highly trained specialists to focus their work on these narrowly defined problems.

The elitism implicit in deference to technical experts is different from the elitism that worried Locke. Disagreements over morality and religion were tearing at the social fabric of seventeenth-century Europe, and Locke believed that the root cause of this upheaval was an unthinking deference to diverse religious and moral authorities. His epistemology sought to address the crisis by defending the idea, daring at the time, that ordinary people, and not just intellectual and religious leaders, have the capacity to form their own opinions about matters of religion and morality. They need only to make proper use of the faculty of reason that God had given them for this purpose.

Whatever one thinks of Locke's views as a response to seventeenth-century religious elitism, they are decidedly not an adequate response to the challenges of twentieth-century scientific elitism. Contemporary elitists plausibly claim that in technical fields many issues are simply beyond the comprehension of nonexperts. Nonexperts lack the training to understand these issues and, moreover, it is often unrealistic for them to acquire the relevant training. It is not as if I can devote my spare time to molecular genetics and expect to have informed opinions about the field. Worse still, nonexperts are often not in a position even to judge the qualifications of the purported experts who make claims in the field.

These kinds of challenges to egalitarianism, which are already serious, are going to become even more urgent in future years, and we need a theoretically adequate way of understanding and treating them. Although Locke's response to religious and moral elitism does not constitute an adequate response to scientific elitism, there is nonetheless one aspect of his response that is fundamentally correct. Locke vastly underestimated the difficulties of being able to make up one's own mind on complex issues, but on the other hand he was right in thinking that there is something profoundly disturbing about the recommendation that nonexperts should simply defer to experts. This is, or at least should be, as disturbing to us today as it was to Locke in the seventeenth century. It is as objectionable to defer mindlessly to immunologists or quantum theorists as it is to defer mindlessly to religious authorities or the tradition of the church.

On the other hand, it is also objectionable, indeed every bit as objectionable, to ignore or reject the conclusions and achievements of modern science. So, there is a balancing act to be performed. One of the most pressing intellectual demands of our age is how to achieve this balance. We need to find a place for our egalitarian convictions in an era of experts and to do so without becoming Luddites. We do not have a fully adequate solution to this problem yet, but it is possible to discern at least the general direction of the solution.

The first step is to recognize that what is potentially dangerous about deference to scientific experts is identical with what Locke found dangerous about deference to religious leaders. Namely, both too easily can become an excuse for not bringing one's intelligence to bear on important issues. A division of cognitive labor with deference to expert opinion produces undeniable intellectual benefits, but there are also intellectual dangers in such a system, especially insofar as it encourages lay people to be passive. Lay people will then tend to have homogenous beliefs on expert topics, and this homogeneity of opinion can contribute to complacency among the experts themselves, who are unchallenged.[37] The dangers here are essentially the same as those that worried John Stuart Mill in his famous defense of free speech in Chapter 3 of *On Liberty*, namely, the dangers of too much agreement. Mill argued that diversity of opinion is in general preferable to unanimity of opinion, because disagreements encourage further evidence gathering and, thus, are in the long-term conducive to the search for truth.[38] A corollary of this thesis is that anything that discourages disagreements is potentially dangerous. Indeed, as mentioned in the previous section, consensus is sometimes a mark that unhealthy pressures are at work on the community.

So, a centrally important question for us in this age of specialization is how to bring our intelligence to bear on issues connected to technical and scientific expertise, given that it is not a realistic option for us to acquire the expertise ourselves. The answer to this question, at least in roughest form, is that it is possible for nonexperts to form credible opinions about the overall workings of the system that produces specialized knowledge claims. Even this is immensely difficult, but it is at least a practicable project, whereas achieving first-hand expertise usually is not.

Moreover, perhaps the single most important thing for nonexperts to know about the practice of science is that it is designed, ideally, to be a self-correcting system. It requires that theories and hypotheses be testable; it requires that the tests be publicly observable and repeatable, thus allowing one inquirer to verify the conclusions reached by other inquirers; it requires the unfettered flow of information among inquirers; and it requires inquirers to be impartial in the evaluation of theories and hypotheses, which, among other things, requires them to be tolerant of new ideas and open-minded about iconoclastic theories. Of course, even when the system is working well, there is no absolute guarantee that errors will in fact be corrected. The claim on the behalf of science is *only* that it is reasonable to think that the system will move us in the direction of greater accuracy when it is operating in accordance with the above requirements.

---

37 Frederick F. Schmitt, "Justification, Sociality, and Autonomy," especially 69–71.
38 For similar and equally energetic defenses of the importance of tolerating diversity, whether in social, political, or intellectual matters, see F. A. Hayek, *The Constitution of Liberty* (Chicago: University of Chicago Press, 1960), Chapter 2; and Robert Nozick, *The Nature of Rationality*, 174.

This is a statement about how the system is ideally supposed to work, but the real world of science, of course, is a different matter, and it is about this real world of science that individuals, even nonscientists, can and should have opinions. In particular, the question on which individuals should strive to have informed opinions is whether science as it is actually practiced is sufficiently close to the ideal to make its results trustworthy. It bears repeating that it is extremely difficult for nonexperts to have credible opinions about even this issue, but – and this is the Lockean point – they can do so if they are prepared to bring their intelligence to bear on the issue. Their efforts need not be aimed at a mastery of the fields and subfields themselves. Rather, their efforts can be aimed at the overall workings of the system of science in that field, with the goal of coming to a credible opinion about its overall trustworthiness.[39]

Once I have come to an opinion on this question, the account of intellectual authority defended above comes into play in the usual way. Like the opinions of others, the opinions of experts on a given issue are prima facie credible for me. Moreover, insofar as the issue is a technical one, I may not have any prior opinion at all, much less a conflicting one. Even so, if I have good reasons to think that the self-correcting mechanisms of science have not been working as well as they should, the prima facie reason I have to believe what the experts believe may be defeated. The reverse is also possible, of course. I may have a conflicting prior opinion, in which case the prima facie credibility of the experts' opinions is defeated. Nonetheless, their opinions will still have specialized authority for me, provided that I have reasons to think that the system of science has been working in this case as it is designed to work.[40]

---

39 See Miriam Solomon, who argues that in some respects, informed lay people may be better positioned than the experts themselves to evaluate the data: "Scientifically literate observers or historians of scientific disputes are often in an epistemically more neutral position than scientists themselves. They rarely have prior theoretical commitments; they are not subject to the particular peer and authority pressures in the community; and their professional rewards are not usually bound up in the outcome of particular scientific disputes. They are in more of a position to evaluate claims of empirical success, since they are less likely to reason with confirmation bias, motivational factors, and so on." M. Solomon, "A More Social Epistemology," in Schmitt, Socializing Epistemology, 229–30.

40 For a discussion of the epistemic relevance of investigations into the social structures of the institution of science, and more generally, investigations into the social structures that confer the status of experts on individuals, see Hilary Kornblith, "A Conservative Approach to Social Epistemology," in F. Schmitt, Socializing Epistemology, 93–110.

Although Locke's three fundamental presuppositions (optimism, egalitarianism, and individualism) are no longer tenable in the strong forms he held them, there is nonetheless an insight at the core of each presupposition that the account of intellectual authority I have been developing preserves. A kernel of Locke's optimism is preserved insofar as the account allows individuals to have trust in their faculties and opinions even though they lack non–question-begging assurances of their reliability. An important aspect of Locke's egalitarianism is reflected in the view that it can be appropriate even for ordinary people to have opinions about the practice of science, opinions that potentially can determine the degree of intellectual deference it is reasonable for them to display toward the opinions of those widely regarded as experts. And, one of the central concerns motivating Locke's individualism is acknowledged, given that the account leaves room for the possibility of individuals dissenting, and doing so rationally, from even the most cherished opinions of their contemporaries.

Of these three presuppositions, it is individualism that is apt to seem most problematic for contemporary thinkers. Locke worried about the threat of overly easy intellectual conformity and correspondingly stressed the need for intellectual autonomy. He was right to be worried. Few things are more difficult than resisting domination by one's intellectual environment. However, he also assumed that the proper use of reason can immunize one against such domination. Not many of us are so confident anymore. We now recognize that even the ways we reason and deliberate are shaped by our intellectual heritage and surroundings. The recognition of this point has made it easy to slide into positions that so emphasize the social construction of our opinions and ways of reasoning that there is little or no room for intellectual independence.

Twentieth-century intellectual life was characterized by an increased emphasis on communities and groups, as opposed to individuals, as the most appropriate or most interesting objects of study. This trend occurred across the social sciences and humanities.[41] It helped create and

41 For example, see Karl Mannheim, *Ideology and Utopia: An Introduction to the Sociology of Knowledge* (New York: Harvest, 1929), 3: "It is not man in general who think, or even isolated individuals who do the thinking, but men in certain groups who have developed a particular style of thought. . . . Strictly speaking it is incorrect to say that a single individual thinks. Rather it is more correct to insist that he participates in thinking further what other men have thought before him."

in turn was reinforced by a public political discourse that increasingly focused on the rights, privileges, and histories of groups as opposed to individuals.

Epistemology has been no exception to this trend. An emphasis on the community of inquirers has become especially common in work on the epistemology of science. This should not be surprising, since science is largely cumulative, with one generation building on the work of previous ones. In addition, its methods emphasize the use of publicly observable and repeatable experiments, thus allowing inquirers to test each other's hypotheses. Moreover, the nature of its problems often require a division of intellectual labor, which brings with it a need to trust the work of others. Observations such as these convinced C. S. Peirce that scientific rationality is essentially social. Scientific theories are justified only because they are products of a method (or set of methods) employed by a community of inquirers over an extended period of time.

The method of modern science is social in respect to the solidarity of its efforts. The scientific world is like a colony of insects in that the individual strives to produce that which he cannot himself hope to enjoy. One generation collects premises in order that a distant generation may discover what they mean. When a problem comes before the scientific world, a hundred men immediately set their energies to work on it. One contributes this, another that. Another company, standing on the shoulders of the first, strikes a little higher until at last the parapet is attained.[42]

More recently, philosophers of science as otherwise diverse as Thomas Kuhn, Bruno Latour, Philip Kitcher, Helen Longino, and Miriam Solomon have also defended the view that the notion of scientific rationality, or epistemic rationality generally, is inextricably social.[43] Feminist epistemologists have also argued for such views and added a political warning; our standards of epistemic and scientific rationality cannot be disentangled from our social arrangements, and just because of this, these standards can be wielded as political tools to empower some groups and disempower others. Some epistemologists go further and suggest that

42 *Collected Papers of Charles Sanders Peirce*, ed. C. Hartshorne, P. Weiss, and A. Burks (Cambridge, MA: Harvard University Press, 1931–1958), 7.87.

43 Thomas Kuhn, *The Structure of Scientific Revolution*, 2nd ed. (Chicago, MA: University of Chicago Press, 1970); Bruno Latour, *Science in Action* (Cambridge, MA: Harvard University Press, 1987); Philip Kitcher, *The Advancement of Science* (Oxford: Oxford University Press, 1993); Helen Longino, *Science as Social Knowledge* (Princeton, NJ: Princeton University Press, 1990); and Miriam Solomon, "Social Empiricism," *Nous* 28 (1994).

questions concerning the rationality of our opinions are wholly social. For example, both Ludwig Wittgenstein and Richard Rorty flirt with positions implying that one's opinions are reasonable only if the manner in which one comes to have the opinions is intellectually acceptable in one's community.[44]

Locke and the generations of philosophers influenced by him over-estimated the ability of individuals to escape the influence of their intellectual inheritance and surroundings. The above movements and positions are effective antidotes to this excessive individualism. However, I have been arguing that there is also a danger of overreaction, of epistemology becoming excessively social. Moreover, as I argued in Chapter 2,[45] it is easy enough to identify one of the principal danger signals. An epistemology has become excessively social if it a priori precludes the possibility of individuals engaging in radical but rational critiques of the prevailing standards, practices, methods, and opinions of their communities or traditions. No matter how entrenched or widely accepted these standards, practices, methods, and opinions may be, our epistemologies ought not to imply that it is utterly impossible for an individual within the community to reject them and yet still be rational in an important sense.

However, it is one thing for an epistemology to leave room for the rationality of intellectual independence, and it is another for individuals actually to succeed in being intellectually independent. Indeed, there is even a question as to how intellectual autonomy is possible, given what we know about the power of one's inheritance and surroundings to shape one's concepts, opinions, and even the way one reasons. We cannot plausibly conceive intellectual autonomy as the ability to cast off wholesale one's intellectual tradition, but then how are we to conceive of it?

The answer, at least in broad outline, is to conceive autonomy as being grounded in our ability to use our existing methods and opinions to examine these very same methods and opinions, the very same ability, not coincidentally, which makes epistemology possible. We have the ability to make ourselves into an object of study, to evaluate and monitor ourselves, and moreover to do so in terms of our own standards, while

---

44 Ludwig Wittgenstein, *On Certainty*, ed. G. E. M. Anscombe and G. H. von Wright, trans. D. Paul and G. E. M. Anscombe (New York: Harper, 1969); Richard Rorty, *Philosophy and the Mirror of Nature* (Princeton, NJ: Princeton University Press, 1979).
45 See especially the discussion in § 2.3.

fully recognizing that these standards have themselves been shaped by our intellectual surroundings and inheritance. The ability to engage in such metacritiques creates a space for intellectual autonomy.

It is only a space, however. Self-monitoring in terms of one's own standards does not eliminate the threat of complete intellectual domination. Marx and Foucault both emphasized that the most effective kind of control is that which is internalized, where we accept as our own the very norms by which we are controlled without realizing we are being controlled. Be this as it may, we can monitor ourselves for intellectual domination just as we monitor ourselves for error. In this respect, the possibility of complete and utter intellectual domination is not much different from the possibility of complete and utter intellectual deception envisioned by skeptical hypotheses. Just as something or someone might conceivably be powerful enough to use our own sense experiences to deceive us thoroughly without our being aware of it, so too something or someone might conceivably be powerful enough to control our deepest intellectual standards and convictions without our being aware of it. Even so, neither of these is a reason for thinking that our intellectual projects are pointless or hopeless.

No amount of self-monitoring will provide us with absolute certainty that a powerful demon is not using our own experiences to deceive us, but in itself this does not imply that perceptual knowledge is altogether impossible for us. To be sure, we need to trust that our faculties and procedures are reasonably well suited to yield accurate opinions if our intellectual projects are to have any point at all. We cannot prove with utter certainty that this optimism is well placed, but despite the claims of some classical foundationalists, it can be reasonable for us to have such trust in our faculties and procedures even if we lack such proofs.

Precisely analogous points hold with respect to intellectual autonomy. No amount of reflection and self-monitoring will provide us with absolute assurances that powerful intellectual forces are not controlling us by means of our very own intellectual standards, but in itself this does not imply that autonomy is altogether impossible for us. To be sure, we need to trust that we have at least some capacity for intellectual independence if our thinking critically about our own and other people's opinions and practices is to have any point at all. However, we are entitled to assume we have a capacity for autonomy, even if we cannot prove with utter certainty that this assumption is correct.

As intellectual beings, we are both social and autonomous. The latter is in tension with the former but also dependent on it. We become intellectually independent despite the influence of others, but also because of it, at least if all goes well. Our intellectual training, which we largely receive from others, develops and hones abilities that allow us to evaluate and at times even radically criticize the views, procedures, and standards of those around us, the very views, procedures, and standards that have intellectually shaped us.

5

Past Opinion and Current Opinion

1. THE DIARY PROBLEM

In rummaging through my attic, I find an unusual diary that I have not looked at since I last wrote in it five years ago. In it is an extensive list of propositions that I then believed. As I look through the list, I see that many of the propositions are ones that I still believe, but some of the entries surprise me. I had forgotten that I ever had such opinions. The diary does not provide information about why I had these opinions or the conditions under which I formed them. All it tells me is that these were my opinions at the time. As I consider the entries, I wonder whether they have any epistemic relevance for me now. Does the fact that I believed these propositions five years ago give me a reason to alter my current opinions? If so, why? Call this "the diary problem."

The diary problem raises the question of how, if at all, one's own past opinions should figure in deliberations about what now to believe, and does so in a way that focuses attention on the intellectual authority of one's own past self. The paradigmatic issues of intellectual authority concern other people. However, questions of authority can arise about one's past self as well, and as I discuss in Chapter 6, they can also arise about one's own future self.

With respect to many matters, my beliefs do not change much over time. I now believe what I used to believe and, hence, questions about the intellectual authority of my past self are not especially pressing. With respect to other matters, my beliefs do change, but I know what it is that I observed or read or heard that changed my mind. Part of the interest of the diary problem is that it provides a framework for thinking about cases in which I become aware that my past beliefs about a topic

131

differ from my current beliefs, and yet I have little or no information about why I believed what I used to believe, and likewise little or no information of what caused me to change my mind. Cases of this sort place issues about the intellectual authority of one's past self into sharp relief. Intellectual trust in my current self is pitted against the authority of my past self. Should my past opinions have any effect on my current opinions? Should I defer to my past self or trust my current self? Moreover, even when there is no conflict with my past self because I currently lack an opinion about the issue, there are still questions about the intellectual authority of my past self to be addressed. Should I rely on my past opinion or should I instead take the trouble to investigate the issue anew?

2. THREE THESES ABOUT PAST OPINION

A general attitude of trust toward one's own past intellectual efforts is an essential part of any remotely normal intellectual life. A manifestation of this trust is that we do not feel a need to go over past conclusions continuously, nor do we feel a need to go over continuously the arguments, procedures, or evidence that led to these conclusions. We trust that our past intellectual efforts have spawned opinions that are generally reliable and, thus, we generally feel no need to review them constantly.

The fact that we by and large trust our past opinions, however, does not resolve the questions of whether such trust is reasonable, and if it is, what makes it so. Nor does it solve the diary problem. If I do not now believe P but then discover in the diary that I used to believe it, should this in any way influence my current attitude toward P? Does it give me any reason now to believe P?

Such questions can also be formulated in terms of degrees of belief rather than beliefs simpliciter. Imagine that the diary lists various propositions and also lists the degrees of confidence with which I then believed them. My degree of confidence in P, I see from the diary, used to be in the range between X and Y, but I now believe P with a degree of confidence that lies outside this range. How is this difference to be treated? Does it give me a reason, all else being equal, to alter my present opinion in the direction of my past opinion?

To get the discussion off the ground, I will introduce three rival theses about the epistemic relevance of past opinion. The first thesis is that it is reasonable to grant authority universally to our past opinions. Thus, even if I have little or no information about the conditions under which

I formed a past opinion, it is prima facie reasonable for me to regard it as credible. If I know from the diary that I used to believe P, then all else being equal this gives me a reason now to believe P. A similar thesis can be formulated for degrees of belief: if I know that I used to believe P with a degree of confidence between X and Y, then all else being equal, this gives me a reason now to believe P with a degree of confidence between X and Y.

To avoid needless controversy, this thesis can be restricted to past opinions that on reflection I would have been willing to stand behind. This is a natural restriction, because with current opinions, it is those that on reflection I would be prepared to endorse, insofar as my goal is to have accurate and comprehensive beliefs, that are epistemically the most relevant. Some current opinions, even some that I believe with great confidence, are such that I would retract them if I stopped to think about them for a moment and, hence, on reflection I myself would be critical of using them in deliberations about what else to believe. But if with respect to current opinions, it is those that I am prepared to endorse on reflection that are epistemically relevant, it should be no different with past opinions. The relevant opinions, if any, are those that I was willing to stand behind at the time.

So, assume that the thesis, call it "the credibility thesis," is to be restricted in this way, and assume also that the opinions listed in the diary are all ones that I was prepared to stand behind five years ago. The credibility thesis says that these past opinions count for something, all else being equal; they are prima facie credible for me now.

For simplicity, the credibility thesis can also be restricted to one's past opinions as a adult, thus avoiding controversy over whether opinions from the distant enough past, for example, opinions from early childhood, are prima facie credible. This restriction won't make much of a difference for those of us who are reluctant to claim any detailed knowledge of what we believed in early childhood, but there are those who are not so timid. Salvador Dali was fond of bragging that he could remember in detail what he was thinking on the day he was born.

There are other questions of detail that can be raised about the credibility thesis, for example, questions about the degree of credibility that attaches to one's past opinions (does the fact that I once believed P give me a sufficient reason, all else being equal, now to believe P, or does it rather generate a weaker reason of some sort?) and questions about how to treat past opinions that conflict with one another (if I believed not-P ten years ago but then believed P five years ago, do the two past beliefs cancel out each other's prima facie credibility, or is it rather the case that the later belief undermines the prima facie credibility of the earlier one, on the principle that, all else being equal, the least distant opinion is the most credible?). For the moment, however, I am going to ignore these and other details, so that the fundamental differences between the credibility thesis and two rival theses do not get slighted.

The first of these rival theses, call it "the neutrality thesis," denies what the credibility thesis asserts. It denies that it is reasonable to grant authority universally to our own past opinions. According to the neutrality thesis, my past opinions do not in general have a presumption in their favor for me now and, thus, in my current deliberations about P, I need not and should not take into account the fact that I believed P five years ago, unless I have special reasons to think that this past opinion is credible. If I have reasons to think that it belongs to a reliable subset of past opinions, for example, perhaps P concerns an issue that I was in an especially good position to evaluate five years ago, then the opinion is relevant to my current deliberations, but in the absence of considerations of this sort, it is not relevant.

The third thesis, call it "the irrelevancy thesis," goes further, claiming that it is never reasonable to grant intellectual authority to past opinions. Thus, the only legitimate way for the opinions in the diary to affect my current opinions is through Socratic influence. If the entries contain enough information about a topic that I come to understand now what I formerly understood, it may be reasonable for me now to believe what I formerly believed. But according to the irrelevancy thesis, it is never reasonable for me simply to borrow opinions from my past self, that is, to come to believe now what I used to believe on the basis of the authority of my past self.

These three theses are analogous to the three theses discussed in Chapter 4 concerning the opinions of other people. One of these theses, the counterpart to the credibility thesis, is epistemic universalism, which asserts that it is reasonable to grant authority universally to the opinions of others. According to universalists, even the opinions of complete strangers are prima facie credible for me. Thus, for testimony to be relevant, I need not have any special information about the reliability of the person giving the testimony. Rather, it works the other way around. I can reasonably rely on the opinions of others unless there are positive reasons for doubting them. A rival thesis is epistemic egoism. It denies that it is reasonable to grant authority universally to the opinions of others. If we are to rely on the testimony of another person, we need special information about the person's reliability. Epistemic egoism thus imposes a burden that epistemic universalism does not. A third thesis, epistemic egotism, makes an even stronger claim. According to egotists, it is never reasonable to grant authority to the opinions of others. The only legitimate way for someone else to affect my opinions is through Socratic influence.

Just as epistemic egoism imposes a burden that epistemic universalism does not, so too the neutrality thesis imposes a burden that the credibility thesis does not. It requires me to have reasons for thinking that there is something special about a past opinion P if I am to trust it, while the credibility thesis imposes only a negative requirement. According to it, each of my past opinions is prima facie credible for me. So, unless there are reasons to discount my past opinion P, it is relevant for my current deliberations. Furthermore, just as epistemic egotism makes a stronger claim than epistemic egoism, so too the irrelevancy thesis makes a stronger claim than the neutrality thesis. According to the irrelevancy thesis, my past opinions never have authority for me now.

However, this is still not exactly the right way to think about the differences among these theses. I have been talking as if it is unproblematic to determine what I formerly believed, but of course this is not always so. Like my opinions about other matters, I can have more or less defensible opinions about what my past opinions were. Because the irrelevancy thesis denies that past opinions ever have any epistemic significance, this point does not affect it, but the point is relevant for both the credibility and neutrality theses. Each of these theses must acknowledge that past opinions reasonably come into play in shaping current opinion only insofar as I have rational beliefs about them. If my past belief P is to give me a reason to alter my current opinion of P, it must be rational for me to believe that I did in fact believe P. Mere belief won't do.

Once again, there is an analogy with the opinions of others. If it is to be rational for me to defer to your belief P, it is not enough for me to believe that you believe P. It must be rational for me to believe this. It is no different with past opinions. To be sure, there are differences between the ways I come to have opinions about other people's opinions and the ways I come to have opinions to my own past opinions. Testimony and the behavior of others ordinarily provide me with the most ready access to other people's opinions, whereas memory and my current beliefs (since much of what I now believe is what I used to believe) ordinarily provide me with the most ready access to my own past opinions. I will return to these differences later, but for the moment the important point is that it is not quite accurate to say that the issue at hand is one of how past opinions should figure in current deliberations about what to believe. The issue, more precisely expressed, and the issue about which the credibility and neutrality theses disagree, is one of how past opinions, as seen by current rational opinion, should figure in current deliberations about what to believe. In what follows, it won't always be convenient to make this qualification explicit, but it does need to be kept in mind.

3. AN ATTEMPT TO MOTIVATE THE CREDIBILITY THESIS

Later, I argue that there are important truths lying in the neighborhood of both the credibility thesis and the neutrality thesis, despite the fact they are rival theses, but before explaining what these truths are, it will be useful to look briefly at an unsuccessful attempt to motivate the credibility thesis.

The motivation I have in mind is one that emphasizes limitations on our time and resources. In making decisions about how to achieve our ends, we often have to make up our minds quickly. There is little time to reflect on our options, and even less time to go over past conclusions or consult with others. The decisions are too pressing. Thus, it might seem as if we have no realistic choice but to trust our past opinions. Even if we were purely intellectual beings, with the freedom to devote all of our time to intellectual pursuits, we would not have the time or cognitive capacity to go over all, or even a very large percentage, of our past conclusions. We have far too many opinions about far too many issues for this to be feasible.

Indeed, it might seem as if we often have no choice but to trust our past opinions even when a single, sharply defined conclusion is at issue. Suppose I have just completed a proof of P, but the proof is long and, hence, I am unable to keep in mind simultaneously all of its steps. In addition, the proof may be lengthy and difficult enough that I do not have the time, much less the patience, to reconstruct the early steps. Unless I can trust the opinions I had when I was working on the early stages of the proof, I cannot regard myself as having come up with a sound proof of P. Thus, it might seem as if we have no choice but to trust our past opinions. Our own limitations force such trust upon us and, moreover, the alternative courts disaster. If we did not generally rely upon our past opinions, all our time and cognitive resources would be taken up in rechecking past conclusions, and there would be no possibility of temporally extended, cumulative intellectual efforts.[1]

Nevertheless, arguments of this sort do not constitute a convincing epistemic defense of the credibility thesis. The arguments are aimed at establishing that we have no realistic choice but to trust our past opinions; but even if this is correct, it at best provides not epistemic reasons in favor of thesis, that is, reasons that are persuasive insofar as the goal is now to have accurate and comprehensive beliefs, but rather reasons that arise from our practical and temporally extended intellectual goals.

Besides, it is not even clear that the argument is correct in presupposing that the only way to address concerns about constraints on our time and cognitive resources is by trusting past opinions. Trusting current opinions is potentially also a way of addressing these concerns. After all, beliefs are generally retained from one moment to the next. No special effort is needed to preserve them. At the current moment, for example, I have an enormous number of beliefs, most of which I have inherited from my past self without any special effort. Why cannot I rely on these beliefs in making decisions and forming new beliefs? Admittedly, a serious question can be raised about whether, insofar as the goal is to have accurate and comprehensive beliefs, it is appropriate for me to rely on my current beliefs if I do not also have trust in my past beliefs. Indeed, I will be making much of this point in the sections that follow, but the immediate, more narrow point I am making is that insofar as the worry is the pragmatic one of having a sufficiently large body of beliefs to rely on in making decisions and forming new beliefs, trusting current opinions is an alternative to trusting past opinions.

In any event, in what follows, I sketch different and explicitly epistemic argument in defense of the credibility thesis. Moreover, it will be argument that attempts to capture some of intuitive appeal of the neutrality thesis even as it endorses the credibility thesis.

---

1 Descartes maintains that if we remember having deduced a certain conclusion step by step from a set of premises known by intuition, then even if we do not recall each of the steps, we are nonetheless justified in saying that the conclusion is known by deduction. See *Rules for the Direction of the Mind*, in Cottingham, Stoothoff, and Murdoch, trans., *The Philosophical Writings of Descartes*, vol. 1 (Cambridge: Cambridge University Press, 1985), 7–78. Norman Malcolm makes a similar claim, only he does not restrict it to deductions. He says: "If a man previously had ground for being sure that p, and he now remembers that p, but does not remember what his grounds were, then he nonetheless has the same grounds he previously had." *Knowledge and Certainty* (Englewood Cliffs, NJ: Prentice-Hall, 1963), 230.

By and large I trust my current beliefs as well as the faculties that produce them, and, as argued in Chapter 1, it is ordinarily reasonable for me to do so. This trust pressures me also to trust my past beliefs, for if I did not, I would risk inconsistency. Most of my current beliefs, as well as the grounds I have for them and even the very concepts out of which they are constituted, are the products of past learning. Thus, unless I am willing to trust by and large my past intellectual efforts, I should not be willing to stand behind my current opinions either.

Likewise, the kinds of methods, faculties, and environment that combined to produce my past opinions are for the most part similar to my current methods, faculties, and environment. Thus, insofar as I trust my current methods and faculties to produce reliable beliefs in my current environment, I am again pressured, on threat of inconsistency, to trust that my past faculties and methods produced reliable beliefs in my past environment.

Accordingly, for a past opinion of mine to be relevant to my current deliberations about what to believe, I do not need reasons to think that there is anything special about it. For example, I do not need information about my past level of training about the issue in question, or information about how thoroughly I collected data about the issue, or information about how deeply I thought about the issue. It is enough for me to know that it was an opinion of mine.

Considerations of the above sort will not move a skeptic. If I am willing to be skeptical about my current opinions, there is no threat of inconsistency in not trusting my past opinions. However, most of us are not skeptics and, thus, for most of us there is a threat.

Admittedly, there are conceivable ways of avoiding this threat short of embracing skepticism. One might try claiming that one's past opinions have not influenced one's current opinions, or that one's past faculties, methods, and environment do not even broadly resemble one's current faculties, methods, and environment. However, such claims lack plausibility for most of us.

There are exceptions. Intellectual revolutionaries sometimes combine a trust in their current opinions with a deep distrust of their past opinions, even if they also think that these past opinions represented a necessary stage in their intellectual development. For instance, Marxists sometimes claim that they would not have been able to see what is wrong with classical liberal thought without so immersing themselves in it that its contradictions became apparent. Only then were they able to rise above it and adopt the correct view. At the end of his *Tractatus*, Wittgenstein makes a similar claim about the philosophical propositions he has advocated earlier in the book. Those propositions, he asserts, are to be dismissed as useful nonsense – useful because they helped him to see the truth, but nonsense nonetheless. He compares these propositions to a ladder that can be used to climb to a higher position but which should then be thrown away.

So, insofar as I regard myself as having recently revolutionized my belief system, I will view my past beliefs as misguided, even if I am also willing to concede that they placed me in a position from which I could appreciate what was wrong with my outlook. If so, I will be willing to admit that there is something to be said for my past opinions, namely, they helped me reach my current, enlightened position. Still, this does not imply that I should take these opinions seriously in my current deliberations about what to believe. On the contrary, it implies that I ought not to take them seriously, because I now understand how mistaken they were.

It is a delicate business, however, to keep a deep distrust of one's past opinions from spilling over into one's current opinions, especially if it is a broad class of past opinions that are distrusted. The more fundamental and extensive the differences between past and current opinion, the more difficult it will be to counter the suspicion that just as current opinion sees past opinion as deeply misguided, so too future opinion may very well see current opinion as deeply misguided. When current opinion sees past opinion as having been largely incorporated into current opinion, this kind of skeptical worry does not easily get off the ground, but when current opinion dismisses past opinion as massively mistaken, such worries inevitably arise.

Much of the literature in philosophy of science following Thomas Kuhn's *The Structure of Scientific Revolutions* focused on just these kinds of worries. If, as Kuhn argues, the history of science is best viewed as a history of revolutions, in which previous theories are rejected as largely misguided, it is difficult to keep skeptical worries from arising about current theories, because on this reading of the history, there are inductive reasons to think that future opinion is likely to regard current theories as largely misguided. On the other hand, if, contra Kuhn, the history of science is read as one in which former theories are revised but largely incorporated into subsequent theories (rather than simply rejected), the inductive pressures against regarding current theories as true, or at least approximately true, are not nearly as strong.

I do not pretend that there are no strategies available to intellectual revolutionaries for keeping such worries at bay. My point is simply that whenever trust of current opinion is combined with a deep distrust of past opinion, there will be worries of this sort, and with these worries comes a threat of inconsistency. In particular, the threat is that one's confidence in one's current opinions is at odds with what one can reasonably infer from one's view about the history of one's own past opinions, namely, that the history is largely a history of error.

Moreover, even if there are conceivable ways for intellectual revolutionaries to avoid being inconsistent, there are not many of us who are inclined to combine a deep distrust of our past opinions with a general trust of our current opinions, at least not with respect to a wide range of topics and not for very long. After all, even those who have only recently revolutionized their opinions will soon be trusting once again their past, though postrevolutionary, beliefs; or at least this is so barring new revolutions. A familiar story is that of youthful political revolutionaries becoming respectable, establishment figures in middle-age. The epistemic analogue of this trajectory is that distrust of past opinions is likely to be only a temporary phenomenon, even for intellectual revolutionaries. On other hand, if the unlikely occurs and one engages in continuous, successive revolutions of one's opinions, skeptical worries about one's current opinions will be all the more difficult to resist.

The conclusion, then, is that most of us do generally trust our past opinions, and we would risk inconsistency not to do so, given that we trust our current opinions and given also that we view our current opinions as having evolved out of our past opinions with the help of faculties, methods, and procedures that are broadly similar to the faculties, methods, and procedures that produced our past opinions. The conclusion, in other words, is that trust in our current opinions pressures us to give credence to our past opinions as well. It may well be that the more distant in the past the opinion and the more we have changed intellectually in the interim, the less this pressure is. Such refinements are consistent with the basic argument, which asserts that our past opinions have at least some initial credibility for us now.

To accept this conclusion is to accept a modest version of the credibility thesis. In its strongest form, the credibility thesis asserts that necessarily our past opinions are prima facie credible for us now. The above arguments, which emphasize considerations of influence and similarity, are not capable of supporting anything stronger than a contingent claim. Past opinions have exerted a major influence upon our current opinions, and most of us would be willing to acknowledge this. Likewise, the methods, faculties, and environment that combined to produce our past opinions have broad commonalities with our current methods, faculties, and environment, and most of us would be willing to acknowledge this as well. Accordingly, trust in our current opinions pressures us to trust our past opinions. The conclusion is not that these pressures are completely unavoidable, or that past opinions are necessarily credible. The conclusion, rather, is the more cautious one that these pressures are extremely difficult to escape. There are broad features of our intellectual situation that pressure most of us, on threat of inconsistency, to trust by and large our past opinions.

5. DIFFERENCES IN THE CREDIBILITY OF PAST OPINIONS

If it is reasonable for me to believe that I once believed P, I have a reason, all else being equal, now to believe P. However, it is often not easy to tell whether all else really is equal. To illustrate this, I here describe some cases in which one should apparently defer to past opinion as well as some cases in which one apparently should not. My ultimate aim is to use these cases to illustrate that the credibility thesis needs to be supplemented by two other theses governing past opinion. Moreover, these other theses capture some of the spirit of the neutrality thesis. This is getting ahead of myself, however. First the cases.

Suppose one of the entries in the diary indicates that I believed that I proved that Q is a tautology. However, I am now unable to recreate the proof. Moreover, Q is complex enough that I am not able to see from inspection whether or not it is tautologous. In addition, its complexity makes it unfeasible for me to work out a truth table for it. Even so, I may very well defer to my past conclusion, and such deference may well be reasonable, especially if I have reasons to think that my past efforts were in some way superior to my current ones. Perhaps I have not done proofs recently. I am out of practice, whereas previously I was doing them regularly. Consequently, it is plausible to think that there is something that I am now not seeing.

To be sure, there are limits on how deferential I should be to my past efforts. If I fail to find the proof despite trying very hard and if I have no reason to think my skills have slipped significantly, I eventually will begin to question whether what I previously took to be a proof really was a proof. Such doubts are especially likely to arise if there was no clear mark at the time that I had the proof right.

Think of Rubik's Cube. The point of the game is to find a way of manipulating the small cubes so that there are uniform colors on all six faces of the large cube. Suppose I cannot now find a solution. I have been working on it for several hours without success. However, I do remember having found a solution last year, and there was a mark of its being a genuine solution. I remember seeing the uniform colors on each of the six sides. Accordingly, I recognize that my current difficulties are the result of my not having hit upon the right combination.

There can be analogous, albeit perhaps less definitive, external marks of success for a past proof. Perhaps a colleague who is more talented than I in logic told me that my proof was a good one, or perhaps I checked my proof against the one given in the manual of a logic book. However, there need not have been any such sign of my having got it right, or even if there was, there need not be any indication in the diary that I was aware of it. But then, if I try very hard to recreate the proof but nonetheless fail, I may eventually come to have reasons for suspecting that I was mistaken when I previously thought that I had found a proof. These reasons will be all the more compelling if it is reasonable for me to believe that I am now more skilled in working these kinds of proofs than I was at the time of the diary.

In this case, I have some idea about how to adjudicate between my past and current efforts. Even if I cannot recreate the exact proof, I still do know the general techniques of proving that something is a tautology, and I assume that it was these techniques, either correctly or incorrectly applied, that convinced me five years ago that Q is a tautology. In other cases, however, I might not have much of an idea of what it was that led to my past belief. Suppose I discover in the diary that I used to believe P, but I do not now have a clear idea of what kinds of considerations prompted me to believe it. Hence, I have no clear idea whether they were the kinds of considerations I would now regard as reliable. Despite this ignorance, the diary entry gives me a prima facie reason now to believe P. I am pressured to trust by and large my past opinions and, thus, I am also pressured to trust, all else being equal, any particular past opinion. On the other hand, whether or not all else is equal depends upon what the proposition P is, what if anything I now believe about P, and what I think has happened in the interim.

Assume that I have no specific knowledge about what changed my mind about P. Even so, given the kind of proposition P is, I may be able to speculate. If P is the proposition that Steven Smith has a sister named Clare, where Steven Smith is a former acquaintance whom I have not seen in recent years, it is probably reasonable for me to assume that I have simply forgotten this fact about Steven. It was not important enough for me to retain. It is probably also reasonable for me to assume that I was in a better position to know P five years ago than I am now. Accordingly, I am likely to regard this entry in the diary as credible, that is, as giving me a good reason to believe that Steven really did have a sister named Clare.

By contrast, if a proposition listed in the diary is important or at least memorable, this kind of explanation of why I no longer believe it will not be as readily available. Suppose the diary includes the propositions that there is highly intelligent life elsewhere in universe and that Richard Nixon and Nancy Reagan had an affair. These are propositions that in the normal course of things I was not likely simply to have forgotten. So, it is probably not reasonable for me to assume that I failed to retain them in memory. A more plausible hypothesis is that I believed them, perhaps only for a very short time, and subsequently dismissed them. Accordingly, I am not likely to regard the fact that I used to believe these propositions as giving me a reason to believe them now, even if I cannot now remember exactly why or when I quit believing them.

Of the entries in the diary that I no longer believe, many will fall between these extremes. It won't be altogether clear whether they are propositions I have simply forgotten with the passage of time, or whether they are instead propositions that I have dismissed. Moreover, with many propositions of the latter sort, I will remember, at least vaguely, what it was that changed my mind. Nevertheless, these are complications that can be ignored for the moment. For immediate purposes, the important point is that it seems reasonable to regard some of the opinions listed in the diary as credible and reasonable to regard others as not credible.

6. THE PRIORITY THESIS AND THE SPECIAL REASON THESIS

At risk of inconsistency, I am pressured, all else being equal, to trust by and large my past opinions and, as a result, I am also pressured, all else being equal, to trust any particular entry in the diary. But then, why are there differences among the various entries? Why it is reasonable for me to take seriously some of the entries but not others?

143

Part of the answer, of course, is that my past opinions are only prima facie credible. According to the credibility thesis, its being rational for me to believe that I did believe P gives me a prima facie reason now to believe P, but this reason, being prima facie, can be defeated by other considerations. It is defeated, for example, if I now have reasons to think that the evidence that convinced me of P was misleading or that I was not careful in evaluating this evidence or that I was biased in some way.

But in addition, there is another common way for the presumption of trust to be defeated. Even if I lack information about the conditions under which my past belief P was formed, the presumption of trust in it is defeated if my current opinion of P conflicts with it. The rationale for this thesis, call it "the priority thesis," is an extension of the rationale for the credibility thesis. The grounds for the latter is that I risk inconsistency if I do not in general trust my past opinions, given that I generally trust my current opinions and given also that my current opinions are largely the products of my past intellectual efforts. Trust in my current opinions exerts a pressure on me to trust my past opinions as well, including those which I had five years ago when I wrote in the diary. However, according to the credibility thesis, I have a prima facie reason to trust not just what I believed five years ago but also what I have believed in the interim. All else being equal, I must by and large trust the opinions that I had four years ago, the opinions I had three years ago, the opinions I had two years ago, and so on. Indeed, what I am most pressured to trust, on threat of inconsistency, is not my opinions at any given moment in the past but rather the overall drift of these opinions, the drift that eventually led to my current opinions. Thus, if a current opinion conflicts with what I believed five years ago, it undermines the prima facie trustworthiness of that past opinion. Because of the commonalities between my current self and past self, trust in my current self creates a pressure to trust my past self, but by the same token, when my current opinions about a topic P conflict with my past opinions about P, this constitutes a relevant dissimilarity between my current self and my past self and, hence, dissipates the pressure to trust my past self with respect to P.

On the other hand, even when the prima facie credibility of the past belief P is defeated by my currently having a conflicting opinion about P, it might nonetheless be epistemically rational for me to defer to my past self. I may have evidence to think that my past self was in a better position to evaluate P than my current self, in which case I have reasons to defer to my past opinion, despite the fact that it conflicts with current opinion. This is the second supplemental thesis to the credibility thesis. Call it "the special reasons thesis."

The special reasons for thinking that my past self was in a better position to evaluate P than my current self are not necessarily ones that imply that I have been irrational or intellectually irresponsible in the interim, because there need not have been any pressing reasons for me to ensure that I remained in a good position to evaluate P. Let P once again be the proposition that Steven Smith has a sister named Clare, where Steven is a former acquaintance. It is easy to explain why I no longer believe P; I have not seen Steven for a long time and the proposition was not an important one for me to remember. It is also easy to explain why I was in a better position to know P five years ago than I am today. I saw and talked to Steven regularly then whereas I do not do so now. Accordingly, it is easy to see why it can be reasonable for me to defer to my past opinion on this question even if I currently seem to remember that his sister's name was Pat.

By contrast, if P is the proposition that there is highly intelligent life elsewhere in the universe, there is not such a ready explanation as to why I would have been in a better position then than now to evaluate its truth. Of course, there are conceivable scenarios in which I would have reasons to think this, for example, perhaps I engaged in an extensive study of the issue five years ago. But without a memory of this sort or something else equally specific, it ordinarily won't be reasonable for me to think I was then in a better position than now to evaluate P, because there is nothing about the proposition itself to suggest that in the normal course of events that this is likely to be so. Thus, there are unlikely to be special reasons for me to defer to my past self on this issue.

The credibility thesis together with the priority and special reasons theses constitute the beginnings of an account of the epistemic relevance of past opinion. The account provides a framework for organizing our thoughts about the issues raised by the diary problem. According to the account, I risk inconsistency if I do not generally trust my own past opinions. This creates a presumption in favor of these opinions. Thus, on the assumption that it is rational for me to believe that I believed the propositions listed in the diary, I have a prima facie reason now to believe these propositions. However, this prima facie reason is defeated whenever there is a conflict between past opinions and current opinions.

So, unless there are special reasons to defer to the opinions I had when I wrote the diary, I need not revise my current opinions in deference to my former opinions.

According to this account, a general attitude of trust in one's own past opinions is not an utterly necessary condition of rationality, as the strongest version of the credibility thesis would assert. On the other hand, the considerations that make it prima facie reasonable to trust one's past opinions are so broad and so pervasive that the pressures to trust them are nearly inescapable. So, the basic intuition lying behind the credibility thesis is correct, namely, in order for a past opinion P to be credible for me now, I do not need know anything special about the conditions under which the opinion was formed. I need not have information about how thoroughly I gathered evidence or how extensively I reflected on the issue or how carefully I considered opposing views. It is enough that it was a past opinion of mine. It being reasonable for me to believe that I did believe P gives me a prima facie reason now to believe P.

On the other hand, if I currently have a conflicting current opinion about P, the prima facie credibility of my past opinion P is defeated, in which case it is reasonable for me to defer to my past opinion only if I have special reasons for thinking that my past self was in a better position than my current self to evaluate P. Thus, for a large and significant set of cases, namely, cases in which past and current opinion are at odds with one another, the neutrality thesis is correct at least in spirit. In these cases, I do indeed need special reasons to trust in the reliability of past opinion if past opinion is rationally to influence current opinion. In this way, the above account, while endorsing the credibility thesis, nonetheless also captures some of the intuitive pull of the neutrality thesis, despite the fact that the latter is a rival thesis to the former.

7. RADICAL CONFLICTS WITH ONE'S OWN PAST OPINIONS

Consider an especially extreme conflict between current opinion and past opinion. Suppose I find an entry in the diary that says at time t, where t is now, my opinions about P will be unreliable. Moreover, the entry adds that these opinions will remain unreliable even if I read the entry and try to correct my opinions in light of the warning.

According to the credibility thesis, I have a prima facie reason to believe this entry in the diary, because, by hypothesis, it is rational for me to believe that I believed it five years ago and I have a prima facie reason to trust by and large my past beliefs. On the other hand, according to the priority thesis, the prima facie credibility of a past belief is defeated if it conflicts with what I now believe. So, if I believe my current opinions about P are reliable, the prima facie credibility of this entry in the diary is defeated. Moreover, it is defeated even if the entry describes what I then took to be the source of my current unreliability. For example, the diary might indicate that at the time I made the entry, I was convinced that I was going to develop certain kinds of biases about P and these biases would be so deep that I would not be able to correct them. Nevertheless, if I am convinced that my current opinions about P are reliable and not the result of biases, the prima facie credibility of my former opinion is defeated.

Even so, it might still be epistemically rational for me to defer to the entry. Although I am convinced that my current opinions about P are reliable, there may nonetheless be considerations which, if I were sufficiently reflective, would persuade me that the worries raised by my past self were legitimate. Suppose that this is in fact the case. Perhaps there is indirect evidence, which I have not sufficiently attended, indicating that I do in fact have biases that make me an unreliable evaluator of P. Then, as the special reasons thesis envisions, I have reasons to defer to my past opinion, and my current beliefs about P are irrational. I should instead withhold judgment on P, at least for the time being.

I say for "the time being," because even in this scenario, I am not necessarily precluded from forming defensible beliefs about P. To be sure, I have very strong reasons to be wary of any belief I might be inclined to form. Still, even under these extreme conditions, it may be possible for me to have rational beliefs about P, provided that I come to grips with the worries raised by my past self. In particular, I may be able to monitor myself against the kind of biases that my past self foresaw, or short of avoiding the biases altogether, I might try to adjust for them by factoring them into my current opinion. If, for example, the diary indicates that my biases tend to make me overly confident of P's truth, I can try to compensate by lowering my confidence in P by an appropriate degree.

Self-monitoring or recalibration is extremely risky, given the above described conditions. Self-trust is being pushed to the limit in this scenario and, hence, the safest strategy is to withhold judgment about P. I mention self-monitoring and recalibration, nevertheless, because at least in principle they are options, despite the fact that the diary and my subsequent investigations provide reasons for doubting not only my current beliefs about P but also about my current ability to correct these beliefs. Whatever strategies or methods I might choose to employ in my attempts at self-monitoring or recalibration, I will be making use of strategies or methods the reliability of which the diary challenges. Even so, this does not categorically prevent me from having defensible beliefs about P. If, while acknowledging my biases, I can somehow manage to find a way of revising my beliefs about P such that even on deep reflection I would be satisfied that I have adequately avoided or compensated for my biases, I can be entitled to the resulting opinions, despite the doubts of my past self concerning my ability to make revisions of just this sort.[2]

In effect, this is to grant my current self and its opinions a special, albeit limited, epistemic status. The status is revealed in two ways, first, by the fact that the prima facie credibility of past opinion is defeated when it conflicts with current opinion, and, second, by the fact that it is my current self that determines whether or not there are special reasons to defer to the warnings of my past self.

If the present is thought of as merely one time among many at which I have opinions, this special status might seem unwarranted. For, it then might seem that when there is a conflict between my current and past opinions, they necessarily discredit one another, with neither taking precedence over the other. From my current perspective, my current beliefs about P may be unimpeachable, even given my past warnings. However, I also realize that if from my perspective of five years ago I could have peered into the future, these same current opinions would have seemed irremediably unreliable. Thus, impartiality might seem to require that inasmuch as my current self and past self are in conflict, it is inappropriate to allow the former to arbitrate the conflict.

In accounts of practical rationality, it is sometimes argued that because we are temporally extended beings, our desires, values, and needs at the current moment cannot take precedence over our desires, values, and needs at other moments. Rationality, it is said, demands that we escape to the extent possible our immediate perspective and take a temporally impartial view of ourselves. Because one's current self is merely one part of a temporally extended self, one should identify equally with the various moments of one's life.[3] In epistemology, there can be similar positions, ones that conceive rationality as demanding that we escape to

2 Compare with the discussions of self-monitoring in §3.3 and §3.4.
3 See Thomas Nagel, *The Possibility of Altruism* (Oxford: Oxford University Press, 1969).

the extent possible our current perspective and take a temporally impartial stance with respect to our past, future, and present opinions.

There is obviously something right about the observation that it is important to keep in mind that one is a temporally extended being and that, hence, one's current perspective on a set of issues can be at odds not only with the perspectives of other people, but also with one's own perspectives at different times. However, whatever philosophical conclusions one tries to tease out of this observation must be tempered by the truism that insofar as one is deliberating about what to do and think, it is one's current self that is doing the deliberating. This means that conflicts between past opinions and current opinions cannot be treated by me as conflicts between a past self and a current self, where the latter is merely one more part of my temporally extended self. To view the matter in this way is to overlook the banal truth that at the current moment, if I am to have opinions at all, they will be current opinions. Correspondingly, if I am to arbitrate between my current opinion and past opinions, it will be my current self that does the arbitration. Thus, it cannot be a demand of rationality that I shed my current perspective and adopt a vantage point from which I treat all of my temporal selves and their opinions identically.

On the other hand, it is a legitimate demand of rationality that one not allow one's surface perspective, the pushes and pulls of the moment as it were, to dominate one's deliberations. Rationality requires depth. Just as whims, impulses, and urges are not as determinative of what it is rational to do as full-blooded, less fleeting, and more deeply seated drives, preferences, and needs, so too hunches, inklings, and other such shallowly held opinions are not as determinative as what it is rational to believe as deeply held beliefs.

In cases like the one described above, which involve a radical conflict with one's own past opinions, one cannot simply assume that one's current, unreflective take on the issues takes precedence over one's past opinions. Such an assumption would constitute a failure to acknowledge that one's current perspective is but one of various possible perspectives that one has taken, will take, or could take on the issues. However, the remedy, as I have been arguing, is not to suppose that one can somehow escape one's current perspective but rather to burrow more deeply into that perspective and to form a judgment that one could continue to endorse even on the deepest, most thorough reflection.

Less radical conflicts between past and current opinion raise similar problems, and the solution to them is also similar. Suppose that an entry in the diary reveals that five years ago I was embarking on an ambitious intellectual project with the aim of confirming or disconfirming a hypothesis H. At the time, I estimated that in order to conduct the inquiry thoroughly, ten years of collecting and analyzing data would be required. I was aware that over the duration of the project, the overall force of the evidence was likely to shift back and forth, sometimes in favor of H and at other times against it. Moreover, I recognized that if I were to allow this incomplete evidence to determine my opinion, I might be seduced into giving up the project prematurely, before all the critical data were in. So, I resolved, no matter how the evidence amassed at various stages of the inquiry, not to form an opinion of H until the ten-year project was completed. However, at the current moment, five years later and halfway through what I originally estimated to be the life-span of the project, the evidence is overwhelmingly in favor of H. Hence, from my current perspective, the truth of H seems well established and, accordingly, there seems little point in continuing my investigations. The right strategy seems to be to accept H as proved and terminate the project.

Michael Bratman has discussed cases that raise closely analogous issues for practical deliberations. Suppose that I am an avid reader of mysteries, and I do most of my reading at night, just before going to sleep. From past experience, I know that I have a tendency to get wrapped up in the plots of especially good mysteries and to read well into the night, with the result that I get less sleep than I need, which in turn adversely affects me at work the next day. So, I form a policy of reading only one chapter a night, as a way of protecting myself against myself. My overall interests, I judge, are best served by such a policy. However, it is now Tuesday night, I have just finished my allotted one chapter, I am intrigued by the story, and when I weigh the pleasures of reading an additional chapter against the cost of being tired at work the next day, I now judge that these pleasures are more than sufficient to compensate for tomorrow's tiredness. So, I now think it best to deviate from my established policy and to read the additional chapter.[4]

Cases of this sort illustrate how well thought-out plans and policies can be at odds with the inclinations of the moment, and in doing so they raise fundamental issues about practical rationality. The stability of

---

4 Michael Bratman, "Reflection, Planning, and Temporally Extended Agency," *The Philosophical Review*, forthcoming. See also Bratman, *Intention, Plans, and Practical Reason* (Cambridge, MA: Harvard University Press, 1987).

plans and policies over time is an important part of any well-ordered life and, thus, an adequate account of practical rationality must allow that it can be rational to stick with plans and policies even when fleeting temptations provide powerful incentives to deviate from them. Well thought-out plans and policies ought to be able to bind one even when the felt pushes and pulls of the moment incline one to deviate from the plan or policy.

An overly rigid way of responding to this challenge is to make it a condition of rationality that one not re-assess a plan that it was rational for one to adopt. Such a response provides an explanation of the rationality of adhering to plans in the face of temptations, but it leaves no room for the rationality of deviating from them once they have been established, which is also an important part of a judicious life. As circumstances change, it is sometimes reasonable to diverge from even the most well-conceived plan.

A better way to address the challenge is to dig deeper into one's current perspective. Rationality demands that decisions about whether to deviate from an established policy not be made simply on the basis of currently activated preferences. Such preferences are too ephemeral. Preferences that one would endorse even on deep reflection are another matter, however. By 'deep reflection' I mean, in particular, reflection that takes into account the fleeting character of one's surface wants at any given time and that also takes into account that these surface wants may be at odds with one's deeper interests, as defined by the wants, needs, and values one would endorse were one to be reflective. An established plan or policy (for example, that of reading only one chapter a night) at odds with the felt inclinations of the moment (wanting very much to know what happens in the next chapter) is a warning marker that one ought not to accede too quickly to one's immediate inclinations. The decision ought to be made in light of one's deep and abiding wants, needs, and values, not just in light of one's currently activated preferences.

The above diary case poses an analogous challenge for an account of epistemic rationality. The challenge is to leave room for the possibility that it might be rational for me to continue to withhold on hypothesis H, as my policy of five years ago dictates, despite the fact that H now strikes me as having been proved. On the other hand, an adequate response to this challenge must also allow that, in some instances, it can be rational to discard or revise a policy that it was rational to adopt five years ago. The solution, as with practical rationality, is not to pretend that I can somehow escape from my current perspective. It is to burrow deeper into my current perspective, and to insist that judgments about whether to deviate from the established policy not be made simply on the basis of my initial, surface evaluation of the current data, but rather on the basis of evaluations that I could continue to endorse even on deep reflection. Specifically, the judgment must go beyond the felt pushes and pulls of currently available evidence and come to grips, in a manner that I could continue to endorse on reflection, with the issue of whether my evidence at this stage of the project is definitive enough to override my considered judgment of five years ago that it would be too risky to take a firm stand one way or the other on H until at least ten years of evidence collecting and analysis had been completed.

This case of conflict between past and current opinion, like the more radical one described earlier, illustrates that my current self has an epistemic standing that my self of five years ago lacks for me now, just as five years from now what will then be my current self will have a standing that what is now my current self will lack then. When the opinions of my current self conflict with an opinion of my past self, the former defeats the prima facie reason I have to trust the latter. I might still have reasons to defer to my past self, but once again it is my current self that assesses whether there are sufficiently strong, special reasons to do so.

The special standing of my current self is sharply limited, however, in that I cannot simply assume that I am now in a better position than I was five years ago to determine the truth about a proposition or hypothesis. On the contrary, this is one of the issues about which I have to make a judgment. I must evaluate, as best I can, given my current abilities and information, whether it is best to defer to my past opinions or best to retain my current opinions or best to withhold judgment about the issue.

The only other option is to refuse to arbitrate the conflict on the grounds that my past self doubted my current abilities to arbitrate. On this way of viewing the matter, I should refuse to have any opinion at all about the issue, not even a probabilistic one. With respect to some propositions, even if I am not prepared either to believe or disbelieve them, I am prepared to make an assessment of their probabilities. For example, when I assess the probability of a fair coin coming up heads to be approximately 0.5, I am taking a definite, albeit probabilistic, position about the chances of the coin coming up heads.[5] The recommendation

---

5 Compare with the discussion in §4.5.

here, however, is that given the nature of the conflict with my past self, even such a probabilistic stance is impermissible. If I begin to be convinced that some such attitude X is the correct one to take, I need only recall the diary entry and this should undermine my confidence in X.

This is not an incoherent position. My reasons for trusting my past self might be compelling enough to undermine any current opinion about the issue that I might otherwise be tempted to form, just as the studies in cognitive psychology discussed in Chapter 3 documenting our tendencies to make unreliable judgments about people we have personally interviewed might be compelling enough to undermine any opinion I might otherwise be tempted to form after such an interview.

Thus, it is possible for conflicts between past and current opinion to leave me with no reasonable option but to have no opinion on the issue in dispute. What I have been arguing, however, is that this is not an inevitable result, not even in cases involving the most extreme conflicts between past and current opinions. Such conflicts are not necessarily paralyzing. The diary tells me that five years ago I confidently believed that nothing I could do five years hence, that is, now, would result in my having reliable opinions about P, but I do not necessarily have to defer to this entry just because it questions my current abilities to determine the truth about P. If after thoroughly evaluating and considering the warning from my past self, I conclude that there is little substance to the warning and, hence, retain my current opinions of P, or if in acknowledgment of the warning I revise my opinions of P to my own current satisfaction, I can be entitled to these opinions. I can be entitled to them, despite the fact that my past self has warned me that my attempts at revision are hopeless.

Given the nature of the warning, there is no possibility of my being able to discharge it in a non–question-begging way, but this does not necessarily require me to defer to it on pains of irrationality, any more than my inability to discharge the evil demon hypothesis in a non–question-begging way requires me to defer to it on pains of irrationality. Contrary to what some classical foundationalists assumed, it can be rational for me to generally trust my current opinions and faculties even if I cannot prove in a non–question-begging way that the warnings of radical skeptics are unfounded. Similarly, it can be rational for me to generally trust my current opinions about P, and my faculties, even if I cannot prove that the radical warnings of my own past self are unfounded.

It is especially disquieting that the source of the radical worries in this case is my own past self. I must generally trust my past self on threat of inconsistency and, thus, I cannot ignore these worries or lightly dismiss them. Even if in the end I continue to trust my current opinions, I will want an explanation as to why and how I went so wrong in coming to have radical doubts about my current abilities to form reliable opinions about P. Nevertheless, it is not an absolute prerequisite of my currently having a rational opinion about P that I find such an explanation. I may not have access to enough information to do more than guess what prompted me to have these doubts. If so, my past doubts will remain a mystery, one that gives me reasons to be especially careful in monitoring my current opinions about P but one that does not necessarily preclude those opinions from being rational.

8. PAST OPINIONS AND THE OPINIONS OF OTHERS

There are striking similarities between the reasons I have to trust my own past opinions and those I have to trust the opinions of others. Likewise, there are striking similarities with respect to the kinds of considerations that defeat this trust in the two cases. Indeed, the account of the epistemic relevance of past opinions defended in this chapter is structurally identical to the account of the epistemic relevance of the opinions of others defended in Chapter 4. Each consists of a credibility thesis, a priority thesis, and a special reasons thesis.

The three theses concerning the intellectual authority of others defended in Chapter 4 are as follows:

Credibility thesis. I risk inconsistency if I trust my current opinions and do not also generally trust the opinions of others, given that my opinions have been thoroughly shaped by other people. Moreover, the kinds of methods, faculties, concepts, and environment that combine to produce the opinions of others have broad commonalities with the kinds of methods, faculties, concepts, and environment that combine to produce my opinions. Thus, once again, if I trust my opinions, I am pressured to trust those of others as well. Accordingly, its being rational for me to believe that you have an opinion X about P gives me a prima facie reason also to have opinion X about P.

Priority thesis. If my opinion about P conflicts with yours, then the prima facie reason that your opinion gives me is defeated.

Special reasons thesis. Even when the prima facie credibility of your opinion X is defeated by my having a conflicting opinion, it can nonetheless be epistemically rational for me to defer to you, but only if I have reasons that indicate that you are in a better position to evaluate P than I am.

In this chapter, I have been arguing that three analogous theses about my own past opinions are also correct:

Credibility thesis. I risk inconsistency if I trust my current opinions and do not also generally trust my own past opinions, given that my current opinions have been thoroughly shaped by my past opinions. Moreover, the methods, faculties, concepts, and environment that combined to produce my past opinions have broad commonalities with the kinds of methods, faculties, concepts, and environment that combine to produce my current opinions. Thus, once again, if I trust my current opinions, I am pressured to trust my past opinions as well. Accordingly, its being rational for me to believe that I had an opinion X about P gives me a prima facie reason now to have opinion X about P.

Priority thesis. If my current opinion about P conflicts with my past opinion, the prima facie reason that my past opinion X gives me is defeated.

Special reasons thesis. Even when the prima facie credibility of my past opinion is defeated by my now having a conflicting opinion, it can nonetheless be epistemically rational for me to defer to my past self, but only if I have reasons that indicate that I was in a better position then to evaluate P than I am now.

Although the system of reasons and defeaters governing the opinions of others is structurally identical with the system governing my own past opinions, this structure produces different results in the two cases. Most beliefs are automatically retained from one moment to the next and, hence, the extent to which my past beliefs are incorporated into my current beliefs tends to be much greater than the extent to which the beliefs of friends, family, and acquaintances are incorporated into my beliefs. Accordingly, whereas it is common for others to have opinions on issues about which I have no opinion, it is less common for my past self to have opinions on issues about which I currently have no opinion. In addition, the number and degree of severity of conflicts between the opinions of my past self and those of my current self tends to be less than those between the opinions of others and myself, and even when there are conflicts with my past self, I usually have first-hand knowledge of the source of the conflict and often enough this knowledge explains why my current self is in a superior position to evaluate the issue in question; for example, I now have data or training that I formerly lacked. By contrast, when my opinions conflict with others, I frequently have little or no information of the circumstances in which they formed their beliefs. For all these reasons, the above structure, when applied to past opinions, generates fewer occasions to revise my beliefs than it does when applied to the opinions of others. Still, the system of reasons and defeaters is the same in the two cases.

This system provides a way of understanding the epistemic reasonability of some of our most pervasive and fundamental intellectual practices, in particular, those that presuppose that we are social beings who persist through time, as opposed to momentarily existing atoms. Our individual belief systems are the products of opinions borrowed from others supplemented by our own past intellectual efforts. The above system explains how it can be epistemically rational to rely so extensively on the opinions of others and on our past selves. The range of people influencing us includes family, friends, teachers, authors, journalists, lecturers, and countless others about whom we know little. All these people have prima facie credibility for us and, hence, it can be reasonable to rely on them. Likewise, our own past intellectual efforts have prima facie credibility for us and, thus, it can be reasonable to rely on them as well, without having to reconsider or reconfirm anew their conclusions.

These two accounts – the account of the epistemic relevance of past opinion defended in this chapter and the account of the epistemic relevance of the opinion of others defended in Chapter 4 – are mutually reinforcing. The case for each is strengthened by the fact that they are structurally identical with one another. In Chapter 6, I argue that this very same structure of reasons and defeaters is again operative when the issue is the epistemic relevance of future opinion. This will be the final piece. Once it is in place, the result will be a theoretically unified way of treating all issues of intellectual authority.

6

Future Opinion and Current Opinion

1. EPISTEMIC ULYSSES PROBLEMS

How should future opinion when known affect current opinion? If I discover that in one year I will believe P, how should this affect my current belief about P?

Ulysses cases offer a compelling way of addressing these questions. Recall the story of Ulysses and the Sirens. The Sirens had the power of so charming sailors by their songs that the sailors were irresistibly drawn to throw themselves overboard, where they drowned in the strong currents surrounding the island where the Sirens lived. Although Ulysses was warned by the sorceress Circe about the Sirens, he nonetheless wanted to hear their songs. Following instructions from Circe, he took steps to protect himself. He had his men stop their ears with wax, so that they would not be able to hear the Sirens, and had himself tied to the mast, so that upon hearing the Sirens sing, he would not be able to throw himself overboard.

The problem that confronted Ulysses, most generally expressed, was that of how to take his future wants and values into account in his current deliberations about what to do. Problems of this sort are especially pressing when the future wants and values are at odds with one's current wants and values. Ulysses, for example, knew that the Sirens' songs would alter his wants in ways he currently did not approve.[1] Epistemic Ulysses problems are the counterparts of these problems within epistemology. They are problems of how to take future opinions

---

1 Thomas Schelling and Jon Elster were among the first to emphasize these problems. See Schelling, *The Strategy of Conflict* (Cambridge, MA: Harvard University Press, 1960); and, Elster, *Ulysses and the Sirens* (Cambridge: Cambridge University Press, 1979).

into account in current deliberations about what to believe, especially when these future opinions are at odds with current opinions. Such conflicts raise questions about the epistemic authority not only of one's future self but also one's current self. If I become aware that my future opinions are going to conflict with my current opinions, I am confronted with the question of whether to trust my current self or defer to my future self.

Notice, however, that although we sometimes speculate about what our future opinions will be, we generally do not base our deliberations about what now to believe on opinions about what our later opinions will be. Thus, epistemic Ulysses problems do not arise with any frequency in our everyday intellectual lives. Nevertheless, they are of significant theoretical interest, in part because the best account of them mimics the account of the intellectual authority of other people developed in Chapter 4 and the account of the intellectual authority of one's past self developed in Chapter 5. The structural similarities among these three accounts suggests that it is possible to develop a perfectly general approach to questions of intellectual authority, that is, an approach that provides an adequate framework for addressing such questions wherever they arise. I return to this point at the end of this chapter.

In addition, epistemic Ulysses problems are intriguing precisely because of their rarity. Why is it that such problems do not arise with any frequency in our everyday intellectual lives? We constantly rely on the opinions of others. Why are we not equally inclined to rely on our own future opinions when we know what they will be? I will propose an answer to this puzzle, but I first need to consider why we might have reasons to take future opinion into account in current deliberations about what to believe.

2. TRUST IN FUTURE OPINION

Most of us have a general attitude of trust in our future intellectual efforts and in the opinions these efforts will generate. The trust is not absolute. We know all too well that we are capable of making mistakes. Likewise, the trust does not extend indefinitely into the future. We know that our intellectual abilities are likely to decline if we live long enough. Still, we assume that we generally will be reliable inquirers in the future, even though we cannot prove this.

There is something short of a proof, however. There are internal pressures on us to trust our own future opinions. We are pressured to do so on threat of inconsistency. The threat arises because we generally trust our current faculties and opinions, and we generally assume that our future opinions will be extensively shaped by our current opinions and faculties. Thus, insofar as we trust our current opinions and faculties, we are pressured to trust our future opinions as well.

Of course, our future opinions will also be influenced by whatever additional information we acquire. However, we generally assume that this additional information will be collected and then processed using faculties and methods not greatly different from our current faculties and methods, and we assume also that these faculties and methods will be interacting with an environment not greatly different from our current environment. Thus, once again, we are pressured to trust our future opinions. If we withheld such trust, we would be hard pressed to explain why it is that our current opinions and faculties are to be generally trusted while our future opinions are not.

Indeed, our intellectual projects invariably presuppose such trust. These projects are temporally extended. They take time to complete and, thus, would not be worth pursuing if we did not assume that our future selves will be generally reliable. Recall an analogous claim made by Peirce, who argued that unless scientists had trust in the community of future inquirers and saw themselves as a part of this community, there would be no point to their inquiries. There would be no point, he thought, because the goal of scientific inquiry is nothing less than the complete truth about the topic being investigated, but given the relative shortness of human lives, there is no realistic hope of individual scientists achieving this goal on their own. Peirce concluded that it is rational for individuals to devote themselves to scientific work only if they view themselves as part of a temporally extended community of inquirers, because it is only such a community that has a realistic chance of achieving the principal intellectual goal in doing science.[2]

My claim about the importance of trusting one's future self is analogous to Peirce's claim about science, only less grandiose and more personalized. No doubt our lives are too short to get the complete truth about very many topics, but on the other hand something less than the complete truth is enough for most of our purposes, even most scientific purposes, and we assume that this is often achievable in a manageably

2 For a discussion of Peirce on these issues, see C. F. Delaney, *Science, Knowledge and Mind: A Study in the Philosophy of C. S. Peirce* (Notre Dame, IN: University of Notre Dame Press, 1993).

short period of time. So, we engage in various intellectual projects. Some are personal projects that do not involve a community of inquirers, at least not in any direct way. Moreover, some are very narrowly defined, balancing a checkbook, for example. But even these small personal projects are temporally extended and, thus, even they would have no point if we did not trust our future selves. It takes time and effort to get the answers we are seeking. If we did not think that we would continue to be reliable for the duration of these projects, we would not have a rationale for engaging in them.

Underlying the above argument for trusting future opinion is a consistency claim. If I generally have intellectual trust in my current self, I am pressured for reasons of consistency to trust my future self as well. The pressure arises because it is reasonable for me to think both that my future opinions will be thoroughly influenced by my current opinions and that my future intellectual faculties and environment will be broadly similar to my current intellectual faculties and environment. To be sure, there are no shortage of considerations that can defeat this trust. I can have reasons to think that my evidence will be misleading or that something will interfere with my normal cognitive functioning, to name just two possibilities. Such possibilities are compatible with the above argument, which asserts only that I have a prima facie reason to trust the opinions of my future self. I have this prima facie reason because I believe that my future opinions will be built out of my current opinions supplemented by additional information, where this additional information will be generated by faculties broadly similar to my current faculties interacting with an external environment that is broadly similar to my current environment. I am thus pressured, all else being equal, to extend the trust I have in my current opinions and faculties to my future opinions.

There are ways of trying to block the general force of this argument, but none of these ways is especially plausible. One strategy is for me to deny that my future external environment will be broadly similar to the environment in which I currently form my beliefs. Another is to deny that my future intellectual faculties will be broadly similar to my current ones.

Most of us occasionally entertain the notion that at some future stage of our lives we will be thinking and processing information differently from how we now think and process information. Even so, in its most radical form, this is not a view that many of us are willing to endorse. In our thoughtful moments, we are willing to grant that there will be broad commonalities between our future selves and our current selves. We assume that in the future we will not be fundamentally different intellectually from what we are now, or, more cautiously, this is so at least for most of us and for most of our future life. If one projects oneself into a distant enough future, assuming longevity, it is not difficult to envision deterioration of one's cognitive faculties. And as the similarities to one's current faculties begin to decrease, so too do the pressures to trust one's opinions at these future times.

Thus, there is nothing inherently incoherent in thinking that one's future intellectual abilities will be vastly different from one's current ones or even that one's future environment will be vastly different. Accordingly, there is nothing inherently incoherent in refusing to grant intellectual authority to one's future self. Yet, it is not an utterly categorical requirement of epistemic rationality that one do so. The claim I am arguing for is more cautious and contingent than this. The claim is that intellectual trust in one's current self normally creates a pressure to trust one's future self as well, a pressure that is extremely difficult to avoid.

This result makes it all the more puzzling that in our everyday intellectual lives future opinion does not play much of a role in shaping current opinion. If, all else being equal, we have reasons to trust our future selves, it seems as if future opinion ought to influence current opinion in much the way that the opinions of others do. Why doesn't it?

I propose an answer to this question in the following sections. Part of the explanation is that the presumption in favor of future opinion is only prima facie and, hence, can be defeated by other considerations. Another part of the explanation is that the prima facie credibility of future opinion is defeated when it conflicts with current opinion. However, a final part of the explanation concerns how we typically get information about what our future opinions will be.

3. REASONS FOR BELIEVING THAT I WILL BELIEVE P

If it is to be rational for me to alter my opinion of P on the basis of your believing P, it is not enough for me to believe that you believe P. It must also be rational for me to believe this. It is no different with my own future opinions. If it is to be rational for me to alter my opinion of P on the basis of my future belief P, it must be rational for me to believe that I will believe P. Mere belief won't do.

What kinds of considerations might give me a reason to believe that

I will believe a proposition P? The most common reason is that I now believe P. I currently believe that water is H_2O, that I was born in the United States, and that hawks are usually larger than finches, and presumably it is rational for me to think that a year from now I will still believe these propositions. Of course, I do not have reasons to think this of every proposition that I currently believe. I believe that I am now wearing a tan shirt, but it is probably safe for me to assume in a year's time I will have forgotten what I was wearing today. Even so, the most routine reason for me to believe that I will believe a claim is that I now believe it. Notice, however, that in such cases, future opinion has no significant role to play in influencing current opinion. These are not cases in which my future beliefs about P give me a reason to alter what I now believe about P. Rather, it is the other way around. The fact that I currently believe P gives me a reason to believe that I will believe P.

Assume, then, that I do not now believe P. Under these circumstances, what might give me a reason to believe that I will believe P? One possibility is that I might have evidence for P itself, evidence that I have somehow overlooked or not fully appreciated. As a result, I do not now believe P, nor do I believe that I will believe P, but this evidence might nonetheless make it rational for me to believe that in a year's time I will have come to appreciate the force of this evidence and, hence, will have come to believe P.

But once again, this is not a case in which my future opinion alters what it is rational for me now to believe. It is precisely the reverse: what I now have reason to believe about P determines what I have a reason to believe about what my future opinion will be. By hypothesis, I do not now believe what it is rational for me to believe about P, but this failure is not the result of my overlooking my future opinion. It is the result of my overlooking my current evidence.

So, if there are to be cases in which it is rational for future opinion to shape or constrain current opinion in some interesting way, they will have to be ones in which my reasons for believing that I will believe P are not derived from my current evidence for P or from my current belief in P. The cases of this sort that come most readily to mind, however, are ones in which I have reasons for thinking that my future opinions will be unreliable. For example, David Christenson describes a case in which I know that I have just taken a psychedelic drug that in one hour will make me very confident that I have the ability to fly. Christenson correctly points out that this does not mean that it is rational for me now to be confident that I will be able to fly.[3] Similarly, Patrick Maher discusses a case in which I know I will be overly confident of my ability to drive home from a party after ten drinks,[4] and Brian Skyrms devises a case in which I know I will be infested with a mind-worm, which will cause me to have a variety of strange beliefs.[5] In each of these cases, my reasons for thinking I will believe P are not derived from my current evidence for P or my current belief in P, but on the other hand the reasons impugn my future reliability and, hence, defeat the prima facie credibility I am pressured to grant, on threat of inconsistency, to future opinion. So once again, these are not cases in which future opinion ought to have an effect on current opinion.[6]

Consider a different kind of situation, one in which my reasons for thinking I will believe P have nothing to do with drugs, mindworms, diseases, and the like. As discussed in Chapter 3, studies in cognitive psychology indicate that a large percentage of normally functioning individuals tend to make certain kinds of mistakes with predictable regularity. For example, in some contexts, we tend to assign a higher probability to a conjunction than to one of its conjuncts; in other contexts, we regularly ignore base rates in evaluating statistical data for causal influences; and in yet other contexts, the way we store data in memory adversely affects in a predictable way our estimates of likelihood.

Suppose I am now attentive to my tendency to make mistakes of this sort, having just read the literature that documents them. As a result, I am currently managing to avoid these errors, but I also know that in a year's time I will have dropped my intellectual guard and, as a result, I will once again be guilty of making such mistakes. Among the mistakes,

---

3 David Christenson, "Clever Bookies and Coherent Beliefs," *Philosophical Review*, 100 (1991), 229–47.

4 Patrick Maher, "Depragmatized Dutch Book Arguments," *Philosophy of Science*, 64 (1997), 291–305.

5 Brian Skyrms, "The Value of Knowledge," in C. Wade Savage, ed., *Justification, Discovery, and the Evolution of Scientific Theories* (Minneapolis: University of Minnesota Press, 1987).

6 Christenson, Maher, and Skyrms develop these cases in criticizing a proposal by Bas Van Fraassen, which implies that one's current degree of belief in a proposition P ought to lie within the range of possible opinions one may come to have about P at a later time, as far as one's present opinion is concerned. For example, if I know that in a year I will believe P with a degree of confidence between .7 and .9, then according to van Fraassen, my present degree of confidence in P ought be between .7 and .9; future opinion in this way constrains current opinion. See van Fraassen, "Belief and the Will," *The Journal of Philosophy* 81 (1984), 235–56; and van Fraassen, "Belief and the Problem of Ulysses and the Sirens," *Philosophical Studies*, 77 (1995), 7–37.

let us suppose, is the belief P. Thus, I might have reasons for thinking that in a year's time I will believe P, and these reasons are not derived from evidence for P or from the fact that I currently believe P. On the other hand, these reasons do impugn my future reliability and, hence, defeat the prima facie credibility of future opinion. Thus, once again, these are not cases in which future opinion ought to influence current opinion.

Suppose it is the testimony of other people whose reliability I have strong reasons to trust that gives me reasons for thinking that I will believe P. The question for me then to ask is why it is that they think I will believe P, given that I do not now believe it? Is their belief based on the presupposition that I will be a reliable inquirer, or do they rather have other kinds of reasons for thinking I will believe P? For example, do they believe that someone will deceive me or that my abilities will deteriorate or that additional information will confuse me, making me prone to errors? If it is reasonable for me to think that considerations of this latter sort have led them to believe I will believe P, my future reliability is again being challenged and along with it the prima facie trustworthiness of my future opinion.

On the other hand, suppose it is reasonable for me to assume that they have no such special reasons for thinking I will believe P, and they are instead presupposing that I will be a reliable inquirer. If so, it is also reasonable for me to think that they themselves believe that P is true and that I as a reliable inquirer will eventually come to agree. But then, there is not a significant difference between this case and an ordinary case of testimony. In effect, their saying that I will believe P, is an indirect way of telling me that P is true.[7]

The lesson that emerges from these various cases is that it is extremely difficult to find situations in which my future opinions should influence my current opinions, and a large part of the explanation for the rarity of

---

7 A minor complication is that it is not altogether impossible for others to think that although I am a reliable inquirer, my reliable procedures will unluckily lead me to the wrong conclusion about P. If so, they may think that I will come to believe P even though they do not believe P themselves and, thus, their telling me that I will believe P is not necessarily an instance of indirect testimony. Nevertheless, the relevant issue is what it is reasonable for me to believe of them, given that it is reasonable for me to assume that they are presupposing I will be a reliable inquirer. Although it is possible that they think I will believe P because my reliable procedures will unluckily lead me to the wrong conclusion, by its nature this is an unlikely possibility. So, unless I have concrete evidence indicating otherwise, it will be reasonable for me to assume that they believe P and have inferred that I, as a reliable inquirer, will eventually come to believe it as well.

such situations has to do with the kind of considerations that can make it rational for me now to believe that I will have a belief P. Sometimes my reasons for believing that I will believe P impugn my future reliability, in which case the prima facie credibility of my future opinion is defeated. In other situations, my reasons for thinking I will believe P are based on my current belief in P or my current evidence for P, in which case my current opinion either does or should coincide with what my future opinion will be, but not because the future opinion in any way affects what it is rational for me now to believe. Rather, it is the other way around; it is my current opinion or evidence that shapes what it is rational for me to believe about what my future opinion will be. Agreement between current and future opinion is a by-product in such cases, not something that itself rationally shapes or constrains current opinion.

Are there any cases in which I have neutral reasons to believe that I will believe P, 'neutral', that is, in the sense that they are based neither on a current belief P nor on current evidence for P nor on considerations that impugn my future reliability? It is possible to imagine some such cases, but they tend to not be realistic and, hence, confirm yet again how unusual it is for future opinion to affect current opinion. Even so, it is worth considering one such case.

Imagine that I am in possession of a device that I know reliably predicts what people will believe, and imagine in addition that the way I come to know this has no obvious implications for the reliability of the beliefs predicted. For example, I have no reason to think that the device is better at predicting true beliefs than false ones, or vice-versa. It occurs to me to use the device on myself, to predict my own future opinions, and when I do so, it tells me that I will believe P in a year's time.

By hypothesis, the belief-predicting device gives me a reason to believe that I will believe P. Since I have a prima facie reason to trust future opinion, its being rational for me to believe that I will believe P gives me a prima facie reason now to believe P. Moreover, by hypothesis again, my reasons for believing that I will believe P do not involve evidence of future unreliability.

So here at last is a situation, although admittedly a highly artificial one, in which my reasons for thinking I will believe P are based neither on my current belief P nor on current reasons for P nor on considerations that impugn my future reliability. Thus, it is a situation in which future opinion might potentially play a role in shaping current opinion.

But even here, future opinion should play this role only if the presumption in its favor is not defeated by my having a conflicting current opinion.

4. CONFLICTS BETWEEN CURRENT AND FUTURE OPINIONS

When future opinion conflicts with current opinion, the prima facie reason I have to trust future opinion is defeated, thus limiting in another way the potential of future opinion to affect what it is epistemically rational for me now to believe. By "conflict" I mean, as in Chapters 4 and 5, something more than a mere difference in doxastic state. If I will believe P but have no current opinion about P, there is no conflict with my future belief P. Alternatively, if P now strikes me as unlikely, but this attitude is little more than the doxastic counterpart of a whim, then once again there is no real conflict.

A conflict with current opinion defeats the presumption of trust in a future opinion, because the presumption is based on trust in my current self. For the most part, my future opinions will be built out of my current opinions using faculties that are not unlike my current faculties. Thus, insofar as it is reasonable for me to trust my current opinions and faculties, I am pressured to trust my future opinions as well. The broad commonalities between my current self and future self create this presumption, but by the same token, trust in my current self defeats the prima facie credibility of my future self with respect to an issue P when there is a conflict between my current and future opinions about P. The credibility of my future self on P is defeated because by my current lights, my future self will be unreliable with respect to P. Trust in my current self creates a presumption in favor of my future opinions, but this same trust dissipates the presumption when there is a conflict with current opinion.

Thus, when my future opinion about P conflicts with a current opinion, my future opinion gives me no reason to alter my current opinion unless I have special reasons for thinking that my future self will be in an especially good position to assess P. By "special reasons" I mean reasons beyond those generated by the general trust I am pressured to have in my future opinions on threat of inconsistency. However, special reasons of this sort are hard to come by when current opinion conflicts with what it is rational for me to believe my future opinion will be. As discussed in the previous section, a more likely scenario is for the considerations making it rational for me to believe that I will believe P to impugn my future reliability. Suppose, however, that the situation is an unusual one. For example, suppose the belief-predicting device mentioned earlier gives me reasons to believe that I will believe P and that I also have reasons to think that I will be in a better position to evaluate P in the future. Perhaps P concerns a future state of affairs, or perhaps P belongs to a field of inquiry in which rapid progress is being made, or perhaps in the future I will be more skilled at evaluating issues of this kind because by then I will have received additional training. In such a situation, even if I currently have a conflicting opinion about P, my reasons for believing that I will believe P can combine with background information about my future reliability to provide me with a reason to alter my current opinion of P.

On the other hand, if I do not have any such special reasons to think that my future self will be in a better position than my current self to judge the truth of P, I have no reason to defer to my future opinion. The prima facie reason that my future belief gives me to believe P is defeated by my having a conflicting opinion, and there are no other considerations giving me a reason to defer.

5. FUTURE OPINIONS AND CURRENT DELIBERATIONS

One reason that future opinion so rarely affects what it is now rational for us to believe, despite the former's prima facie credibility, is that its credibility can be so easily defeated. It is defeated if there is a conflict with current opinion or if there is evidence of future unreliability. This can be only a partial explanation, however, because the same is true of the opinions of others. The prima facie credibility attaching to the opinions of others is defeated when our own opinions conflict with theirs or when we have evidence of their unreliability. Yet, we commonly do rely on the beliefs of others in our deliberations about what to believe. What, then, is the difference?

The biggest difference is in the way we get information about our own future beliefs as opposed to the way we get information about the beliefs of others. The most common reason I have for thinking that I will believe a proposition P is that I now believe P, but in such cases there is not much point in taking future opinion seriously in my deliberations about what to believe. My future belief P, like my other future opinions, is prima facie credible, but because I already believe P, it does not provide a motivation for revising my current opinion. Nor does it add force to my current reasons for P, given that my reasons for thinking that I will believe P are derived from my now believing P.

By contrast, when I have reasons to believe that you believe P, there usually is a point in my taking your opinions seriously. If I have no opinion about P myself, your belief P gives me at least a weak reason to believe P myself. And even if I already believe P, the fact that you also believe P can provide me with additional assurances that P is true, if the considerations leading you to believe P are independent of those leading me to believe P.

Admittedly, there are situations in which my reasons for thinking that I will believe P are not based on my currently believing P and likewise not based on current evidence for P. They are based instead on the likelihood that my memory will by then be unreliable or on the prospect of my then being depressed or even on the knowledge that I will then be under the influence of a drug. In such situations, I am viewing myself more from the outside than is usual, and in extreme cases, I may come close to regarding my future self as a distinct other self rather than an extension of my current self. But, it is precisely in these cases, where my future self most resembles a distinct self, that I have the most reasons to doubt the reliability of my future self. Thus, it is not epistemically rational for these future opinions to influence what I now believe, despite the fact that my reasons for thinking I will have these opinions are independent of my currently having them. This independence potentially makes my future opinions relevant to my current deliberations in much the way that the opinions of others are relevant, but the independence comes at a price, namely, evidence of the unreliability of my future opinions.

6. SELF-TRUST RADIATES OUTWARD

The above account of the epistemic relevance of future opinions is identical in structure with the account of the epistemic relevance of the opinions of others defended in Chapter 4, and also identical in structure with the account of the epistemic relevance of past opinions defended in Chapter 5. The system of reasons and defeaters is the same in all three cases.

At the heart of this structure is a credibility thesis, asserting that we have a prima facie reason to trust the opinions of others, our own future opinions, and our own past opinions. In each instance, the credibility thesis is made plausible by a combination of self-trust and consistency constraints. It is reasonable for most of us to trust, by and large, our own current opinions, but these opinions have been extensively shaped by the opinions of others and our own past opinions, and in turn they will extensively shape our own future opinions. Thus, insofar as we reasonably trust our current opinions, we are pressured, at risk of inconsistency, also to trust the opinions of others, our future opinions, and our past opinions. Moreover, there are broad commonalities between our current selves on the one hand and other people, our future selves, and our past selves on the other. The kinds of methods, faculties, concepts, and environments that combine to produce the beliefs of other people, the beliefs of our future selves, and the beliefs of our past selves are broadly similar to the kinds of methods, faculties, concepts, and environments that combine to produce or sustain our current beliefs. Thus, once again, insofar as it is reasonable for us to trust our own current opinions, we are pressured to trust also the opinions of others, our own future opinions, and our own past opinions.

At the next level in the structure is a priority thesis, which describes an especially common way for the prima facie credibility of the opinions of others, future opinions, and past opinions to be defeated. Namely, their credibility is defeated by conflicts with current opinions. Trust in my current self creates for me the presumption in favor of the opinion of others, my own future opinions, and my own past opinions, but by the same token, trust in my current self defeats this presumption when there is a conflict with current opinion. So, for the prima facie credibility of someone else's opinion about P to be defeated, I need not have information about the specific conditions under which the person formed the opinion. It is enough that I have a conflicting opinion about P. Similarly, for the prima facie credibility of my past or future opinion about P to be defeated, I need not know anything special about the conditions under which I formed or will form the opinion. It can be enough that I currently have a conflicting opinion.

However, the structure also incorporates a special reasons thesis, which acknowledges that it can be reasonable to defer to the opinions of others, future opinions, and past opinions even when their prima facie credibility is defeated by a conflict with current opinion. It is reasonable for me to defer if I have reasons to think that the other person, my future self, or my past self is better positioned than my current self to assess the truth of the claim at issue.

This structure produces very different results when applied to the opinions of others, our own future opinions, and our own past opinions. The opinions of others rationally influence our current opinions much more frequently than do our own future or past opinions, but this is because we normally get information about the opinions of others in a different way than we get information about our own past and future opinions. The most common reason I have for thinking that I will or did believe P is that I now believe it, but in such cases there is no point in taking future or past opinion seriously in my deliberations about what to believe. My future or past belief P, like my other future and past opinions, is prima facie credible, but since I already believe P, it does not provide any motivation for revising my current opinion. Nor does it provide me with independent, additional assurances that P is true, insofar as I believe that I will or did believe P only because I now believe P. On the other hand, when considerations other than my currently believing P give me a reason to believe that I will or did believe P, these considerations frequently also give me reasons to doubt my future or past reliability, thus defeating the prima facie credibility of my future or past opinions. For example, if I think that I will believe P because I will be drunk or severely depressed, the prima facie trustworthiness of my future opinion is undermined. Similarly, if I recall that I formerly believed P because of a newspaper article that I now recognize to have been misleading, the prima facie credibility of my past opinion is undermined.

So, there are sharp differences in the ways we typically get information about what we will believe or did believe as opposed to the ways we typically get information about what others believe, and these differences help explain why our own future and past opinions rarely give us adequate reasons to alter our current opinions, whereas the opinions of others frequently do so. Nevertheless, the overall structure of reasons and defeaters is identical in all three cases.

These three accounts are mutually supporting. The case for each is made stronger by the fact that the same structure is operative in the other two cases. This structure, with its three characteristic theses – the credibility thesis, priority thesis, and special reasons thesis – constitutes a theoretically unified approach to questions of intellectual authority. It provides a framework for thinking about issues of intellectual authority wherever they arise.

As to be expected, within this framework there are many complications that I have only hinted at and that a complete account of intellectual authority would have to treat in detail. One of the more important of these complications is that the prima facie reasons to trust the opinions of others, as well as past and future opinions, come in different degrees of strength, which vary in accordance with factors that I have mentioned only in passing.

For example, the opinions of others, future opinion, and past opinion give me a reason to alter my current opinion only if I have reasons for believing that others have the opinion in question, or that I will or did have it. However, these reasons come in varying strengths and, hence, the strength of my prima facie reason to believe what they believe, or what I will or did believe, varies accordingly.

Moreover, the basic argument in favor of the credibility thesis varies in strength in accordance with the force of the similarity claim on which the argument in part relies. According to the argument, the kinds of methods, faculties, concepts, and environments that combine to produce the beliefs of other people, our future selves, and our past selves are ordinarily broadly similar to the kinds of methods, faculties, concepts, and environments that combine to produce our current beliefs. Thus, insofar as it is reasonable for us to trust our own current opinions, faculties, methods, and procedures, we are pressured, on threat of inconsistency, to trust also the opinions of others, our own future opinions, and our own past opinions.

Similarities come in degrees, however. The methods, faculties, concepts, and environments that combine to produce the beliefs of the Masai, for example, are less similar to mine than those that combine to produce the beliefs of my two brothers. Likewise, the methods, faculties, concepts, and environments that will combine to produce my beliefs twenty years from now are likely to be less similar to my current ones than those that will combine to produce my beliefs twenty days from now. Analogous claims are true of my past methods, faculties, concepts, and environments. Those of the recent past are likely to be more similar to my current ones than those of the distant past.

The strength of the prima facie reason referred to by the credibility thesis thus varies in accordance with the strength of the relevant similarity claim. In particular, it varies as a function of distance in time, place, and circumstance. The smaller this distance, that is, the more extensive the similarities of time, place, and circumstance, the stronger the force of the argument. Correspondingly, the prima facie reason to trust the opinions of others, future opinions, and past opinions is also stronger. On the other hand, the greater the distance, the weaker the force of the argument is and the weaker the prima facie reason is.

The basic argument for the credibility thesis also appeals to considerations of influence. My own past opinions and the opinions of others have influenced my current opinions, and my current opinions will in turn influence my future opinions. Thus, insofar as it is reasonable for me to trust my current opinions, I am pressured to trust the opinions of others and my own past opinions, because they have influenced current opinion, and to trust as well my own future opinions, since current opinion will influence them. However, influences, like similarities, come in degrees. The opinions of the recent past and the opinions of those people in my immediate environment ordinarily have a greater degree of influence on my current opinions than do opinions of the distant past and opinions of those far removed from me. Analogously, my current opinions are likely to have a greater degree of influence on my opinions of the near future than those of the distant future. Accordingly, the prima facie reasons I have to trust the opinions of others, my own past opinions, and my own future opinions once again vary as a function of distance.

The varying strengths of such reasons is just what one should expect, given the account of intellectual authority I have been defending. According to this account, trust in the overall reliability of our current opinions and in the faculties, methods, and procedures that produce or sustain these opinions is a nearly inescapable feature of our intellectual lives. This self-trust, which can be reasonable even if we have no non-question-begging assurances that we are reliable, radiates outward to make trust in others, our own future selves, and our own past selves prima facie reasonable as well. For, insofar as we reasonably trust our current selves, we are pressured, on threat of inconsistency, to trust also the opinions of others, our own future opinions, and our own past opinions. However, as self-trust radiates outward, the force of the reasons it produces diminishes as a function of the distance between our current selves on the one hand and our own future selves, our own past selves, and other people on the other hand.

Conclusion

Issues of intellectual trust, both in ourselves and in others, are of fundamental importance for how we conduct our intellectual lives, but in
general these issues have not received the attention they deserve from
epistemologists, in large part because of the influence of classical foundationalists, whose aim was to develop an epistemology that would
provide guarantees that our beliefs are generally accurate. Within such
an epistemology, there is no need for, and indeed no room for, a basic
trust in one's intellectual faculties and the opinions they generate. However, the classical foundationalist project has failed. There are no non–
question-begging assurances that our faculties and opinions are largely
reliable. As a result, all of our intellectual projects require a significant
leap of intellectual faith in ourselves, the need for which cannot be
eliminated by further argumentation or inquiry.

With the fall of classical foundationalism, the way was cleared for a
greater appreciation of this point, but various trends in contemporary
epistemology continue to mask the importance of intellectual self-trust.
Some epistemologists take for granted that the theory of natural selection
is capable of providing us with assurances that our opinions are largely
reliable. Others try to provide assurances of reliability by arguing that
skeptical hypotheses are necessarily self-refuting. Still others narrowly
focus on the project of defining knowledge and thereby bypass questions
of how epistemological problems look from an internal, first-person
perspective; to the extent they concern themselves with issues of rational
belief, it is because they stipulate that the properties that make a belief
rational are the same properties that make a true belief into a good
candidate for knowledge.

These trends have made it difficult for epistemologists to acknowledge the full implications of classical foundationalism's demise, one of the most important of which is that self-trust is an unavoidable element in our intellectual projects. Contrary to what is sometimes assumed, it is not unnatural to worry that our most fundamental faculties and methods might not be reliable. Moreover, try as we may to expunge this worry, we cannot altogether do so. We want to defend the overall reliability of our faculties and methods, but the only way to do so is by using these same faculties and methods, which means that we will never succeed in altogether ruling out the possibility that our opinions, unbeknown to us, might be largely mistaken. Skeptical worries are inescapable, and the appropriate reaction to this fact is not denial but rather an acknowledgment that inquiry always involves a substantial element of fundamental trust in the reliability of our intellectual faculties and the opinions they generate.

Evil demon and brain-in-a-vat hypotheses dramatically illustrate this truth about our intellectual lives as well as one of its most significant corollaries, namely, that our beliefs can be rational in an important sense even when they are by and large unreliable. If, unbeknown to me, I am a brain-in-a-vat, then I am being deceived into having unreliable beliefs about my environment, but in being denied knowledge of my environment, I am not thereby also automatically prevented from being rational in at least one important sense, a sense that is closely associated with having beliefs that from my perspective are invulnerable to criticism, insofar as my goal is to have accurate and comprehensive beliefs. Even if I am a brain-in-a-vat, I can nonetheless be a brain-in-a-vat who is in this sense rational.

An adequate epistemology will acknowledge the centrality of intellectual self-trust, but it will also recognize that such trust should not be unlimited. There are countless ways for something to go wrong in forming opinions, and when warnings signs of error occur they are not to be ignored. For example, if I become aware that my opinions are inconsistent, I know that not all of them can be true. I am thus put on my guard, and I will need to investigate how the inconsistency arose and what might be done to eliminate it. Nevertheless, it is not a categorical imperative of epistemic rationality that I eliminate inconsistencies whenever and wherever I become aware of them. As the lottery and the preface cases illustrate, it sometimes can be reasonable to tolerate inaccuracy in one's opinions. More generally, intellectual trust in the overall reliability of one's opinions can reasonably coexist with a recognition that one's opinions are less than ideally accurate.

Similarly, empirical studies that indicate that in general people are not reliable inquirers in certain kinds of situations place me on guard about my own opinions and, thus, also constitute a challenge to self-trust. The proper response to the first-person worries raised by such studies is analogous to the proper response to the discovery of inconsistency. I am not entitled to ignore the challenges that these studies pose to my own opinions. In particular, I cannot simply assume that unlike others, I am reliable about the matters in question. I must instead reexamine as best I can how I came to have the opinions I do about the topics in question and monitor myself in light of the warnings implicit in the studies. But just as intellectual self-trust can sometimes coexist with a recognition that my opinions are inconsistent, so too it can sometimes reasonably coexist with a recognition that some of my beliefs are such that people in general tend to be unreliable in forming beliefs of this kind.

These issues of intellectual self-trust are inextricably intertwined with issues of intellectual authority, both in a concrete and theoretical way. Whenever my opinion about a topic conflicts with the opinion of someone else, I am faced with the concrete question of whom to trust, myself or the other person? But in addition, there is a theoretical interconnection between self-trust and issues of intellectual authority, because the materials for an adequate account of the intellectual authority of others are to be found in the trust that most of us have in our own faculties and opinions.

Insofar as I trust my own faculties and opinions, and insofar as this trust is reasonable, it not being a condition of rationality that I have non–question-begging assurances of my reliability, I am pressured to grant intellectual authority to others. I am pressured to do so because the cognitive equipment that others use to form their opinions and the environments in which they form these opinions are broadly similar to my own. In addition, almost everything I believe has been deeply influenced by the opinions of others. So, unless others were generally reliable, I would not be either. Thus, if I trust my own faculties and opinions, I risk inconsistency if I do not also trust the faculties and opinions of others.

On the other hand, the prima facie authority of others on a topic is defeated when I have a conflicting opinion about the topic. Trust in myself creates a presumption in favor of other people's opinions, even people about whom I know little, but trust in myself also defeats this presumption when there is a conflict between me and the other person. To be sure, it might nonetheless be reasonable for me to defer to the person, but if the person's prima facie credibility for me has been defeated by my conflicting opinion, I need special reasons to do so, for example, information to the effect that the person is in an especially good position to have reliable opinions about the issue in question.

These theses explain how it can be reasonable for me to rely on the opinions even of people about whom I know little or nothing and, moreover, they provide this explanation without recourse to an a priori claim that testimony is necessarily credible. Moreover, because the prima facie credibility of other people's opinions is defeated when they conflict with my opinions, the theses also capture the kernel of truth in the Enlightenment's emphasis on the importance of intellectual self-reliance, that is, of making up one's own mind on important issues.

Exactly the same structure of reasons and defeaters is applicable when the opinions are not those of another person but rather those of my own past self or my own future self. Because the ways I ordinarily get information about the opinions of others differ from the ways I ordinarily get information about my own past and future opinions, the latter make it rational to revise my current opinions much less frequently than do the former. Nevertheless, structurally, the relation between my current opinions on the one hand and my past and future opinions on the other is identical with the relation between my current opinions and the opinions of others.

For example, the same kinds of considerations that pressure me to trust the opinions of others also pressure me to trust my own past and future opinions. In each instance, it is a combination of self-trust and consistency constraints that creates the pressure. My current opinions have been extensively shaped by the opinions of others and my own past opinions, and in turn they will extensively shape my future opinions. Thus, insofar as I reasonably trust in the overall reliability of my current opinions, I am pressured, at risk of inconsistency, also to trust the opinions of others, my future opinions, and my past opinions. Moreover, there are broad commonalities between my current self on the one hand and other people, my future self, and my past self on the other. The kinds of methods, faculties, concepts, and environments that combine to produce the beliefs of other people, the beliefs of my future self, and the beliefs of my past self are broadly similar to the kinds of methods, faculties, concepts, and environments that combine to produce and sustain my current beliefs. Thus, once again, insofar as it is reasonable for us to trust my current opinions, I am pressured to trust also the opinions of others, my own future opinions, and our own past opinions.

Just as this argument helps explain why it can be epistemically rational to rely so extensively on the opinions of people about whom one knows little, so too it helps explain why other fundamental intellectual practices are epistemically rational. For example, we do not feel a continuous need to go over past conclusions or the arguments, procedures, and evidence that led to these conclusions. In general, we trust that our past intellectual efforts have spawned opinions that are by and large reliable and, thus, we feel no need to review them constantly. Given that our past opinions have prima facie credibility for us, this is a reasonable practice; and it is reasonable not just from the pragmatic point of view that rechecking past conclusions would swallow up all of our time, leaving no time for other pursuits, but also from a purely epistemic point of view, that is, insofar as the sole concern to have accurate and comprehensive beliefs. In an analogous manner, our intellectual projects presuppose the reliability of our future selves. Even our small, personal intellectual projects, balancing a checkbook or doing a logic proof, are temporally extended and, thus, presuppose trust in our future selves. They take time to complete and, hence, would not be worth pursuing if we did not assume that our future selves will be generally reliable. Given that our future opinions have prima facie credibility for us, this is a reasonable assumption to make.

The kinds of considerations that pressure me to trust the opinions of others also pressure me to trust my own past and future opinions, and in addition the same kinds of considerations defeat this trust in each instance. In particular, the prima facie credibility of the opinions of others, future opinions, and past opinions is defeated by conflicts with current opinions. So, for the prima facie credibility of someone else's opinion to be defeated, I do not need to have information about the conditions under which the person formed the opinion. It is enough that I have a conflicting opinion about the topic. Similarly, for the prima facie credibility of my past or future opinion to be defeated, I do not need to have information about the conditions under which I formed or will form the opinion. It is enough that I currently have a conflicting opinion. Nevertheless, even in cases of conflict, it can be reasonable for me to defer to the opinions of others, my own past opinions, and my own future opinions. The prima facie credibility of these opinions is defeated when they conflict with current opinion, but I may nonetheless have information indicating that the other person, my future self, or my past self is better positioned than my current self to assess the truth of the claim at issue. If so, it is reasonable for me to defer to the opinion of others or to my own past or future opinion.

The result is a unified way of treating issues of intellectual self-trust and intellectual authority wherever they arise. It can be reasonable for me to have trust in the overall reliability of my faculties and opinions even though I lack non–question-begging assurances of their reliability. This intellectual trust in myself then radiates outward in all directions, making it reasonable for me also to have prima facie trust in the opinions of others, and in my own future and past opinions.

In radiating outward, intellectual self-trust creates an atmosphere of trust in which our intellectual lives are played out. This atmosphere allows us to makes sense of what would otherwise be puzzling aspects of our intellectual practices in much the way that an invisible ether was once postulated by physicists to make sense of what would otherwise be puzzling aspects of the physical universe. The ether was conceived as permeating all space, thus providing a medium for the transmission of light waves and other forms of radiant energy. Analogously, intellectual self-trust radiates outward, permeating the intellectual atmosphere, creating a general climate of trust in other people and in our own past and future selves. It is this climate of trust that explains why it makes intellectual sense, all else being equal, to borrow opinions from complete strangers, to rely on past conclusions without reconfirming them, and to engage in intellectual projects that extend well into the future. Within such a climate, it becomes possible for the transmission of opinions across peoples and times to be epistemically rational.

Index

Adler, Jonathan, 107n28
Alston, William, 97
Anonymous example, 84–5, 117–20
Asch, Solomon, 116
Audi, Robert, 92, 107n29
authority, intellectual: credibility thesis
   concerning, 154; direct and indirect
   exercise of, 85; earned, 86–7;
   granted to future opinions, 161;
   granted to opinions of others, 85–6,
   100–7, 134–5, 154–6; granted to
   past opinions, 85–8, 132–4; Hume's
   view of, 94; Locke's view of, 89–92;
   openness of experts to, 118–19; priority thesis concerning, 154; reasons
   and defeaters structure in questions
   of, 170–1; Reid's view of, 92–4;
   specialized, 85–8, 111; special reasons thesis concerning, 155; universal, 85, 88
autonomy, intellectual, 128–9
Ayer, A. J., 5

beliefs: accuracy of, 15–19, 51–3, 61;
   automatic, 34–5; constitute perspective, 29; contradictory, 48–9; Davidson's view of, 104–5, 112; degrees
   of, 113–14; diversity of, 102–5; externalist accounts of, 13, 37–8, 53;
   inconsistent, 48–52; modularity of,
   49; perceptual, 26; reasons distinct

from rationalizations for, 77–8; responsible, 32–3; testimony-based, 93–
   7, 116–17. *See also* opinions
beliefs, rational: but unreliable, 174; di-
   vorced from theory of knowledge,
   21; invulnerability to self-criticism,
   27–37
Bradley, F. H., 94n14, 105
brain-in-a-vat hypothesis, 6, 37–8, 174
Bratman, Michael, 150
Burge, Tyler, 97, 107n29

Carnap, Rudolf, 5
Cartesian circle, 19, 73, 77
causal theory of knowledge, 10–11
Cherniak, Christopher, 50
Chesterton, G. K., 40
Chisholm, Roderick, 42–3
Christenson, David, 107n29, 162–3
circularity, 73–4
Coady, C. A. J., 96–8, 107n29
cognitive diversity, 102–4, 124
coherentism, 23
color blindness, 70
conflict, intellectual: with future self,
   166–7; with others, 78–80, 108–17;
   withpast self, 148–53
consensus, 120–1, 124
consistency, 49, 160
contradictory beliefs, 48–9
Craig, Edward, 97

179

credibility thesis, 132–41, 167, 168–72
cultural influence on opinions, 44, 112

Dali, Salvador, 133
Davidson, Donald, 7, 40n9, 104
decisions, rational and irrational, 29–31
defeaters of intellectual trust, 108–12,
    117, 144–7, 167–71
deference: to experts, 122–3; of experts
    to others, 119–20; to opinions of
    others, 110–13; to past opinion, 144–
    8
Delaney, C. F., 159n2
Descartes, René, 4, 7–8, 13, 15, 19, 21–
    3, 73, 76–7, 90, 137n1
diary problem, 131–2, 149–54
division of intellectual labor, 119, 122–7
doubt. *See* method of doubt
Duhem, Pierre, 41

egalitarianism: challenges to, 122–3; of
    Locke, 89–92, 122, 126
egoism: epistemic, 86–8, 99–108, 111–
    12, 134–5; ethical, 87–8, 100–101
egotism: epistemic, 86–8, 99–108, 111,
    135; ethical, 87–8, 100–101; pure,
    89
Elgin, Catherine, 45
Elster, Jonathan, 157n1
evidence, 68–9, 71, 89–90
evil demon hypothesis, 6, 174
evolution, 15–17, 60–6
experts: deference to opinions of, 122–3;
    openness to intellectual authority,
    118–19; opinions of, 125; using So-
    cratic influence, 115–16
externalism, 11–13, 22–3

Field, Hartry, 43n13
Fodor, Jerry, 104n23
Foucault, Michel, 40, 44, 129
foundationalism, classical, 5–6, 18, 22–
    25, 76–8, 90, 173–4
Fricker, Elizabeth, 107n29
Frost, Robert, 28
Fumerton, Richard, 5n1, 23n25

Gettier, Edmund, 9–10
Gettier-style counter examples, 20–1
Gibbard, Alan, 85
Goldbach's conjecture, 49–50
Goldman, Alvin, 10–12, 107n29
Goodman, Nelson, 43–4

Hardwig, John, 107n29
Hayek, F. A., 124n38
holism, 103–4
Holton, Richard, 107n29
Hume, David, 89, 94–8

inconsistency, 47–53, 174
independence, intellectual, 98, 112, 126–
    30
individualism, 90–2, 122, 126, 128
inheritance, intellectual, 112
internalism, 11–13, 22–3, 39
interviewing studies, 55–9, 68–72
introspection, 69–70. *See also* self-
    monitoring
irrelevancy thesis, 134–5

justification: as condition for knowl-
    edge, 10–11; epistemic, 11–12, 92,
    120; of externalists and internalists,
    12; sources of empirical, 42–3;
    testimony as source of, 93–7, 116–
    17

Kitcher, Philip, 17n19, 86, 127
Klein, Peter, 38n7, 40, 104n25
knowledge: analyses of, 8–13, 21; causal
    theory of, 10–11; reliability theory
    of, 11–12
Kornblith, Hilary, 21n24, 70n8, 77n11,
    78n12, 107n29, 125n40
Kuhn, Thomas, 127, 139

Latour, Bruno, 44, 127
Lehrer, Keith, 20n23, 26n1, 47n20,
    119n36
LePore, Ernest, 104n23
Lewis, C. I., 5
Locke, John, 13–16, 19, 21–2, 89–91,
    122–3, 126, 128

Longino, Helen, 127
lottery case, 50–1, 53, 174

McGinn, Colin, 38n7, 104n25
Mackie, J. L., 92
Maher, Patrick, 163
Malcolm, Norman, 137n1
Mannheim, Karl, 126n41
Marx, Karl, 129
method of doubt, 22–3, 73, 76–8, 90
Mill, John Stuart, 124

Nagel, Thomas, 148n3
Naturalized Epistemology, 10–11, 16–17
neutrality thesis, 134–6
Nozick, Robert, 53n29, 77n10, 124n38

opinions: accuracy of, 16–19, 38, 46, 60, 89; consensus, 120–1; deep and shallow, 26–27; inconsistent, 48–51; recalibration of, 71–2; social construction of, 92–9, 126; that are matters of value, 115–16. *See also* beliefs
opinions, current: conflict with future opinions, 166–7; conflict with past opinions, 144–54; influence on future opinions, 160; priority thesis concerning, 143–6, 152–4, 169; role of past opinions in shaping, 135; trust in, 137, 140–1, 144
opinions, future: conflict with current opinions, 166–7; defeating credibility of, 166–7; prima facie credibility of, 167; special reason thesis concerning, 166–7, 169
opinions, past: access to, 135–6; conflict with current opinions, 146–54; defeating credibility of, 138–41, 148–54; influence on current opinions, 135, 141; prima facie credibility of, 132–4, 140–6, 155; special reasons thesis concerning, 155–6, 169
opinions of others: conflict with one's own opinions, 108–12; defeating credibility of, 138–41, 148–54; in-

fluence on our opinions, 77–9, 98–9; prima facie credibility of, 125, 134–5, 154; special reasons thesis concerning, 154–6, 169
optimism, intellectual: of Descartes, 90; of Locke, 14–15, 90–2, 122, 126
overconfidence bias, 57

Pascal, Blaise, 61
Peirce, Charles S., 44, 127, 159
perception, 41–4
perspectives: in assessment actions, beliefs, and decisions, 29–31; of groups, 29; of individuals, 29–32
Plantinga, Alvin, 16n5, 96n16, 98n22, 107n29
Pollock, John, 113n30
preface case, 50–1, 53, 174
Price, H. H., 106
prima facie reason, 36
priority thesis, 143–6, 169
prisoner's dilemma, 78
probability, 19, 90–1
proportionality (Locke's principle), 89–90
Putnam, Hilary, 7

Quine, W. V. O., 8–9, 41

rationality: constituted by social practices, 44–5; practical, 29–31, 78, 148–51; strong and weak sense of, 29
rationality, epistemic: notion of, 28–9, 33–7, 50–3, 78, 177–8; social aspects of, 127
rationalization: distinct from genuine reasons, 77–8
Rawls, John, 44
reason: distinct from rationalization, 77–8; Locke's idea of natural, 14, 126; prima facie (epistemic), 36, 110
recalibration, 71–2
reflection: beliefs that survive, 32–5; deep, 151; on one's current opinions, 26–7, 45–7
reflective equilibrium, 43–4
Reid, Thomas, 92–8, 115n32

reliabilism, 11
responsible belief, 32–3
Root, Michael, 107n29
Rorty, Richard, 44, 128
Russell, Bertrand, 5, 23, 24

Schelling, Thomas, 157n1
Schmitt, Frederick, 96n16, 107n29, 119n35, 124n37
Schweitzer, Albert, 100–101
science: interpretations of the history of, 139–40; as self-correcting system, 124; social aspects of, 127
selection, natural, 15–17, 64–7
selection tasks, 65–6
self-criticism: invulnerability to, 4, 27–37, 48, 53–4
self-monitoring, 69–76, 129
self-reliance, intellectual, 91–2, 98–9, 176
self-trust: appropriate degree of, 47–51; coexistence with intellectual conflicts, 53–4; generates presumption of trust in others, 106, 108, 120, 168–72, 178; limits of, 25, 47, 174; necessity of, 78; radiates outward, 106, 120, 168–72, 178
skepticism, 6–8, 13, 17–21, 37–47, 55
Skyrms, Brian, 163
social epistemology, 126–8
social influences on opinion, 92–9, 126
Socratic influence, 86–9, 92, 110–11, 135

Solomon, Miriam, 125n39, 127
Sosa, Ernest, 96, 107n29, 113n30
specialization, 122
special reasons thesis, 143–6, 169–70
Stich, Stephen, 17n20
Swinburne, Richard, 97

testimony, 92–8, 105–6, 116–17
theology: Descartes' reliance on, 7–8, 13, 15, 73; Locke's reliance on, 13–16
tradition: influence on opinion, 44, 112
trust, intellectual: even when proof is lacking, 129, 175; in faculties of others, 106–8, 175; in future opinions, 158–61, 176–8; in one's current self, 3–4, 20, 24–39, 48, 55, 99–101, 137–8, 143–6, 159, 173–5; in opinions of others, 102, 106–7, 176; in past opinions, 135–9, 143–6, 154, 176; toward past intellectual efforts, 13

Ulysses case, 157–8
universalism: epistemic, 87–8, 134–5; ethical, 87–8

van Frassen, B., 163n6
Vygotsky, L. S., 44

Wittgenstein, Ludwig, 5, 44, 128, 139
Wolterstorff, Nicholas, 89–90

Lightning Source UK Ltd.
Milton Keynes UK
UKOW041346021012

199940UK00001B/95/A